OPPORTUNITIES THAT PASS

OPPORTUNITIES THAT PASS

An Historical Miscellany

CECIL ROTH

Editors
Israel Finestein
Joseph F. Roth

Foreword by
Raphael Loewe

VALLENTINE MITCHELL
LONDON · PORTLAND, OR

First published in 2005 in Great Britain by
VALLENTINE MITCHELL
Suite 314, Premier House, 112–114 Station Road, Edgware, Middlesex HA8 7BJ
and in the United States of America by
VALLENTINE MITCHELL
c/o ISBS, 920 NE 58th Avenue, Suite 300, Portland, OR 97213 3786
Portland, Oregon, 97213-3644

Website http://www.vmbooks.com

Copyright collection © 2005 Vallentine Mitchell

Chapter 34 reprinted from the Menorah Treasury, © 1964,
The Jewish Publication Society with the permission of the publisher,
The Jewish Publication Society

British Library Cataloguing in Publication Data:
A catalogue record for this book has been applied for

ISBN 0 85303 575 X (cloth)
ISBN 0 85303 576 8 (paper)

Library of Congress Cataloging-in-Publication Data:
A catalog record for this book has been applied for

Typeset in 11/13pt Sabon by FiSH Books, London
Printed in Great Britain by MPG Books Ltd, Bodmin, Cornwall

To the memory of Cecil Roth
(5 March 1899 to 21 June 1970)
and
Irene Roth
(17 March 1904 to 4 December 1996)

Contents

Foreword

A glance is sufficient to show that the pieces assembled here – most of them specimens of the author's Jewish literary journalism prior to his appointment in 1939 as Reader in Post-Biblical Jewish History at Oxford – have an internal coherence. Although this circumstance makes it convenient to gather them between the covers of a book, it would not, in itself, have justified their exhumation. That they are worth publishing is due to the fact that with the passage of time they have become something of an historical source in their own right. An aspect of Roth's genius which, as his academic stature as a Jewish historian grew, both complemented and fructified it was his enterprise as a traveller and his capacity to note things that, taken for granted in the Jewish world as commonplace, might all too easily disappear, recorded inadequately or not at all. In the 1920s and 1930s rail travel was still comparatively cheap. The availability (at prices still uninflated by retrospective sentimentality) of Hebrew manuscripts, early printed books and ritual artifacts that were still considered as accoutrements of Jewish domestic life and communal life rather than as museum pieces or, indeed, investments meant that although Roth commanded no private means, he was able to visit the main centres as well as the byways of Sefardi Jewry, and also to lay the foundations of what would become an important library and art collection. In addition to this, in the years immediately following the First World War and the establishment of the British Mandate for Palestine, the Jewish scene (apart from Eastern Europe) was both serene and hopeful. It is possible that one who, as a soldier, had witnessed the terrible casualties of that war had his awareness sharpened to the precariousness of those cultural and traditional frills that individualise local Jewish life and can enhance its aesthetic expression. But little could he have imagined that Hitler's war, by the enormity of the catastrophe that accompanied it, would so emphatically and so tragically endorse his intuition that many of the things which Jewry took for granted ought to be documented before it was too late.

These articles – the dates of all of which are indicated, and should be noted – exhale the atmosphere of the period, and also reflect the tenacity of Jewish memory, and the vigour of what may be called the cultural superstructure of Jewish ritual observance, before the clouds descended and it was still possible for a Jewish writer to speak ironically about Hitler's antisemitic policy. Even though these references must now provoke an involuntary shudder in the reader, to have deleted them editorially would have defeated the object of preserving, as it were in amber, authentic specimens of the atmosphere of the time. The only one of the communities which the young Roth visited that is still recognisable as the integral continuation of its own self half a century ago is Gibraltar. In addition to the hurban of European Jewry, demographic changes stimulated by the emergence of Israel have standardised much of Jewish ritual observance, blurring local distinctiveness or casting it into complete oblivion save for the historian. To read these pieces now brings into sharp focus the words with which Roth himself concluded the preface to his *History of the Jews in Italy* (dated 1945): 'At one time the writing of these pages could have been a sheer joy to me. Under the shadow of the recent tragedy, it has been sheer agony. I would inscribe this work to the memory of those dear Italian friends who have fallen victim to the Nazi fury.'

Since these articles were produced for a popular readership and so many appeared in the *Jewish Chronicle*, references to antiquarian items, historical events, and so on were not provided with indications as to the sources or other supportive evidence. To have added such apparatus now would have been to alter the flavour of the original in a significant way, and in point of fact Cecil Roth subsequently made such an undertaking superfluous because of the way in which he planned what is possibly his greatest monument, the English *Encyclopedia Judaica* – the first Jewish encyclopedia to have included an index which marshals in magisterial manner a mass of detailed information. If the appetite of readers of this volume is whetted to follow it up by reference to the relevant articles (and the bibliographies that they carry) in the *Encyclopedia*, that would surely be the very thing that he would have wished. Perhaps I may refer to one supplementary source, since it has appeared since the date of the publication of the *Encyclopedia*. In Chapter 12 Roth discusses the *yom ha-hesger*, the custom in some places of subjecting the local Jews to house arrest at Easter-tide, and the liturgical poems to which this institution gave rise. My facsimile edition of *The Rylands Haggadah* (1988), which includes one such poem, provides it in full translation.

Raphael Loewe
Former Head of the Department of Hebrew and Jewish Studies,
University College London

Introduction

Poetry is not limited to verse. Historians have sometimes been compared to poets. The historian's role may in some cases prove to be not only to tell what happened but at the same time to entertain, move, and instruct his or her readers. It is of course a matter of personality, circumstance, and flair. Cecil Roth was one such historian, as this collection of articles by him amply demonstrates.

This London-born scholar was from 1938 to 1964 Reader in Post-Biblical Jewish History at Oxford, where he and his wife, Irene, were popular among many generations of Jewish students. In addition to his many well-known historical works, Roth wrote numerous articles of Jewish interest in journals published in Britain and overseas. He and Irene loved to travel. Roth travelled widely in Europe while single, and was accompanied by his wife after marriage. There were frequent visits to centres of past or then current Jewish residence.

He was an acute observer of scenes, people, atmosphere and change. Roth was intensely curious about everything that he saw and heard, and his impressions are recorded in characteristically felicitous style. He reflects on the history and on the contemporary state of the Jewish communities, examining local legends, ancient customs, and the then contemporary hopes. In addition to pieces of traditional Jewish lore, there are also telling sketches of Jewish events and personalities. They speak for themselves, well reflecting his own sense of somtimes impish humour. But at every turn the volume reveals the author's Jewish commitment and his instinctive and informed shaping of the joys and sorrows of his people.

We have retained Roth's language as he left it. Liberty has been taken to adopt English spelling. Editorial footnotes have been kept to the minimum consistent with clarity.

We are aware that there are a few passages of an especially sensitive nature which may evoke memories of events during the period 1933–45 and indeed possibly beyond. Following careful consideration it was decided not to delete such passages. Each article belongs to its place and time, as readers will readily appreciate. To each article is appended the name of the journal and where and when it first appeared.

Israel Finestein
Joseph Roth
London, 2005

Cecil Roth: A Vignette

Joseph Roth

Cecil Roth was one of the world's most outstanding historians. His first love was for Italy and Italian history – and Italian Jewish cultural history in particular – over the period from the beginning of the medieval era until the end of the seventeenth century. He was born in London, England, in 1899 and died in 1970 Jerusalem, where he is buried in the Sanhedria cemetery.

Following active service in France in the First World War, Cecil studied at Merton College, Oxford. His interest in history was first aroused at the City of London School before the war, but it was while he was at Oxford that he was drawn towards the Italian Renaissance period and more specifically to Florence. As he was studying the age of Dante his tutors suggested that it would be to his benefit to spend part of the long vacation in Italy. So during the summer of 1920 he first visited Florence, laying the seeds of his intellectual and emotional involvement with the history of Italian Jewry. During this and many later visits he stayed in a pensione on the second floor of an old Palazzo (No. 2, Piazza S. Firenze, just behind the Piazza della Signoria), the proprietress being a tiny wizened lady by the name of Signora della Pergolia, affectionately known to her guests as Signora Giulia. Life at the pensione was never dull, for it was frequented by interesting guests from many countries. Here Cecil met a profusion of colourful characters and was introduced to many Italian Jewish traditions. Later the pensione moved to an apartment building in a busy shopping street close to the River Arno.

The drama and colour of the Italian Renaissance period appealed to Cecil's flair for the dramatic. His interest soon focused on sixteenth-century Italy and more specifically the period of the last Florentine Republic, which developed into the subject of his doctorial thesis for which he was awarded his doctorate on 24 November 1924. This work formed his first major publication in the following year under the soon famous title *The Last Florentine*

Republic. It was translated into Italian a year later. It was as a result of the many periods he spent in Florence, some quite lengthy, that he made the transition from a general historian specializing in the history and culture of Florence to a student of Florentine and Italian Jewry. In appreciation of services he performed for the local Jewish community during the summer of 1924 some friends in Verona enabled him to acquire various papers of historic interest which led him to the life and times of a long forgotten Jewish worthy of the eighteenth century – Rabbi Menahem Navarra of Verona – subsequently forming the source for a series of published essays and so laying the foundations for future similar research work.

It was during his initial visits to Florence that he first became interested in Jewish ritual art and acquired the first pieces of what eventually became an extensive collection of religious and general art objects, most of which is now housed in the Beth Tzedec Synagogue in Toronto, Canada. Probably his most cherished exhibit are the fifteenth-century keys with their leather pouch to Florence's old Porta San Gallo, obtained at an auction in 1935 at Sotheby's in London and which he deemed should in due course be returned to their place of origin.

In 1935, Cecil published *The Ritual Murder Libel and the Jew: The Report by Cardinal Lorenzo Ganganelli*, a timely publication as the libel had been once again revived. The book concerned the investigation in 1759 at the request of the then Pope Benedict XIV which demonstrated that the libel was a baseless lie. On 29 March 1935 Cecil presented a specially bound copy to the Pope (Pius XI) in private audience at the Vatican when the Pope congratulated him on his excellent command of Italian and was relieved that he could conduct the audience in that language with no need for an interpreter.

For Cecil, history was like a detective story – from the most insignificant of clues and by dint of constant and painstaking investigation and research, a thrilling picture emerges of a long lost episode in all its glory. It was the byways, the oddities, the minutiae of life, the discovery of the unexpected or unexplored, the revealing of unknown characters and personalities that really interested him. Yet from these often ostensibly insignificant pointers he could follow the trail, to see where the story might lead, fitting the pieces together not by some abstract theory but like a jigsaw puzzle.

Cecil was an expert on things Italian. He wrote many books and articles regarding both general Italian and Judeo-Italian subjects. But this was just one aspect of his interests and his scholarship. As an Anglo-Jewish historian he has no equal and has delved deeply into the history of the Jews in England, revealing many features previously overlooked or forgotten. He drew on his vast learning to produce volume after volume on various aspects of Jewish history in a style which immediately appealed to the general public at large and through his concise, colourful descriptions found history to be as enthralling and exciting as any detective novel. He never tired of championing the Jewish contribution to civilisation – the title of one of his books. He had an encyclopedic knowledge and his list of publications runs to over 700, among which is probably his greatest legacy – the monumental 16 volume *Encyclopedia Judaica* which he edited. Sadly, he never actually saw the final production, for the first volume came off the press on the day following his death.

In recognition of his work regarding Italian history, Cecil was elected to a number of Italian learned societies before 1939 but he resigned his memberships as a protest against Mussolini's anti-Jewish legislation. Immediately after the war in 1945, under the auspices of the British army, he toured Italy giving lectures to the Allied troops on aspects of Italian history and culture. Whilst there, he was also invited to lecture at various Italian Universities and learned societies, being the first 'foreigner' to do so for many years. After 1965 he was re-elected a corresponding member of the Accademia Colombaria of Florence and in 1969 he was appointed a commendatore of the Order of Merit of the Italian Republic for services to Italian culture.

Acknowledgements

The conception and germination of this book goes back over many years. Some 20 years ago Cecil's widow, Irene, mentioned to a frequent friendly visitor, Bill Soloway, that in a cupboard in her apartment in New York, there was a collection of articles which Cecil had put together, possibly with the intention of revisiting them at some point with a view to their republication. In turn Bill Soloway asked Andrew Gluck for an opinion and as the latter recorded at the time he 'was amazed by what he found'.

Andrew Gluck attempted to bring this collection to the attention of various publishers but met with little success until he turned to his good friend Larry Ambush. He was President of the publishing house Moody and Bickerstaff and he agreed to publish the collection. That proved to be no mean task, for it was necessary first to track down the various copyright holders and obtain their permission for the republication. This was somewhat akin to a detective's exploration for many of the original publishers had long since disappeared or had passed their rights to others. His search took him to various countries and many individuals gave of their time to help him amongst whom must be mentioned Daniel Rose and Joe Maleh.

Unfortunately Larry Ambush died before he could finish the preparatory work and his son, Joshua Ambush an attorney, valiantly assumed the mantle of his father but he again was unable to obtain an undertaking from a publisher. Subsequently Martin Schwarzschild, a great friend of both Cecil and Irene and executor of their estate, introduced Joshua Ambush to Cecil's nephew Joseph Roth who then explored the opportunities in England. He was delighted when Frank Cass – the talented, well known publisher of fine books of Jewish interest – agreed to publish this work. The editors are grateful to him and his team at Vallentine Mitchell for their expertise and unstinted efforts in bringing this venture to fruition and in so doing fulfilling the promise made by Larry

Ambush so long ago to Cecil's widow, Irene, in the twilight of her life.

It is to all of the above, and to others who one way or another have helped in the planning, preparation and production of this volume, that the editors give their thanks. Without their invaluable participation, this might indeed have become one of those 'Opportunities that Pass'.

The editors are grateful to Professor Raphael Loewe for his telling foreword.

1 Opportunities that Pass

Jewish scholarship has been over-concentrated hitherto on the written or printed word. This was the reaction, presumably, from the uncritical pre-Mendelssohnian era, when everything traditional was accepted on trust. But at the same time it is in a sense a survival of the old ideals of the exclusive study of a Talmudic text, extended in scope and applied to a wider field.

The *cause* of the phenomenon is, however, a matter of very minor importance. The significant fact is that Jewish scholars and Jewish institutes of learning throughout the world have been directing their attention almost exclusively, during the past half-century of feverish activity, upon texts old and new, and the information to be derived from them. Nothing wrong, of course, in this. Historical and literary studies must always remain based predominantly, if not over-whelmingly, upon documents, whether printed or manuscript. A point, however, which needs accentuating, and more in Jewish than in non-Jewish circles, is that there are other records than these. There are archeological fragments; there are artistic monuments; and, above all, there is human memory.

There is no need to go into the comparative importance of these various sources. It may be conceded, perhaps, that the conventional books and manuscripts are the most valuable. They have, however, a quality that the others lack: they are not likely, excepting by sheer accident or deliberate carelessness, to be destroyed. After they are housed in a great library, they are reasonably safe. No opportunity should be lost of enriching the various great collections with fresh material. But once such acquisitions are made, there is no peculiar urgency to hasten research and publication.

So far as non-documentary sources go, matters are very different. They are frequently less tangible. They are always less transferable. And what is most significant, they are of such a nature that the present feverish march of 'civilization' is in many cases imperilling their very existence.

Let us take the most obvious and (it would seem) the most
indestructible category – that of architectural monuments. It would
seem that no great anxiety need be felt concerning their future. They
are to all intents and purposes imperishable, and in ten, or twenty,
or a hundred years' time, they will still be awaiting the investigator.
That was once true, perhaps (though only to a qualified degree), up
to a few years ago. However, since the Great War a mania for
reconstruction has swept over the whole of Europe. As it happens,
the Jewish quarters in the medieval world always tended to be in the
centre of the city – most convenient for business as well as for
surveillance. Hence, they have suffered disproportionately in the
course of the recent alterations. At Rome, the last vestiges of the old
Ghetto have disappeared within the last decade. At Rovigo, not only
the Jewish quarter, but also the old synagogue have been
demolished. Most tragic, perhaps, has been the case at Verona,
where the Via dei Portici – the old Ghetto – with the Corte
Spagnuola where the Sephardic synagogue was situated, and the
Vicolo Sagatino where the *shochet* plied his craft, and the Ghetto
Nuovo which was added when the area became too small for its
inhabitants, have all been replaced during the course of the past
couple of years by brand-new edifices laid out rectangularly, on the
American plan, so that even the names and the configuration of the
picturesque old streets have been entirely submerged.

In Italy, perhaps, the matter is of minor importance, for (in the
north of the country at least) archeological remains of the sort date
in the main from the Renaissance period and after. Germany can
no doubt be left to look after itself. England has little or nothing
to look after. But the mania for reconstruction is nowhere so
advanced as it is in Spain, where in some places the whole of the
old centres of the cities has recently been razed to the ground in
order to be rebuilt in the approved modern style. Here the Jewish
quarters and synagogues, if they exist, go back to the fifteenth
century at the very latest; but this antiquity and this unique
interest are not likely to affect the minds of those responsible for
the reconstruction. It is to be feared, accordingly, that more than
one ancient Spanish synagogue, of great archeological importance,
has disappeared within the last couple of years. At the close of the
nineteenth century, two pre-Expulsion places of worship, both
subsequently devoted to Catholic purposes, were to be seen at
Segovia. Now one has been burned down, and the other has

disappeared. At Saragona the case is much the same. At Tomar, in Portugal, an enthusiastic Jew was just in time to purchase, for a trivial sum, a thirteenth-century synagogue which was on the point of being sold to the Seventh Day Adventists, who are hardly likely to have been interested in its architectural amenities. Another, of rare beauty, is lying in ruins at Oporto. There is another, according to report, at Ronda. These are only one or two tragic instances which have come to the notice of the present writer, but there must be dozens more. The old *Juderias*, which served as the scene of the Jewish life which is now stilled forever, is, of course, threatened to an equal or greater extent.

The actual archeological significance of all these edifices is not, perhaps, great from the secular point of view. However, for the Jewish world, monuments of the sort have a unique importance. Those which are still standing are all too few, and steps should be taken to study and investigate them before it is too late. It may not be possible in every instance to save them from destruction. But they can at least be recorded, described, and photographed, and the material thus amassed will be of immense value to the Jewish historian in the future. With every year or month or even week that passes, the opportunities may become fewer.

Just as the former Jewish quarter occupied, frequently, a valuable position in the centre of the city, the Cemetery on what was formerly its outskirts has often come to acquire a considerable value as a potential building site. In more than one instance in recent years, it has been expropriated, and dwelling-houses constructed on the hallowed soil. At Verona, for example, the two ancient cemeteries – one of them dating back to the sixteenth century at least – were recently condemned to this fate. More important is the case of Salonica, where the 'House of Life' which served the community throughout its period of glorious supremacy, and where scores of persons renowned in the Jewish past were laid to rest, is now under sentence. It is not likely that execution can be averted. Before the final desecration takes place, however, the inscriptions on the tombs ought to be carefully copied, and the more important ones photographed. Four and a half centuries ago, when the Spanish communities lay under the sentence of expulsion, an enthusiast at Toledo copied out the epitaphs which were to be found in the time-honoured burial ground of that city. Later generations of scholars have had occasion to be grateful for this antiquarian zeal. It will be a curious sign of decadence if, after all this lapse of time, the present generation shows itself apathetic in a similar matter.

It is not only stones and bricks and mortar which are threatened by the tendencies of today. Folklore, in its fullest and widest meaning, is in an equally precarious condition. Until comparatively recently, a specific Jewish dress was to be found in many parts of the world. Now, it is rapidly becoming discarded in favour of ordinary European clothing: in some lands, indeed, it has already entirely disappeared. It would be disastrous if all memory and record of it were to be lost. That, however, is far from unlikely if modern tendencies continue. Up to little more than a century ago, tens of thousands of Jews living throughout Italy wore a specific red or yellow hat as their statutory badge of shame. For half a dozen years, the present writer has been attempting to trace a specimen, with the collaboration of influential and well-informed persons throughout the country. He has utterly failed. Steps should be taken without delay to safeguard against complete disappearance of the same sort in other quarters of the globe.

The Jewish costume for all occasions and everywhere – in Poland, in India, in Arabia, in North Africa – should be photographed and minutely described in every detail. Puppets should be prepared and dressed by those in whom the old tradition is still alive. Ideally, an Ethnographical Collection might be formed, with life-size models dressed from top to toe in the actual wardrobes of those whom they are intended to depict. Thus, future generations would have before them faithful and permanent records of the Polish Rabbi of the generation which is passing, with his fur hat and gabardine, and the Hassidim in their white Sabbath robes, and the Jews of Salonica with their finery brought with them long centuries ago from Spain, and the Moroccan Jewish brides with their weighty and picturesque finery, and the oppressed Jews of the Atlas with their black skull caps and jackets and *ganephs*, and the women of Cochin in far-off India, with their traditional wedding garments and jewellery. Some of these categories may possibly retain their old traditions for a generation or so more. Others are disappearing before our very eyes. Steps must be taken at once, if any permanent record is to be preserved.

Along with picturesque costume, one associates picturesque legend. It is to be found everywhere, from New York to Bombay, and from Stockholm to Sydney; tales of the establishment of the community, of departed worthies, of half-forgotten persecutions, of providential deliverances, of presumptive miracles, of strange local usages. More than one of the present writer's historical sketches has been based to a large extent upon legendary material collection on the spot, and he is convinced that a systematic enquiry might elicit more material, some possibly of the greatest interest and importance. One may find it among the Gentile population, too, in Spain or in Italy, whose credulous anti-Jewish legends are as important for the reconstruction of our past as any other, more sympathetic record of our own. In the Peninsula, indeed, the Passion Plays which still linger on in some places, retain the medieval conception of the Jew, and the costumes and language associated with them deserve a close study from the point of view of Jewish history. The same applies to local celebrations, such as that of Corpus Christi at Segovia, commemorating the most tragic episode in the history of that community.

But all of this is now disappearing fast, and something should be done to record it. The same applies to local ballads and songs, and hymns and tunes; the same applies, of course, to synagogal melodies, though something has been done through American enthusiasm in this direction. It is not out of place to mention also, in this connection, the Jewish dishes and delicacies of a former age, which a delicately-minded Italian publisher has recently entitled 'Hidden Poetry'.

More important than all of this is, of course, language. Every part of the Jewish world formerly had its own dialect, combining its vernacular, or its former vernacular, with typical Jewish turns of expression, of language, of pronunciation. Yiddish, or Judeo-German, and Ladino, or Judeo-Spanish, are likely to survive for some time to come, and both have recently formed the object of scientific studies (though in both of these dialects one hears of curious local expressions, of unique philological significance, which are fast disappearing). The same applies, to a certain degree, to Judeo-Arabic. Judeo-Italian, no less characteristic than any of these, is, however, dying before our eyes. Fortunately, competent scholars are at present engaged in a serious study of the subject. What, however, of Judeo-Provencal, spoken formerly by the isolated communities of the Papal possessions grouped about Avignon in southern France? This, too, was once spoken generally by some thousands of persons. Now it is almost entirely forgotten. There cannot be more than half a dozen men and women now alive from whom any valuable guidance on the subject might be elicited. In ten years' time, perhaps they may not be even one. Even more extraordinary than the specific way of speaking the vernacular which prevailed in these parts, was the specific way of pronouncing Hebrew, which changed all of the sibilants into f's and pronounced a familiar word like Zizith as fifith. Today there is perhaps only one person to whom this extraordinary system is completely familiar. Nothing is needed but a little patience and a couple of gramophone recording discs to insure that this amazing relic should not be lost to posterity.

The foregoing sketch touches only on a few outstanding examples of the records of the Jewish past, which are today rapidly becoming submerged. No doubt there are many more similar categories. However there is no need to enlarge the list, for it is extremely unlikely that anything will be done to remedy matters. The professional Jewish scholars are profoundly indifferent, the non-professional are completely overlooked, and those who might subsidize research are another phenomenon fast disappearing from modern Jewish life. The time will come, however, when the value and the importance of these records will be recognized, and it is western Jewry of the twentieth century which will stand indicted before the bar of history for criminal negligence, without extenuating circumstances.[1]

First published in *Views*, Vol. 1, No. 1, 1932.

EDITORS' NOTE

1. Cecil Roth had a lifelong concern for the care of Jewish memorabilia of all kinds as well as Jewish historical sites. It was not antiquarianism. It reflected his interest in the preservation of Jewish historical sources. This was exemplified nearer home by his role in the development of the Jewish museum in London from its inception in 1932. He had the scholar's sense of duty to protect the records and indications of Jewish life and thought of former times. This was perceived as desirable not only because of the sheer human interest but also for the better understanding and the further appreciation of the many-sided Jewish legacy among generations to come. His concern was greatly enhanced by circumstances of war and especially the ravages in Jewish life in the Nazi and Fascist years. During the Second World War, as President of the Jewish Historical Society of England, he convened private and public meetings in London of scholars and others to consider what

might be done in Europe in pursuit of Jewish religious, educational and cultural rehabilitation. He welcomed the post-war operations in this direction on the part of the Claims Conference on Jewish Material Claims against Germany and in particular the work of the separate but associated Memorial Foundation for Jewish Culture established though reparations funds in 1965.

2 Sabbath in Jerusalem

Some zealots complain of the degree of unobservance in Israel, and they may be right. But I want to speak of something diametrically different – of the degree of observance, especially in the capital city. For a Sabbath in Jerusalem is a spiritual experience such as is not to be known anywhere else in the world.

On Friday afternoon the streets begin to empty, the shops put up their shutters, and well before nightfall the last buses stop. From now on, the next twenty-four hours, the Princess Sabbath takes possession. As you go through the streets, you may see the Sabbath candles in almost every window; and later, on every side, you can hear the chanting of the Kiddush and the singing of Zemirot; no chance of forgetting for a single moment that you are in a Jewish city.

But in Jerusalem, it is the day, rather than the eve, of the Sabbath that to my mind conveys the Sabbatical spirit most intimately. Synagogue services are early – many of them are over by nine o'clock, the latest not long after ten – so you must get up betimes if you want to savour the flavour of the Holy City at its best.

I don't advise you to go to the 'modern' suburbs – Rehavia or Talbieh – but to visit the older parts of the city without the walls, Machaneh Yehudah and Meah Shearim, where the spirit of tradition is to be found at its most characteristic. No need to ask where there is a synagogue – people are hurrying to them on every side, with prayer books and Tallit bags under their arms, and it is enough to follow. But indeed, even this is unnecessary, for you can be guided by your ears; there is a synagogue here in every lane and alley – I have been told that there are over four hundred all told in Jerusalem, most of them, of course, only converted rooms. What a treasure for an ethnographer, the folklorist, the student of popular music – not to mention the ordinary inquisitive Jew like myself who is interested in all aspects of Jewish life!

There are synagogues for the Ashkenazim and the Sephardim and the Kurds and the Persians and the Bokharians and the Yemenites and the Moroccans and the Iraqis and almost every other tribe of the Diaspora, all with their specific traditions and customs. Of late they have even transported to Jerusalem an exquisitely lovely little synagogue from a deserted community outside Venice, where the congregation follows the Italian rite. So you may please your fancy. You can be occidental or oriental, just as you please. You may go to the superb Yeshurun Synagogue and imagine that you are in England, or you may go to a Yemenite conventicle and take off your shoes, sit on the ground, and imagine that you are in Arabia.

The latter, rather, is my fancy. It is not only because of the attraction of the exotic, but also for another reason: because I find the physical types of these Oriental and Eastern European communities to be so fascinating. You will see them all parading through the streets after the services, or on the Sabbath afternoon when the sun has lost its fierceness. Once upon a time – and not long since – a stroll through the Bokharian quarter on some festive occasion gave you the impression that a page of the Arabian Nights had come to life. Stately old men with glorious grey beards paced slowly up and down, dressed in long robes of all the colours of the rainbow. Their demure wimpled wives, walking a little behind them, could hardly vie with all this glory, though sometimes they wore little fortunes in ancient jewellery round their necks and in their ears. Now, alas, European costume has made distressing headway even among this conservative element – the first thing that newly-arrived immigrants from any Eastern Community try to do is to buy themselves a cloth cap and a pair of boots. Nevertheless, on High Days and Holydays, you will still sometimes see the Bokharian quarter aglow with colour. And as you stand in the street, the whole pageant will pass you by – an occasional Iraqi in his turban, Sephardi rabbis from Turkey with their characteristic black tarbushes, Yemenites with olive skin and melancholy eyes, followed by their trousered wives, perhaps even some of the newly-found Jews of the Hadramut, in the Arabian Peninsula, with their long hair and exquisite features.

But in Meah Shearim the scene is dominated by the Chassidim, with their earlocks and fur-edged hats, known as shtreimels, and long kaftans and their court shoes, and sometimes knee-breeches with white stockings. Experts can, I believe, distinguish one category of Chassidim from another by their costume, though I have not arrived at such a standard of erudition. But how lovely they are sometimes, the glorious old men with their long white beards, and the young ones with flashing eyes, and the adolescents with their cheeks just beginning to be covered with a soft down, and the little children dressed just like their fathers – but children none the less for all that. They are glorious to look at, and from the way I have sometimes seen some of the young men curl their earlocks about their fingers, I have the impression that they are sometimes well aware of the fact.

The groupings are often extraordinarily effective. One Sabbath morning on my way to synagogue, I met a Chassid all in black, except for a little grey in his beard and pink in his cheeks, and brown in the fur of his shtreimel. Walking a foot or so before him, almost like a trained dog, was a snow-white goat. It looked like a picture by Chagall which had stepped out of the frame.

After the Sabbath is over, on moonlight nights early in the month, you may see a group of Chassidim in some open space, performing the ceremony of the Sanctification of the New Moon. It is a fantastic scene in the silver light: and no words of mine can describe how impressive, in such a setting, is the music of their wordless songs.

I have spoken of the Sabbath only. But I do not wish to end without alluding briefly to the Day of Atonement, as I experienced it here. On my way to synagogue early in the morning, I went out of my way to pass through the same quarters that I have just described. It was tremendously impressive. Not a car in the streets, not a shop open, not a soul about, except for those hurrying to synagogue, perhaps already unconcernedly wearing the Tallit. From every side and in every possible variety of Hebrew accent and intonation, there came the words of the time-honoured prayers. It was not that services were being held in the city, but that the whole city itself was praying. Such a thing I had never seen before; such a thing can assuredly not take place anywhere else in the world today – and I do not speak of the Jewish world only. Jerusalem, the city of the prophets, is after all, true to its tradition.

First published in *Orthodox Jewish Life*, Vol. 21, 1954.

3 Was Hebrew Ever a Dead Language?

It would not be easy to exaggerate the significance of that marvellous revival which, within living memory, has restored Hebrew to its position as the language of the Jewish nucleus in Palestine and the medium of communication between thousands of Jews all the world over. Yet in justice to the idealists of past generations, who endeavoured to maintain the Hebraic tradition in the long night which preceded the present dawn, it is only fair to view the question in its proper perspective. Was Hebrew ever, in fact, a dead language?

There is no need to embark here upon an account of the phenomenally advanced educational system which obtained among the Jews in former generations, based of course upon the study of the Hebrew language and the Hebrew literature – a system which was abreast in many ways of the most modern education ideals. But it must be emphasised that every Jew was introduced to the study of Hebrew at an extremely early and impressionable age. 'At the age of three,' a fond sixteenth-century father jotted down on one of the fly-leaves of his prayer-book, in the collection of the present writer, 'my son Joseph recognised his Creator, for he began to study.' That wayward prodigy, Leone da Modena, was even more precocious, for at the age of two-and-a-half (I write the words in full to make it quite plain that there is no misprint) he chanted the *Haphtarah* in synagogue. Now to persons introduced to their studies so early, it is obvious that Hebrew must have become second nature – more intimate, in its way, even than the language in everyday use. Indeed, the Hebrew alphabet alone was generally familiar in Jewish circles, with the result that in almost every country the vernacular was written, and even printed, in Hebrew characters.

That the use of the ancestral tongue was not confined to the synagogue and the house of study, is abundantly clear. Throughout the Middle Ages and after, it was customary for Jews to keep their accounts in Hebrew. Governments occasionally intervened to secure the adoption of a more intelligible system. When a marriage, betrothal, or death took place in some prominent family, in the smallest Ghetto, a flood of Hebrew verses, unimpeachably correct in diction and prosody, was poured out by the local poetasters, who could plainly count upon a wide and appreciative audience. On the long winter nights – especially during Purim and Hanukkah – every household diverted itself with enigmas, riddles, parodies, charades, mainly in Hebrew. Every community had its notary who drew up wills, contracts of betrothal, deeds of sale, articles of apprenticeship, and all manner of similar business documents, for which Hebrew seemed to be the natural medium.

It goes without saying that synagogal business and rabbinical correspondence was transacted in the same tongue. We have a whole series of English private letters (written to Nottingham, of all places!) dating back to the thirteenth century. Prisoners carved their names and personal notes on the wall of Winchester Castle or the White Tower of Issoudun in the same tongue. Indeed, it may be said that in northern Europe at this period, whatever language Jews spoke among themselves, it seemed natural for them to slip into Hebrew as soon as they took pen or chisel in hand. After the Renaissance, the inroads of the vernacular became more pronounced. Nevertheless, throughout the seventeenth and eighteenth centuries the sumptuary laws and regulations for communal taxation at Mantua (to cite only one place) were drawn up and circulated in pure Hebrew. In these instances the most implicit communal obedience was requisite, and was indeed enforced by every physical and spiritual sanction available. The use of the so-called 'sacred tongue' for the purpose was plainly, therefore, no antiquarian diversion; it was assumed that every member of the community, with no exceptions or very few, could understand every intricate detail without interpretation. All this, it should be added, was long before the days of the *Meassefim*[1] and the Mendelssohnian[2] revival, the importance of which, outside Germany, has been greatly exaggerated.

It is true that by now Hebrew had partially been displaced as a popular medium by Yiddish in Northern Europe, and by Ladino in the Levant. Yet these dialects themselves bore eloquent testimony to the vitality of the old inheritance. Not only were they written or printed in Hebrew characters, but they contained very large numbers of Hebrew words. Sometimes, indeed, the proportion of the latter element was enormously high. The first clause in the code of laws drawn up by the Western Synagogue, London, in 1809, though its syntax was Teutonic, contained upwards of 90 per cent of Hebrew words and phrases. This was exceptional. But the language used in her memoirs by Gluckel von Hameln, the German-Jewish Pepys, was similarly tinged with Hebrew to an extraordinarily high degree, between 25 and 33 per cent of her total vocabulary being taken from that language; and in this case, be it noted, the writer was a woman. Persons to whom a hybrid so constituted was intelligible, cannot have been entirely divorced from the Hebraic tradition.

A further point worth noting is that the development of the Hebrew language, during all this period, was not entirely suspended. Much of what was written was indeed severely, even slavishly, based upon Biblical or Talmudic models, but not all. The prose used by the best medieval stylists is as fine, in its way, as anything which the previous centuries produced, but it was essentially mediaeval in structure and in feeling. (Some of our most beautiful prayers, in fact, date from this period.) Moreover, the language was becoming enriched by a continuous influx of new words. The Ibn Tibbon family, in translating various philosophic classics from Arabic into Hebrew, were compelled to invent a new terminology which has since become an unquestioned part of the vocabulary of the Hebrew language. Other words in everyday use were either adapted or else invented. Thus the term *Memron* (probably from the Latin Membranum) came to be used for a note of hand, and *Perahim* ('flowery coins,' as it were) for Florins, named after the City of Flowers; while *Epiphior*, *Hashman*, and *Hegemon* (terms already found, with a different significance, in the Bible or Talmud) were applied to Pope, Cardinal, and Bishop, respectively.

We have been dealing thus far with the written language. It remains to be discussed how far Hebrew was spoken during the period in question. Unfortunately, reliable documentary testimony now becomes extremely scarce. Nevertheless, it is possible to adduce one or two significant facts and, on the basis of these, to hazard certain conjectures which admit of little doubt. It is known, for example, that there was a great deal of intercommunication in the Jewish world from a very early age. Rabbis from one country were treated with the utmost veneration in another, where their opinions would be listened to with deference; and they would frequently be invited to teach or to preach in the synagogue. What, however, was the medium of communication? A Rabbi from Baghdad would indeed find himself at home in Arabic-speaking Cordova, just as a scholar from Vilna does in Yiddish-speaking circles in New York. But in what language did a sage from the Rhineland (for example, Judah ben Asher, who with his sons revived Talmudic studies at Toledo in the fourteenth century) communicate with his colleagues or his disciples in Spain? When pilgrims went from Germany or France to Palestine, via Italy and Northern Africa, what tongue did they speak to the hosts who entertained them so lavishly on the way? And how did they get on with the miscellaneous handful, from every corner of the Jewish world, who kept the banner of Judaism flying in the Holy City? And, when the Palestinian Jewish settlement had grown and sent out the 'Emissaries of the Merciful' to collect funds on its behalf, in every community from Persia to New York, what language did they use on their journeys?

There is only one possible answer – Hebrew, the ancient *lingua franca*. It may not have been spoken fluently; indeed, the experiments may sometimes have been halting and even ungrammatical. Yet no person who had been introduced to the study of the Holy Tongue in earliest infancy, and had continued to frequent the *Beth haMidrash* morning and evening, can have been entirely unable to make out what was said to him, and even to frame one or two broken sentences in that language.

Nor are clearer indications entirely absent. The greatest of the Emissaries of the Merciful was Hayim Joseph David Azulai, who has left behind him a detailed diary of his travels (including, by the way, a graphic account of London). In 1754, he paid his first visit to Italy, where he records that he delivered a sermon at Pesaro. In what language? In Ladino? they would not have understood him. In Italian? he had not been in Italy long enough to learn it. The conclusion forces itself that on this occasion, as on many others subsequently, he must have spoken in Hebrew; and it is to be assumed that his audience understood what he said.

Now and again, information is given which permits conjecture to be crystallised into certainty. There is, for example, no more intimate picture of Jewish life in Germany in the twelfth century than that mirrored in the anecdotes contained in the 'Book of the Pious'. (Sefer Tsaddikim) Here, in episode after episode, we find the speaking of Hebrew referred to in terms which leave no room for doubting that it was, at that period, the habitual medium of communication between native and foreign Jews. Thus we are told (§799) of the elder who attributed his longevity to the fact that, when a stranger who did not understand his own language stayed in his house, he never spoke to him in Hebrew in the bath-house or in any similar place. Again (§902), there is the story of the pious Jew who was taken captive into a distant land, and saved by two Jews whom he heard speaking Hebrew together; the latter requesting him not to speak to them in that tongue lest the inhabitants should realise that he too was a Jew. Then (§1368) we are told of the sage who, speaking in Hebrew, advised the physician not to disclose the secrets of his art to a priest who happened to be sitting near. Finally (§1923) we read the recommendation that, if a man who is sent to betroth a damsel is unable to speak Hebrew, he should be carefully coached in some language that she understands.

It may be assumed that in Southern Europe and the Sephardi world, familiarity with Hebrew was certainly no less. Here, indeed, we are able to leave the legendary element behind and deal with definite historical facts. When that romantic Messianic adventurer, David Reubeni, was in Italy in 1524, he spoke and pretended to understand no language other than Hebrew – the ordinary medium of communication, as he alleged, amongst those lost tribes of Israel whose representative he was. Be that as it may, he found no difficulty in making himself understood, and he travelled about Europe using no other tongue than this. It was worth while quoting his own artless account of his first meeting with a Jew in Venice, which shows not only how readily he assumed that any chance acquaintance could speak Hebrew, but also how justified he appears to have been in his assumption. 'After I finished my prayers,' he says, 'I saw a man standing behind me. I spoke to him in the Holy Tongue and said, 'Who are you?' He replied: 'I am a Jew.' I said to him, 'Who told you that I was here?' He replied, 'Your servant Joseph, who told me that you are an emissary to do a good deed.''

Rabbi Isaac Luria,[3] 'the Lion of the Kabbala', refused at one stage of his life to speak any language other than Hebrew – on the Sabbath, at least – and it may be assumed that his example was followed by many of his disciples in sixteenth and seventeenth century Safed. Indeed, even in London, within living recollection, there have been religious enthusiasts of the old school who did the same. In the famous *Ets Hayyim* Academy of Amsterdam, in which Menasseh ben Israel and Spinoza had their early education,[4] Hebrew was actually taught by the 'direct' method. According to the account of Shabbettai Bass,[5] the children in the fifth class were allowed to speak no other language than Hebrew, excepting that they interpreted the Laws in Spanish. The result of this was that in the Amsterdam Jewish community, there was a succession of young men who, having had the advantage of the entire educational scheme, could always speak Hebrew if the necessity arose.

There is an additional piece of evidence which proves that, two hundred years ago, Hebrew speaking was not unknown even among the London Sefardim. In the Portuguese memorial sermon delivered by Dr. Isaac Sequeira Samuda in memory of the recently deceased Haham David Nieto in 1728, the following passage occurs: 'Most learned in the understanding of the Hebrew tongue, *he was no less eloquent in speaking it* or writing it in prose, than in composing it in verse.' Since the person responsible for this statement was a Fellow of the Royal Society, its scientific accuracy may be accepted without question.

It may, of course, be objected that all this was not very different from the position of Latin, which continued to be spoken by clerics, written by statesmen, and studied by schoolboys throughout the Middle Ages and after. Even though this were the case it would not materially affect the question under discussion, for it can be maintained quite plausibly that Latin, too, was at no time a 'dead' language in the fullest sense of the term. But even so, there was an enormous difference between the two. Latin, at the best, was partially familiar to only a tiny proportion of the total population of those countries where it formed part of the educational system. But among the Jews, education was universal to a degree not equalled in any European country until the present generation; and knowledge was refreshed by the long succession of evening and morning classes in the *Beth haMidrash* or Synagogue, which so strikingly anticipated our modern system of adult education. Hence the knowledge of Hebrew was spread all but universally, whereas that of Latin was the prerogative of only a small minority. Moreover, as we have seen above, it was used – unlike Latin – for the most ordinary and most strictly secular activities, as well as for the polished and erudite.

It is not, however, desired for one moment to minimise, by what has been said above, the importance of the modern development of Hebrew as a spoken language. Now, for the first time perhaps since the close of the Biblical canon, it is the tongue in which the Jewish child, in a Jewish land, babbles its first halting syllables. Now, for the first time for twenty centuries, Hebrew speech and Hebrew writing have become natural and spontaneous, instead of being based on a sense of duty on the one hand, and vague literary reminiscence on the other. Brethren of the land of Israel, we thank you!

First published in *Views*, Vol. 1, No. 1, 1932.

NOTES

1. Followers of Moses Mendelssohn involved in the promotion of *Meassef* (Collection), a pioneer Hebrew literary journal, and the cultivation of that language.
2. 1729–1786. A pioneer in enlightened German philosophy and generally regarded as father of the Haskalah movement for Jewish enlightenment.
3. Jerusalem-born mystic.
4. In the seventeenth century.
5. 1641–1718. Founder of Hebrew bibliography and through his printing business (founded in 1688 in Lower Silesia) an influential promoter of Hebrew printing.

4 The New Year in History

If you happen to possess a really old edition of the *Selihot*, it is worth turning up at this season of the year, no less for its human than for its liturgical value. You will find the first hymns printed in the largest possible type, and the pages are covered with yellow stains which turn out, on inspection, to be due to blobs of wax, sometimes still detachable. Then, if God has gifted you with an imagination, you may picture the whole scene.

Our pious fathers did not wait until the prescribed New Year had arrived to begin their supplications for forgiveness, but opened their campaign of prayer a week or ten days before. Long before dawn, the Ghetto would be aroused by the *schulklopfer* going his rounds, pounding on every door with his elaborately carved hammer and accompanying the tattoo with his curious, plaintive cry. The whole Community – men, women and children – answered the summons as one. In the pitch darkness, they stumbled their way along the cobbled street until the Synagogue was crowded in a manner which we of a degenerate age associate only with the greatest solemnities; and the *Hazan*, with bated breath and in the melody reserved for the High Festivals, led the first cry of penitence. It was still dark outside, the Synagogue was badly lighted, and it was a not unnatural demonstration of forethought on the part of the printer to set up this part of the Service in the largest characters available to him, as a relief for strained eyes. Nevertheless, some of the worshippers took the precaution of bringing candles with them, which they held a little precariously in their hands as they swayed backwards and forwards over their prayer books. Hence, the splashes of wax, dropped over these pages by pious ancestors perhaps three centuries ago.

The *Selihot* were the luxury of the pious, but as the day of the New Year approached, even the most sluggish soul was stirred and the most indifferent Jew did his utmost to join himself with his brethren in the synagogue for prayer. (Those who consider the Yom Kippur Jew a modern phenomenon will be surprised to learn that overflow Services on that occasion were customary in the Great Synagogue, London, even in the eighteenth century). So in all the quarters of the world, in the most remote and unlikely places, Services have been extemporised for the first time for the New Year, continuing in most cases over the Day of Atonement; and homesick young Jews, cut off from Jewish intercourse for nearly twelve months, would do their best to remember and reproduce the soul-stirring melodies which they had heard at their fathers' side. The files of the *Jewish Chronicle*, in the pioneering days of the last century, contain report after report of prayer meetings of this description held in the middle of the veldt, with the collaboration of worshippers who had trekked fifty or a hundred miles in order to take part. Some of the extemporised prayer-meetings formed the origins of established Congregations which are now of high standing. Indeed, it would not be much of an exaggeration (for it is a matter of common-sense, rather than of demonstration) to suggest that half of the Jewish Congregations in the world today owe their origin to extemporized assemblies on the *Yomim Noraim*.

Two outstanding examples concerning communities of vast historic importance may be quoted. For many centuries, without any but the briefest intermission, the Jews had been excluded from Venice. Then in 1508 began the War of the League of Cambrai, when the Venetian possessions of the *terra firma* were overrun by predatory armies. Large numbers of refugees crowded into the capital, including many Jews. When the New Year and the accompanying solemnities came round, they were formally permitted to hold Divine Service – a privilege hitherto strenuously withheld. Accordingly, extemporised places of worship were set up in several houses. This may be reckoned the birth of the Community of Venice, subsequently one of the most important of the Jewish world.

A century and a half later, Menasseh ben Israel was engaged in his negotiations for the return of the Jews to England. As a recent discovery has shown, he left Amsterdam on September 2nd, 1655. The Jewish New Year, 5416, was to begin on September 22nd, and it may be assumed that Menasseh insisted on celebrating it in due form. The conclusion is obvious. On the High Festivals that autumn, Jewish Services were held in London with all due formality. Samuel ben Israel, perhaps, read the Service, and for the first time since the Jews had been driven out by Edward I, 365 years before, four walls in the City of London re-echoed the long wail of the ceremonial ram's horn. And while we are speaking of London, let us recall that the first permanent home of the Great Synagogue was opened for Service for the New Year of 1722, and the Spanish and Portuguese Synagogue in Bevis Marks a couple of days only before the New Year of 1701. Similarly – *lehavdil* – the Community of Penzance first met for prayer in its diminutive Synagogue in New Street on the New Year of 1807.

But the associations of the New Year in Jewish history have not been uniformly bright. That of 1553, for example, was the occasion of grief and mourning for the Jewish people at large. It was at the height of the Catholic Reaction, and the position of the Jews, in Italy especially, had gradually become more and more precarious. At this stage, a couple of the apostates who are so often responsible for Jewish suffering intervened to bring the matter to a head. Vittorio Eliano (grandson of that eminent scholar of the previous generation, Elias Levita), in association with his brother, Solomon Romano, and a couple of other converts from Judaism, publicly denounced the Talmud as pernicious and blasphemous. Cardinal Caraffa (later to win unhappy notoriety as the arch-persecutor, Pope Paul IV) eagerly fostered the agitation, which coincided so precisely with his own desires, and the ruling Pontiff, the mild but yielding Julius III, had not alternative but to acquiesce. The great work – notwithstanding the fact that it had been published so recently under the patronage of Pope Leo X – was immediately condemned. A perquisition was made in the houses of the Jews of Rome, and all copies of the Talmud and of subsidiary works – sometimes, owing to the ignorance of those responsible, including even Bibles and Prayer Books – were seized. The day of the New Year, which fell that year on September 9th, was chosen for the execution of the sentence; and on that solemn day, while the Jews were assembled in their Synagogues praying for a year of peace and weal and freedom from sin, their most precious treasure was being burned on the Campo dei Fiori – on the same spot subsequently to be hallowed by the execution of Giordano Bruno. But the Talmud's spirit could not be extinguished by burning, any more than his; as the martyred Rabbi had said, so many centuries before: 'The parchment burns, but the letters range in the air.'

First published in the *Jewish Chronicle*, 11 September 1936.

5 Apples and Honey

It is not altogether remarkable that precisely the most important celebrations of the Jewish year are least signalised by domestic rites. The Synagogue service on the High Festivals – the New Year and the Day of Atonement – is all-important so that, for example, no time can be spared and accordingly little attention has been devoted to rendering the domestic celebration more attractive. On the other hand, no child could possibly forget the impression made by the Seder at home on Passover eve, even if he or she did not go to Synagogue.

We humdrum northerners, indeed, have restricted this New Year domestic expression to little more (in addition, of course, to the ordinary Sabbath ritual, when appropriate, and to some extra-ordinary but otherwise non-essential culinary preparations) than partaking of a slice of apple dipped in honey. This is typical of how certain of the more picturesque Jewish usages have progressively dwindled while their observances have become more onerous, for this hurried trifle is in fact the solitary survivor of a domestic New Year's rite which was formerly as elaborate, if not as picturesque, as the *Seder* service itself.

The origin of the whole idea appears to go back to Talmudic times. In the Gemara (*Keritot, 6a*) we find it recorded how Abbaye opined that since it was generally agreed that attention should be paid to symbols, a man should eat pumpkins, fenugreek, leeks, beets, and dates upon the New Year. The *Mahzor Vitry* of the twelfth century informs us that the current practice in France was to signalise the day by consuming sweet red apples. In Provence, on the other hand, men ate white grapes, white figs, and a lamb's head.

By the beginning of the fifteenth century at the latest, our modern practice had begun to establish itself, for the pious Maharil (Rabbi Jacob ben Moses Moellin) attached great importance to eating a sweet apple dipped in honey on the eve of the New Year. As the main dish, it was apparently customary to have a ram's head – partly in memory of the frustrated sacrifice of Isaac, partly as a symbol. Other customary components of the meal at this period were leeks and cucumbers.

One thing, however, was rigorously excluded from the menu. The word for nut, in Hebrew, is '*Egoz*', which has the numerical value of 1+3+6+7=17. The word sin, or '*Chatah*' has precisely the same total. On the day when we attempt to rid ourselves of our sin, it appeared inadvisable to absorb its equivalent into the system, so that pious householders preferred to await the Feast of Tabernacles before sampling the new season's walnuts.

What with all these various prescriptions and customs and recommendations, a whole elaborate dietary ritual grew up in course of time. Rabbi Joseph Caro's precedent is still followed in Italy and the Levant. After the sanctificatory *Kiddush* and Grace before meals, a long succession of symbolic species of food is partaken of, one after the other. Each has its own special benediction and little prayer, generally embodying a little pun on the name of the comestible in question. They begin with the universal apple and honey, or else new figs, in the hope of a goodly and sweet New Year. Then came leeks (in Hebrew, '*Karti*') in token that God's enemies may be cut off (Hebraic, '*YiKaratu*'). Beet ('*Selek*') provides occasion for expressing the hope that the impious may depart ('*Yitalku*'); dates ('*Tomrim*'), that they may end ('*Yitmu*'); pumpkin ('*Ka'ra*'), that the adverse judgments against us may be torn ('*Yika'Rua*'); fish, the symbol of fertility, or many-seeded pomegranates, afford an ample pretext for expressing the hope that our merits may increase; while a lamb's head suggests the prayer that we ourselves may be as a head and not a tail. The stranger, present at one of these elaborate ceremonials for the first time, wonders why the courses that evening are so numerous and the helpings so small. He does not realise that this is in fact nothing but a spiritualised *hors d'oeuvre*, and that he is expected to do full credit to the Festival meal which follows afterwards.

In Italy (in Provence, too, so long as the ancient local communities still existed), there was one other picturesque domestic usage associated with the New Year – one which obviously goes back to the earliest antiquity. A few days before, it was customary to place a handful of corn in a bowl and cover it with water. It naturally sprouts very quickly, and by the Eve of the New Year the bottom of the bowl is concealed by inch-high green sprouts, which form the central ornament of the table during the meal. They are kept a least until Kippur, if not until the end of Tabernacles. (In Provence, in addition, another bowl was prepared with various seasonal fruits, while grains of corn were scattered over the table).

This practice certainly goes back for at least a thousand years. In his commentary on the Talmudic tractate Sabbath, f. 81a, where it is discussed whether one may move about a parsipa on the Sabbath, Rashi interprets the term thus: – 'In the Responsa of the Geonim, I have found that it is customary to make baskets of palm-leaves which are then filled with earth and manure. Two or three weeks before the New Year, they prepare one for every boy and girl in the house and sow it with Egyptian beans or pulse, which soon sprout. On the Eve of the New Year, each one takes his own, passes it round his head seven times, and says: 'This in place of that; this is my substitute, and this my replacement.' After this, they throw it into the river.'

These last details plainly link up with the more modern practices of *Kapparah* (when a chicken, or else its money equivalent subsequently given to charity, is passed about the head), and *Tashlich*, (when sins are symbolically cast into running water).

But there is another analogy, more remarkable by far. For these little pots with their sprouting corn are almost identical with the Gardens of Adonis, well known to antiquity and still manufactured in rural places in Italy and Provence – in precisely those areas, that is, where the practice flourished in Jewish circles. The most common forms which that ancient usage now takes is Christian, for many Catholics still prepare saucers with growing corn in precisely the same manner as has been indicated above, in the middle of Lent. They are bound with ribands and placed round the Holy Sepulchres in the Churches, just as the original Gardens of Adonis of antiquity were placed around the bier of the dead deity. There does not appear to be the slightest doubt that both the Jewish practice and the Catholic are to be linked up with this ancient pagan rite. Not, of course, that this in any way detracts from their value today. It is the *object* of the observance, not its origin, which gives it spiritual and religious importance. As the Jewish proverb puts it: 'It is the heart which God requires.'

6 Kippur Reading

It was the custom of the learned and devout Rabbi Jacob ben Moses Moellin, otherwise known by abbreviation as Maharil, who lived in the Rhineland in the fourteenth and fifteenth centuries, to take a book of non-devotional legalisms with him to Synagogue on the High Festivals, wherein to glance while the Chazan was indulging in his vocal acrobatics. So, at least, we are informed by his pupil, Solomon of St. Goar, who set down his master's practices for the information and guidance of future generations. This is one of the details in which his precedent is still potent, whether consciously or not.

Many, even of the most pious of us, make a point of taking some emergency reading matter to Synagogue on the High Festivals, and especially on the Day of Atonement. Our pretexts are varied. Some of us glance at it during the musical interludes, others as an alternative to the more involved *piyutim*, or to those passages which the Chazan repeats after they have been recited once (or more often) by the Congregation. A few shameless individuals take refuge in it as an alternative to listening to the exhortations of the preacher. But, whatever the reason, a glance round the Synagogue (even the Reform Synagogue, as I am credibly informed) is sufficient to demonstrate that) *Yom Kippur* synagogal reading has continued to be an established institution.

Our fathers were more fortunately situated, in this respect, than we are. Any one Hebrew book, after all, looks to the casual observer as devotional as any other. Accordingly, it was easy for them to find ethical works, commentaries, legalistic compendia, and so on, for their diversion. Most popular of all were, of course, the passages of Midrash Rabba relating to the Day, together with the Talmudic tractate *Yoma*, which deals with the Day of Atonement. The latter, indeed, was often printed (its Mishnaic portions, at least) in the *Yom Kippur* liturgy. The Sefardic prayer book was enriched also by Solomon ibn Gabirol's magnificent cosmological rhapsody, the *Keter Malkhut*. In addition, the commentaries and Dinim (laws) printed in the old prayer books provided an ample field for literary browsing without straying from the volume in actual use.

Our modem editions of the liturgy are more severely utilitarian, and for that very reason are not quite so useful. Hence the feverish search, on *Kippur* eve, for 'something to look at in Synagogue tomorrow.' There is, of course, one obvious choice – the Chief Rabbi's marvellous little compendium, the *Book of Jewish Thoughts*, which contains more devotional matter than half-a-dozen specific religious treatises, and cannot fail to leave the Jewish sentiments of the reader – even if he has read it a dozen times before – on a higher plane than before.[1] The bijou india paper edition of the work, which measures only 5$\frac{1}{2}$ ins. by 3$\frac{1}{2}$ ins. and can easily be slipped into the vest pocket or the handbag, or placed over another book without ruining it, is ideally suited for the purpose under consideration. For children, the late Nina Salaman's collection, *Apples and Honey*, is similarly useful. *The Legacy of Israel*, with its essays in every branch of Jewish lore, is more specifically cultural in character, and by that fact not quite so suited for Synagogal perusal. On the other hand, Israel Abraham's two delightful little books, *The Glory of God* and *Permanent Values in Judaism*, or Alice Lucas's *Songs of Zion*, are ideally suited for the purpose, both in format and in contents. The only criticism against them is that these can be read through too soon.

An alternative possibly is a pocket edition of the Apocrypha, which notwithstanding its hoary antiquity and its Jewish authorship, is unknown territory for most of us. The Book of Maccabees had better be reserved for Hanukkah; but Ecclesiastes is full of the *Kippu*r spirit – and indeed, in the last chapter but one, of the actual phraseology of the *Kippur* liturgy.

Many persons, however (and rightly, in the present writer's opinion) object to perusing in Synagogue any volume without a corresponding Hebrew text, which seems so much better attuned to the spirit of the Jewish place of worship. The English Rashi, or to an even greater extent the Chief Rabbi's Pentateuchal Commentary, can of course be enlisted for the purpose. In the latter, for example, the spirited annotations on Leviticus, chapters xvi–xix, or the excursus upon *Kol Nidrei* which is included in the Book of Numbers have the advantage of *Inyana de Yoma*, or current interest. Is it too much to hope that Dr. Hertz will follow up his next volume with one for the Festival Readings,[2] which will include fields so admirably suited for his talents as the Five Scrolls (Megillot) and the Book of Jonah?

The requirements of *Kippur* reading seems to have been envisaged by the late Jacob Schiff when he endowed the series of Schiff Jewish Classics, published by the Jewish Publication Society of America. With the Hebrew texts and their translations facing one another on corresponding pages, and with their handy format, these are admirably suited for the object. A number of the titles, too, almost seem to have been chosen with an eye to *Kippur* requirements. No words are required to demonstrate the appeal of the triple galaxy of medieval Hebrew poets; though it may be pointed out that Zangwill's IBN GABIROL contains long selections, exquisitely translated, of the *Keter Malchut*, long associated in the Sefardic tradition with the Atonement liturgy.

Malter's edition of the Talmudic tractate, *Ta'anith*, on Public Fasts, is one of the best of the whole series, in execution as well as in value. Its current interest is obvious, and he who reads it reverts in some measure to the practice of former generations, who never hesitated to indulge in the luxury of Talmudic study in the intervals of prayer. Israel Abraham's *Ethical Wills* has no flaw, excepting that it is in two volumes. The texts which it contains are accessible to students only with the utmost difficulty. They are generally couched in translation language so simple that even those of us whose Hebrew is rustiest can make out the meaning of the original, provided that we keep one eye on the Editor's mellifluous rendering. Above all, the subject – illustrations of the simple piety of our fathers and on the spiritual counsels which they set on record at the supreme moment of earthly existence – attunes perfectly with the spirit of the day.

Only one work has been omitted from this list – the Bible, the finest of all. The reason is plain. Incredible though it may seem, the five million English-speaking Jews in the world today do not yet possess any handy edition of the Book of Books, with a faithful vernacular version facing the honoured original.[3]

First published in the *Jewish Chronicle*, London, 14 September 1934.

NOTES

1. The Chief Rabbi mentioned here was Dr H. Hertz.
2. This hope was not realised. Dr Hertz published an annotated edition of the daily prayer book with translation and commentaries.
3. Several such issues have appeared since this was written.

7 Kippur in History

It was one evening in the autumn of 1596. The burghers of Amsterdam, as they sauntered along the banks of the canals after the day's work, were perturbed to see some of the swarthy merchant-strangers who had settled in their midst recently enter, one after the other, into one of the gabled houses and afterwards to hear a muffled chant through the windows. The great struggle of the Netherlands for independence against Spain was still in progress, and the horrors of the Inquisition were still fresh in their memory. A Roman Catholic was, in their eyes, a traitor, and no Roman Catholic services were allowed to take place in their newly-redeemed city.

What, then, could be the object of this gathering of persons not long since arrived from the Peninsula, other than one for holding a Catholic religious service? The hymn singing, too, sounded religious, not unlike what they had been accustomed in the past to hear during the celebration of Mass.

One citizen voiced his doubts to the others, shaking his grave, steeple-hatted head and pulling his dignified beard; and some of them, more patriotic or more suspicious than the rest, insisted on taking drastic action. Knocking on the door of the house, they demanded admittance. There was nothing very incriminating to be found inside, except this telltale gathering of men and women, mostly Portuguese. It was the safest course to haul them before the magistrates, through the gathering twilight. The city fathers demanded an explanation, but none was forthcoming, or could be for the strangers spoke no Dutch.

At last, one of them plucked up his courage. It was a certain Manuel Rodrigues Vega, and he asked, in Latin, what was the matter. In those days, this linguistic achievement was not so rare an accomplishment in a town council as it probably is today, and someone told him what was suspected. His face immediately lightened, for it was easy for him to reply. They were not papists, he and his friends, he explained, though they came from the Peninsula. They were far from it.

They were children and grandchildren of Jewish parents who had been driven by force to embrace Christianity ('Marranos' we would call them today), who had submitted to ferocious persecution by the Inquisition and had left their homes because they desired to worship the God of their fathers in their own fashion. They had come together that evening to celebrate the most solemn day of the Jewish year, the Day of Atonement, as prescribed in the Law of Moses.

This put a different complexion upon matters. No Jews were as yet known in Holland, indeed. But it was difficult for the kindly Dutch to refuse toleration to men so persecuted by their common enemy – all the more so, it may be added, if they comprised among their number so many solid merchants who would be useful to the country.

Further explanations were added. The name of the interpreter was, he said, Jacob Tirado. This was his Jewish name, to which he had reverted only recently; for business purposes, he was still known by his Christian appellation, Manuel Rodrigues Vega. Among the others, there was a beautiful young woman named Maria Nunez, who had left home with all her family in order to be able to find some place where they might practice Judaism without danger; had been captured by an English vessel and brought to port; had refused the hand of an English noble; and had driven about London with Queen Elizabeth.

Others of the party had equally romantic histories. They were now allowed to go back and resume the interrupted service; and next day they assembled again, less furtively, to complete the solemn rites and to express their thanks to God for having brought them at last to a land where they might worship Him as their hearts desired.

One may imagine the heightened feelings of devotion which filled the heart of the little group as they went back to Synagogue on that first Kippur after the disturbance. One can understand why, thereafter, in the Communities of Amsterdam and London (as also, by a curious coincidence, among the Marranos of Portugal as well), it remained customary to interpose in the *Kol Nidrei* service, a special supplication on behalf of 'our bretheren who are in the hands of the Inquisition' a phrase which was recited till recently in Portuguese. One can appreciate with what thankfulness they repeated at night that apt last quotation which concludes the Atonement Service according to the Sefardi rite, though so unaccountably omitted by the Ashkenazim: Go, *eat thy bread with joy, and drink thy wine with a merry heart; for God hath already accepted thy works.*

In some such way as this, according to ancient legend, was born the famous Jewish community of Amsterdam – mother of all those of Holland, and ultimately of England and of the New World, too. There are many other Jewish communities, too, which trace their origin back to the Day of Atonement, or the *Yamim Noraim* of many generations ago. This is not indeed mere imaginativeness.

Throughout the year, the Jewish pioneers in a new land lived their lives of toil, sometimes barely aware of one another's existence, of many miles away from the nearest other Jew. But with the approach of autumn, they became restive. How would they be able to observe the traditional rites on Rosh Hashanah and Yom Kippur? They counted anxiously the number of Jews they knew in the region; they scanned one another's faces as they passed in the streets; they got in touch with friends in nearby villages; and at last, when the great solemnities arrived, they were able to conduct divine service in accordance with full traditional rites.

It was out of this first meeting for prayer that the Jewish congregation ultimately arose in place after place. Thereafter, services would perhaps be held at regular intervals. Moreover, once worship was organised and a congregation established, a synagogue would be built, and later on perhaps the existing one enlarged. No effort would, of course, be spared to have it ready for the High Festivals, even if some of the incidental work still remained to be done. Thus, it is not a coincidence that one after the other of the historic places of worship all over the world – beginning with the Bevis Marks Synagogue and the Great Synagogue in London – were first consecrated and first used for worship either on, or immediately berore, the High Festivals.

Indeed, is not a moment's pondering on the Day of Atonement in history a survey of Jewish history itself, in its most dramatic and most intense moments? The stately solemnities in the temple, which we still recall in our liturgy, when the very appearance of the High Priest struck awe in the hearts of the worshippers. The ritual during the last siege by the Romans, when it was performed with all its rites uncurtailed, although the enemy stood at the gates. The service in the academies in Babylonia, with the great scholars expounding every detail of the former observances, as preserved in poetical form in our Avodah services. The former assemblies of the Marranos in Spain and

Portugal, determined to forego no detail of their ancient ancestral tradition on this day of days, sometimes disturbed by incursions of familiars of the Inquisition, with a tragic sequel at an *auto-da-fe*. The meetings for prayer at this season, which inaugurated congregation after congregation, as we have seen, in Northern Europe, in America, in remote corners of the British Empire. The services yesterday in a hundred military camps of Jewish soldiers fighting for the world's freedom, in the colonies of a renewed Palestine, is what is left of the appalling ghettos of Central Europe.

Another historical association of Kippur is also naturally significant. It was, for example, on Kippur that Sabbetai Zevi died at Dulcigno, Turkey, in 1676, an exiled apostate. But another scene associated with the same day is even more arresting. It was in Recanati, Italy, in the autumn of 1558. Pope Paul IV, arch-enemy of the Jews, had recently ascended the throne of St. Peter, and anti-semitism was rife throughout his dominions. Philip (previously Joseph) Moro, one of the group of apostates to whom had been due the burning of the Talmud a few years earlier, happened to be in the city, armed with a Papal licence to preach to the Jews. Recollecting that it was the Day of Atonement, he saw his opportunity. Forcing his way into the Synagogue, he set up his crucifix in front of the Ark and began to deliver a conversionist harangue to the white-robed worshippers. This was more than flesh and blood could bear. With one accord, the congregation turned against him and forced him to leave the sacred precincts. This opportunity was, no doubt, what the fanatic had desired. Summoning the townspeople round him, he accused the Jews of having molested him and insulted the sacred symbol which he bore. They gathered round the Synagogue en masse, and a general massacre was avoided only by the energetic measures taken by the Governor. It was not long after that the Jewish Community suffered complete and final banishment.

The biblical warning is true, in a very literal sense. He who does not observe the Day of Atonement is cut off from his people.

First published in *Liberal Judaism*, New York, September 1946.

8 Dwelling in Booths

The most distinctive of the three ancient Hebrew Pilgrim Feasts is assuredly Succoth. The associations of *Pesach* and *Shavuot* have become usurped to some extent by the Christian solemnities of Easter and Pentecost. Their autumnal sequel, however, has no Gentile counterpart; and when the Jew goes to dwell in booths for seven days, he is safe at least against imitation, if not always against rain.

The idea is, of course, agricultural in origin. It was natural, during the vintage season, for peasants to transfer themselves from their villages for a few days to booths erected in the midst of their vineyards and olive groves. The conception, indeed, was spiritualised by its association with the Exodus – 'for in booths did I make the children of Israel dwell, when I brought them forth from the Land of Egypt'; but the agricultural associations remained obvious.

Nevertheless, from a very early date the Succah became a little sophisticated, special pains being taken to imbue the observance of the Biblical precept with some of the solemnity, as well as the beauty, of holiness. It is not difficult to picture the scene during that epoch-making revival under Nehemiah, when the people gathered 'olive branches and branches of wild olive, and myrtle branches and palm branches and branches of thick trees' from the hills about Jerusalem, and made themselves booths, 'every one upon the roof of his house, and in their courts, and in the courts of the House of God, and in the street of the water gate, and in the street of the gate of Ephraim.'

Later on, towards the close of the days of the Second Temple and the succeeding generations, the idea of the grandiose Succah and its adornment seems to have become current. Already in the time of the Mishnah, one reads of the practice of decorating the Succah with fruits, tapestries and bottles containing wine and oil. That noble proselyte, Queen Helena of Adiabene, built herself at Lydda a Succah more than twenty cubits high – an exaggeration to which the sages who thronged to visit her tactfully forbore to call attention. There can have been no such luxury, however, in the Succah made by the stern Shammai for his new-born grandson, by the simple expedient of laying bare the rafters over the mother's bed and covering them with boughs. Less luxurious still, if more picturesque, was the Succah constructed by Rabbi Akiba on the poop of the ship on which he was journeying to Rome on an urgent mission to the Imperial Court. Rabbi Gamaliel, who was with him, hardly approved. On the next morning, when they arose, they found that the frail construction had been carried away overnight by the wind. Rabbi Gamaliel was mildly amused. 'Akiba,' said he, 'where is your Succah now?'

But it was in the Middle Ages and immediately after, that the Succah reached its greatest development as an institution. Almost the whole expanse of the Ghetto or Judengasse became covered with the leafy bowers, occupying every vacant piece of ground and every flat roof, and introducing an unwonted touch of verdure into those dreary courts. Immediately the Day of Atonement was over, even before he broke his fast, the pious householder would set to work, thus going straight on from Mitzvah to Mitzvah. In Germany, in the Middle Ages, it became customary to provide a crown-shaped wreath to hang from the middle of the roof, decked about with autumn fruits, while choice curtains and tapestries would conceal the walls.

In wealthier centres, the Succah would sometimes attain great magnificence. Picart's admirable engraving of the observance of the Feast of Tabernacles at Amsterdam, at the close of the seventeenth century, shows us a handsome domed construction, capable of seating a dozen people and adorned with great ornamental festoons, Chinese lanterns, fruits and sconces. A striking contrast to this must have been the simplicity of the Succah made in London by the semi-furtive Community during the Protectorate when 'one year in Oliver's time they did build booths on the other side of the Thames, and kept the feast of Tabernacles in them.'

The materials chosen for the *Sekhakh* (or green boughs to cover the Succah) was generally left to choice or to chance. The Karaites, indeed, insist on palm-branches, and, in the courtyards of their Synagogues you may see the gaunt skeleton of last year's Tabernacle standing from one autumn to another. The Germans in the Middle Ages, had a predilection for willows of the brook, though the Rabbis, with delicate feeling, insisted that a token payment at least was made to the owner of the land, so that the Mitzvah should not be vitiated by even the remotest suspicion of dishonesty. Of the Sefardim, after the Expulsion of 1492, a touching tale is told: how, long afterwards, they sought for their Feast of Tabernacles branches of the orange trees under whose verdant shade they had reposed in Spain and Portugal, and how even in the seventeenth century, Jews travelled to Spain to obtain branches of these hallowed trees for their Synagogues. It is more likely, though, that it was the Spanish *Etrog* which was so valued and sought after.

London Succahs for many years displayed a striking similarity among themselves, as far as their covering was concerned at least. Large numbers of them were covered by boughs distributed from his Gunnersbury estate, to almost all who cared to apply, by that prince of philanthropists, Leopold de Rothschild. And, as we are talking of London, let us remind ourselves of that most historic of London Succahs – that of Dr. Nathan Marcus Adler, Chief Rabbi, in Finsbury Square, in which, at a breakfast party given in 1866 to the Wardens of the three City Synagogues,[1] he mooted that friendly union which developed into the United Synagogue.

There is a favourite story about the Succah which belongs to the Jewish folk lore of more than one country (it is recounted about one of the Grand Dukes of Tuscany, and a Dutch judge, and more than one East End magistrate); how, on receiving a complaint from non-Jewish householders of the nuisance caused by the booths erected by their Jewish neighbours, he tactfully ordered the obstruction to be removed *within eight days*! History recounts a somewhat similar, but more serious, episode at Gibraltar, where in the middle of the last century, a new governor of pronouncedly anti-Jewish tendencies had the Succah pulled down forcibly by the police, ostensibly because of the danger of fire, and forebade their erection outright on the following year. The commotion which resulted took on the nature of a public issue: representations were directed to Whitehall, and engaged the attention of the Board of Deputies of British Jews. In the end, the order was withdrawn.

In the course of time, a whole art grew up in connection with the embellishment of the Succah – wall decorations embodying verses of good omen; elaborate Mizrachs to show the direction of the Holy City; and greetings for the Patriarchal guests or Ushpizin, whose spirits were supposed – charming conception! – to grace the frail construction with their presence. These, of course, were retained from year to year. As soon as the feast was over, on the other hand, the children made bonfires of the boughs and leaves, adding thereby to the hilarity of the Rejoicing of the Law. This was the practice in Germany in the fifteenth century. It is to be recommended for revival today. Why, after all, should Guy Fawkes have all the fun?

First published in the *Jewish Chronicle*, London, 2 October 1936.

NOTE

1.   The Great, Hambro and New Synagogues.

9 The *Etrog* Compote

There was a time when the homely citron, 'the fruit of a goodly tree', played a part more important by far in Jewish life than it does today. This fact becomes obvious when one examines the various symbols which were considered as characteristic of Judaism at the period of the Second Temple and in the first centuries after. In the old Synagogues and sarcophagi, on coins and in catacombs, one of the objects which is repeated time after time, by the side of the Menorah itself, is the *Etrog*, of which the Jews were accustomed to make use on the Feast of Tabernacles. Subsequently, it would seem, the importance attached to this particular symbol waned, but, in the old Synagogues of Avignon and the Comtat Venaissin,[1] a trace of its former importance remained. According to the architectural convention which here prevailed, a niche was left on each side of the Ark. On the right there was placed the Chair of Elijah, used in circumcisions; that on the left was reserved for the *Lulav* and *Etrog*, which the congregation thus had before their eyes during divine worship throughout the autumnal Pilgrim Feast.

One reason for the change of attitude is perhaps to be traced in the increasing difficulty which prevailed among the Jews, in their far-flung Diaspora in Europe, in obtaining the characteristic Palestinian fruit which their Fathers had been wont to pluck. The palm-branch and other adjuncts could, of course, be found in most countries. But the *Etrog* had to be imported, year by year, from warmer climes. At the close of the Middle Ages, according to contemporary Rabbinical sources, the *Etrogim* were brought to Germany from southern Italy – Apulia and Rome – being transported through Marburg to Wiener Neustadt. Hence they were distributed throughout Germany by the intermediary of merchants who assembled for this purpose, though, naturally, the members of the local community had the first choice. In 1389, we find Albert III, of Austria, giving a safe conduct to a certain Jew named Elijah who proposed to cross the Alps into Italy with this object in view. In some places – for example, in the

Salzburg region, from the fifteenth or sixteenth century down to the eighteenth – a special import tax was levied on all *Etrogim* brought across the frontier by the Jewish merchants, this being specifically mentioned in the old toll-books.

BRAVING THE INQUISITION FOR A CITRON

Thus, the *Etrog* merchant from northern countries became a familiar figure in the Italian ghettoes. When in 1641 the pious David Verlengo made his will in Verona (according to Cecil Roth at the time of writing), he left instructions that his younger son should be taken back by them (the *Etrog* merchants) to study at Cracow, on the next occasion that they passed through the city on their return journey. Another source of supply, according to Buxtorf, was Spain, whither sixteen Jews went every year (notwithstanding the Inquisition and the edict of expulsion!) to bring back the palm-branches and citrons for distribution. In Central Europe, 'Esroger' was formerly found sometimes as a surname. It is hardly to be doubted that in the first place it was used to designate the citron merchants who made such venturesome journeys into foreign lands in order to satisfy the religious needs of their co-religionists.

Ultimately the main source of supply was Corfu. This continued to be the case until the anti-Jewish riots of 1891, when under the leadership of Rabbi Isaac Elhanan (called Citron) a movement was inaugurated to boycott the Corfiote *Etrog* growers and to seek an alternative supply in Palestine. Nowadays there is an increasing tendency to ensure that the ritual appurtenances of this exquisitely Jewish feast should all be furnished, as far as possible, by the labour of Jewish workers in the reborn Land of Israel.

Under conditions such as have been outlined above, it was inevitable that the *Etrog* should have been enormously expensive – sometimes all but unobtainable. In Germany, one year in the fifteenth century, the winter was so hard that there was a frost at Pentecost. Barely a single perfect *Etrog* was to be found for love or money in the whole country; even a small green one, hardly fit for use, cost fifteen ducats. The records of the Spanish and Portuguese Community in London show that in 1674 the 'citron and palm that came by post' cost no less than £2 14s – an almost prohibitive sum for those days. In Padua, on one occasion notwithstanding all efforts, only a single *Etrog* could be obtained for the use of the whole community. During the course of the Feast, while it was being brought from the Ashkenazi Synagogue for use in one of the other places of worship, the University students (notorious in that city for their anti-Semitism as well as for their high spirits) stopped the bearer, and kidnapped his precious burden; and they would not give it up until they were paid a high ransom. A similar dearth occurred in Alsace in the autumn of 1680. Asher Levy of Reichshofen recounts in his diary what difficulty there was in his village in obtaining the goodly fruit, how at last he managed to get hold of a single specimen for the use of the entire Community, and how, after the Feast, when he cut it open, he found to his disgust that it was after all not an *Etrog* but an ordinary lemon.

In Central Europe, greedy rulers regarded this – like all other Jewish ritual observances, from the Sabbath candles downwards – as a useful source of revenue. This was without doubt in imitation of the practice of the Jewish communities themselves, which raised a portion of their income for charitable purposes from a levy imposed upon these indispensable adjuncts of religious observance. In 1744, the pious Empress Maria Theresa ordered the Jews in her dominions of Bohemia, Moravia and Silesia to pay her the sum of 40,000 florins yearly, in addition to their manifold other dues, for the right of importing their palm branches and citrons for the Feast. It is regrettable to have to add that it seems that this came about as a direct consequence of the rapacity of a group of Jewish merchants, who a short while before had offered a similarly high sum for an *Etrog* monopoly for Her Imperial Majesty's dominions. Fired by this example, in 1797 certain Galician Jews offered to pay a considerable amount annually to the Imperial treasury in return for an *Etrog* monopoly. Though the reigning Emperor, Francis II, was in general narrow and intolerant, he refused to interfere further with the observance of a religious practice and the idea of a tax was finally abandoned.

OLD ENGLISH CONGREGATIONS

In the Western Synagogue of London (founded in the middle of the eighteenth century) financial considerations entered into the question from quite a different aspect. In the by-laws of 1809, it was laid down (§vii) that a special levy of 6d. in the £ as *Etrog* money should be raised on all seat rentals. Thus, every member could participate in the religious duty, in accordance with the literal wording of the passage (Leviticus xxiii, 40): 'And ye shall take *to yourselves...*' In pursuance of this (§vi), it was enjoined that the heads of the community were to purchase, at a cost of two guineas, four *Etrogim*, two of which should always be in the Synagogue at service time. From the amounts mentioned, it is plain that the price of these ritual appurtenances had considerably diminished by now. We know that in the distant Community of Penzance, the citron for Tabernacles at this period cost one guinea, though its transmission by express came to 8s 7d., with a shilling more for postage. Here, by the way, the statutory functions of the communal factotum included binding the *Lulav* on the Feast of Tabernacles and procuring willow-twigs for *Hoshanna Rabba*.

True to the old adage that the service of the most high should be 'beautified' to the utmost limit of a man's ability, there sprang up in the course of time the custom of having special boxes in which to keep the *Etrog* while not in actual use. The specimens extant are in no case very old (none, perhaps, antedates the eighteenth century), and they come almost without exception from Central and Eastern Europe. The most interesting are made in the shape of an actual citron, perfect down to the last detail. The metal generally used for the purpose is silver. Examples of this are to be found in most of the great Jewish collections (the Jewish Museum in London has one or two admirable specimens), but they do not vie, either in number or in workmanship, with the categories of Jewish ritual art associated with other occasions of the religious year, such as Passover or Purim. In the Levant, on the other hand, the custom has obtained of gilding the citron. As well paint the lily!

FOLK LORE AND FABLE

In Jewish folklore the *Etrog* played a notable role. In Talmudic times, to see one in a dream was regarded as an indication that a man was precious before his Maker. Later there came into existence a widespread popular belief that a pregnant woman who bit into one would bear a male child. After the feast, the dried fruit was sometimes used as a handle for the knife used in the *B'rit Milah*.

Many householders, on the other hand, made a sort of lemonade essence with it, which they kept for regaling distinguished guests (particularly, of course, the learned) throughout the year. Those of especial piety preferred to keep the shrivelled fruit for use, with the *Hoshanna* twigs, for kindling the oven in which their *Matzot* were baked for the following Passover.

In the days of the Second Temple and immediately after, the *Etrog* was associated with some spectacular events in Jewish history. On one occasion, when the warrior king Alexander Jannaeus (103–76 BC) was officiating at the altar, he scandalised public opinion by pouring the water libation contemptuously at his feet. The assembled peopled, shocked at this public spurning of Rabbinic tradition, pelted the King with their *Etrogim*. This was the prelude to a bloody civil war in which thousands lost their lives. After the destruction of the Temple, Rabbi Akiba once attracted attention by coming to Synagogue with an *Etrog* so huge that he had to carry it over his shoulder. This was no doubt in compensation for that other occasion when he had travelled to Rome with a number of eminent colleagues, and was still at sea during the Feast of Tabernacles. Of course, they had erected their Succah on the deck. But they only had one *Lulav* and *Etrog* between the lot of them, and formally presented them to one another after use, so that each could perform his religious duty with articles which actually belonged to him.

Since it is a Holy-day, let us wind up with a story – one of those tales of wonder which are neglected nowadays simply because they are to be found in that marvellous treasure house of Jewish lore, the Midrash, but which cannot fail to come into their own again amongst the new generation in Eretz Yisrael. We know from other sources that on *Hoshanna Rabba*, immediately the adults had finished with their *Etrogim*, the children used to seize them and eat them. It is upon this that the legend is based. Once upon a time, there was a certain pious ne'er-do-well who could never deprive himself of the pleasure of doing a good deed or performing a charitable act. Once, on *Hoshanna Rabba*, his wife gave him some money and told him to go out and do the *Yom Tov* shopping for her. He had not gone far on his way to market, when the Charity Collectors met him and invited him to subscribe towards some office of beneficence for which they needed funds. Of course, he let them have every penny in his pocket. Being now ashamed to go home, he turned his steps in the direction of the Synagogue. Here he found a heap of the *Etrogim* with which the children had been pelting one another. Hardly knowing what he was doing, he filled his wallet with them. Then he went down to the quay and stowed himself away upon a ship which was about to sail.

Ultimately, he disembarked in a far country where no Jews were to be found. As it happened, the King of that place was suffering from some severe internal trouble. He had consulted all the available physicians, but none could help him. At last he had a dream, from which he learned that the only cure for his complaint was to eat some of those *Etrogim* wherewith the Jews prayed upon the day of *Hoshanna*. He sent to all the provinces under his rule to search for this marvellous fruit, but none could be found. Ultimately, on the quay side, his emissaries found the poor Jew sitting all dejected upon his sack, wondering whence his next meal would come.

'What have you got there?' they demanded.

'Nothing,' he replied. 'I am a poor man, and have no property.'

Nevertheless, they searched the sack and found a curious mass of fruits inside, doubtless considerably the worse for wear.

'What are these?' they demanded.

'Oh, nothing,' he said, 'only the *Etrogim* wherewith the Jews pray on the day of *Hoshanna*.'

Their joy can be imagined. The sack was immediately taken to the king, who emptied it of its contents (by which he was immediately cured where of his ailment) and filled it with gold. The owner was subsequently allowed to have any further favour he asked. He chose to be sent in affluence to his original home, he scored off his surviving relatives in a somewhat heartless manner. This being a Jewish fairy story, he omitted to marry the King's daughter, but notwithstanding this unaccountable lapse, there is no reason to doubt that he lived happily ever after.

First published in the *Jewish Chronicle*, London, 21 September 1934.

NOTE

1. Area in south-eastern France ceded to the Pope. Papal territory from 1294 to 1791, it included local Jewish communities, notably in Avignon and Carpentras. It became a refuge for fleeing Jews, including North African Jews in the twentieth century.

10 The Great Hoshanna

For a full week the pious Jew has dwelled in his booth, re-evoking thus the memory of the days when his fathers were agriculturists and farmers, tilling the soil in the Land of Promise. Each day, in Synagogue, he has taken in his hand the stately *Lulav* and scented citron so that, while the Hallel or thanksgiving psalms are recited, the building has looked almost like a Palestinian palm grove. Then, towards the end of the Service, a Scroll of the Law is taken out of the Ark, and round it (as round the Altar in the Temple of old) he has gone in procession, with the rest of the Congregation, each bearing his verdant trophy. 'Hoshanna!' they cry, fervently, rustling the boughs. 'Hoshanna! Save us Now!'

As the Succoth week draws to its close, we are introduced to a different atmosphere. The observance of *Hoshanna Rabba* – the Great Hoshanna – has unfortunately fallen into considerable neglect in this decadent age, but for sheer picturesqueness, few occasions of the Jewish year can vie with it. In origin, of course, it is bound up with the famous Feast of the Water Drawing in the Temple of Jerusalem, which reached its climax on the seventh day. The stately courts were thronged throughout the night by an enormous festive throng, and even Rabbis of the profoundest learning did not disdain to perform torch dances before the eyes of the assembled multitude. Every street of Jerusalem was lit up by the illumination from the giant golden candelabra, fed continually by young priests from vessels of oil. Libations of water were solemnly poured out round about the altar. 'He who has not witnessed the joy of the Feast of Water-Drawing,' the old proverb ran, 'does not know the meaning of joy.'

Among the Sephardim, *Hoshanna Rabba* has all the pomp and circumstance of a major Holy Day. The beauty of the seven-fold circuit with *Etrog* and *Lulav*, to the accompaniment of mysterious hymns and repeated blasts of the Shofar, is unforgettable. Among the Ashkenazim, too, the Synagogue catches an echo on this occasion –

in its music, its vestments, its hymns – of the High Festivals, which have just passed. For on this day, according to Rabbinical fancy, the yearly judgment, decreed on the New Year and sealed on the Day of Atonement, receives its final confirmation. Hence, the *Hallot* or special loaves for this day, as those for the eve of Kippur, were customarily made in the form of a ladder, symbolising the union between earth and Heaven.

According to the folk lore of past ages, it was now possible to obtain an inkling of the Divine judgment: If a man was fated to die in the succeeding year, his shadow when thrown by the moon on the night of *Hoshanna Rabba* would be headless! Other family disasters were indicated by the absence of other parts of the body. In medieval Spain, those who wished to know what fortune had in store for them would wrap themselves in shrouds and go out to some spot where the light of the moon shone brilliantly. There they would strip themselves naked, and stretching out their limbs, would timidly observe the results. This fantasy received artistic expression in the old *Minhag* books, where the conventional scene for this occasion of the Jewish year might depict a man with shadow in complete working order – save for the head, which is absent!

This superstition had a curious extension. Since a man might always be confronted with a headless shadow on this night, many persons preferred to stay indoors from sundown to sunrise. It is possible – though the point has been overlooked – that this is the origin of the Watch-Night Service which is still widely observed on this occasion, when (as on the eve of Pentecost) select readings from the Bible and later literature are systematically studied; for, once they had come together, persons preferred to stay indoors, even at the price of their night's rest.

On the following day, of course, the distinctive feature in the Synagogue is the little bundle of willow-twigs which are held in the hand towards the close of the Service, and then beaten on the benches. This plainly recalls the willow-boughs which, in the Temple of Jerusalem, were set up by the side of the Altar. But in later days of superstition, men furtively inspected their twigs before discarding them, imagining that the number of leaves still attached indicated the proportion of their sins which remained unatoned for!

Generally speaking, the Jew prefers that material used for ritual purposes should not pass through non-Jewish hands, and still less be prepared by non-Jews. *Hoshanna Rabba* provides a solitary exception. If no Jew went abroad on the previous night, how could fresh willow-twigs be provided? Only by Gentiles! And it was regarded as proper that, though *Etrog* and *Lulav* were prepared for use under Jewish supervision, the *Aravah* should be supplied by non-Jews. (Another possible explanation of this custom is, of course, that this was prescribed in order that the material for the performance of the Mitzvah should be formally acquired by purchase, and not, as might otherwise have been the case – informally appropriated.) But whatever the cause, this was good for trade. Within living memory [at the time of writing], the streets of the Jewish quarter of Leghorn would be thronged on *Hoshanna Rabba* by peasants selling little bundles of willow-twigs for synagogal use. When they were finished with, it was the custom in medieval Germany to burn them and to roast apples in the flames. The Rabbis did not quite approve; they thought that it was derogatory. Instead, they recommended that they should be kept till the following spring (together with the willow-twigs in the *Lulav*) and used to light the fire in which the Matzot were baked. Thus the Jewish year was linked up from harvest to seed-time and from seed-time to harvest, in a continual chain of charming ceremonial. We have forgotten so much of it today; the loss is ours.

First published in the *Jewish Chronicle*, London, 9 October 1936.

11 Rejoicing in the Law

There is no celebration of the Jewish year which appears to the casual eye so spontaneous and so simple as the Rejoicing of the Law. But like all other Jewish celebrations, it has a long history behind it, apart from which it cannot be properly appreciated.

The characteristic feature of the day is, of course, the institution of the Bridegrooms of the Law and of the Beginning. Not many of those who take on these functions nowadays realise their real significance. The modern honeymoon has tended to deprive Jewish life of what used to be one of its most happy institutions – the 'seven days of rejoicing' which followed upon every wedding, culminating in the jubilant reception of the bridegroom in Synagogue on the Sabbath. On that day, he was the hero. Special hymns greeted his arrival to the seat of honour reserved for him; sweetmeats were showered down on him as he passed; and a special formula was recited when he was called up, crowned with myrtle, to the Reading of the Law. With him he bore a second Sefer Torah, which had been taken out of the Ark specially for his benefit, and which he had with him in his place. From this, there was read the chapter in Genesis which recounts the story of the marriage of Isaac, accompanied by the Aramaic paraphrase. He then returned to his seat again, bearing his Scroll.

Our present day Simhat Torah institution of the Bridegrooms of the Law and of the Beginning follows so closely upon this nuptial model that it might almost be termed a parody of it. Special hymns are recited in the hero's honour, and he has a special seat reserved for him. Formerly, sweetmeats were showered down upon him as he passed (nowadays, the place of these is taken by a distribution to the children after the Service). When he is called to the Law, a special formula is recited – that delightful, hyperbolical *Mereshut*, which asks the permission of the Almighty, of the Elders, of the Learned, and of the whole Congregation for the formality. This is an almost exact paraphrase of a similar *Mereshut* for the ordinary bridegroom by Rabbi Simeon the Great, formerly recited in the Franco-Jewish communities and found in some old manuscripts, as well as in the Mahzor Vitry (§484). The original has fallen into oblivion, but the parody remains.

The Bridegroom of the Law, like his everyday prototype, goes up bearing his own Scroll, from which a special portion is read. When he returns, according to the Sephardic usage, precisely the same little roundel is chanted as that with which the wedding service was enlivened. A number of other little usages, which we today consider to be typical of the Rejoicing of the Law, are similarly to be traced back to the marriage celebrations on which the ceremonies are based.

CROWNING THE BRIDEGROOM

Some of these have fallen into desuetude in our sophisticated age, for the glories of the Bridegroom of the Law (as of his colleague, the consort of the Book of Genesis) are now, alas! sadly diminished. In former days, for example, when he chanted the concluding portion of the Pentateuch, the silver crown was removed from the Sefer Torah itself and placed upon his head. (It is significant that this procedure was forbidden when an ordinary bridegroom, with a bride of flesh and blood, was in question). Sometimes, as was the case with the Scroll itself, wreaths of myrtle were used for the purpose. It is highly likely, indeed, that the practice of adding a crown to the decorations of the Scroll of the Law (a custom which can be traced back no further than the fourteenth century) owes it origin to the festal usage on the day when the Law was considered a veritable bride and treated as such.

Nowhere, probably, did the Simhat Torah celebrations assume such proportions in former times as in Italy, and especially in Venice. Here the Ghetto, on this day, took on something of the spirit of the secular Carnival. The apostate, Giulio Morosini,[1] writing in the middle of the seventeenth century, goes into picturesque detail in recounting how, on this occasion, the Synagogues were kept open all day and all night. On the eve of the great day, girls and young women used to mask themselves in order not to be recognised, and visited all the Synagogues in turn to see the decorations; while many Christians of every class used to go to the Ghetto as onlookers. During the Service, special hymns were chanted. Meanwhile, some of the congregation endeavoured to supply the want of instrumental music by performing all the motions of musicians to accompany the singing. Once, about 1629, an orchestra was introduced into the Spanish Synagogue for the occasion by the two Hatanim, both devoted lovers of music. In consequence, the press of people, both Jews and Christians, was so great that it was found necessary to summon the police to keep order at the doors. The only instrument cavilled at was the organ, which was ordered to be removed as being too specifically reminiscent of Church usage. The experiment, however, does not seem to have been repeated.

CONTROLLING OSTENTATIOUS FESTIVITY

Rabbinic responsa and similar sources of different lands and different ages supply us with other Simhat Torah usages. In the Middle Ages, it was customary for the children to signalise the occasion by tearing down the Tabernacles used during the previous week, and making a bonfire of the materials. In the Levant, the guests of the Hatanim were sprinkled with scent-sprays. Nearer home, after the invention of gunpowder, salvoes were sometimes fired in honour of the day. As far as Italy is concerned, we may obtain delightfully intimate glimpses from the Sumptuary Laws passed periodically in every community to limit extravagance and ostentation – as rife in those days as in our own. Here, it seems, the wives of the Hatanim were known (not quite logically) as the Bride of the Law and of the Beginning respectively, and received among the women much the same honours as their husbands did among the men. According to the code which was in vogue at Modena, they might not be accompanied to Synagogue by an escort of more than eight ladies, excluding relatives and visitors from other towns. Those of Rome forbade the Kalot to serve any refreshments in the rooms or loggias from which they surveyed the festivities in the Synagogue. Most picturesque of all, though they omit reference to this detail, were the regulations laid down in 1766 at Ancona:

> §xiv. On the evening when the Bridegrooms of the Law (known as Hatan Torah and Hatan Bereshit) are drawn by lot, they may not serve either coffee or sweetmeats or any other species of refreshment. On the evenings when they exercise

their functions, they may be accompanied by six torches only, in addition to the ordinary candle-bearer. Their consorts may be accompanied by only two torches. The latter, when they leave their house and return on the day of Simhat Torah, may be accompanied by only four women. Both on the eve of Simhat Torah and on the day, only coffee and a cake (Pizzola) may be served to the women, and on the evening after Simhat Torah, only coffee both to men and to women. It shall not be permitted to any person to place a candle or torch at his window on this occasion; this shall be permitted only at the house where the function of the Hatan Torah and Hatan Bereshit is being held, and in a single apartment only.

This reference to illuminating the houses, and to a torchlight procession (another distinction shared also by the ordinary bridegroom, as we are informed in this same code), brings us to another forgotten but once invariable Simhat Torah practise. It was the universal custom for the Hatanim to be accompanied to their houses by the Wardens of the Community, with an escort of torch-bearers. Picart's engravings of Jewish life in Amsterdam at the beginning of the eighteenth century comprise one plate which gives a vivid impression of the scene as it was enacted in Northern Europe. Even in England, the same usage prevailed. Lucien Wolf left it on record how, as late as the nineteenth century, the bridegrooms used to be escorted home from Synagogue after the evening Service by a procession of congregants, singing lustily and bearing banners and torches. Nowadays, the faint shadow of this prevails in some places, in the custom of formally ushering the happy pair as far as the door of the Synagogue – but no further.

MR. PEPYS SHOCKED

England, too, appears to have known, at one time (as this record shows), something of the carnival spirit which prevailed on the Continent. Samuel Pepys famously proves it in the classic passage of his Diary for October 13th, 1665:

> After dinner my wife and I, by Mr. Rawlinson's conduct, to the Jewish Synagogue: where the men and boys in their

vayles, and the women behind a lattice out of sight: and some things stand up, which I believe is their law, in a press to which all coming in do bow; and at the putting on their vayles do say something, to which others that hear the Priest do cry Amen, and the party do kiss his vayle. Their service all in a singing way and in Hebrew. And anon their Laws that they take out of the press are carried by several men, four or five several burthens in all, and they do relieve one another; and whether it is that everyone desires to have the carrying of it, thus they carried it round about the room while such a service is singing. And in the end they had a prayer for the King, in which they pronounced his name in Portugal; but the prayer, like the rest, in Hebrew. But Lord! to see the disorder, laughing, sporting, and no attention, but confusion in all their service, more like brutes than people knowing the true God, would make a man foreswear ever seeing them more; and indeed I never did see so much, or could have imagined there had been any religion in the whole world so absurdly performed as this.

It has been pointed out repeatedly that this passage obviously refers to the Rejoicing of the Law, this fact explaining the ebullience of spirit which so unfavourably impressed the diarist. But no one seems hitherto to have noticed that the service to which it alludes is nowadays unknown to the ritual of Bevis Marks, where the *Mincha* on this day is as decorous and as uneventful as on any other Yom-tob afternoon. Plainly, the Community still observed then the old custom, which still prevails at some Sefardi communities in Italy, where the afternoon Service on Simhat Torah is one of the great occasions of the year. The Scrolls of the Law are taken out of the Ark and escorted round the Synagogue to the accompaniment of various hymns chanted to exquisite old-world Spanish tunes, brought with them by the exiles from the Peninsula. (One of the most lovely, by the way, substitutes *Amen, shem nora*, 'Amen, redoubtable Name,' for what obviously read, in the original *Ah! mea senora!*). It is plain from Morosini's account that this same custom had prevailed at Venice in his day, and it is presumable that the London Sephardi congregation modelled itself on the usage of the parent community of the Marrano diaspora in this, as in so much else.

IN THE OLD LONDON SYNAGOGUES

The congregational records provide no inkling as to when the old practice was abandoned. They show plainly, however, the attempt made to prevent extravagance on this occasion. Thus in 1674, 'the Senhores of the Mahamad, considering the tumult and disorder which the decorations made on Simhat Torah...and on Sabbath Bereshit cause, agreed from this day henceforth it be not permitted to the Bridegrooms of the Law to decorate the Synagogue with wreaths of myrtle nor of anything, but it is only allowed them to decorate it with landscape tapestries or gilt leather, as also flowers on the candelabra.' In the Ashkenazic Synagogue in Duke's Place, Simhat Torah received statutory mention in 1735 when the sale by auction of the office of Bridegroom was discontinued, and it was decided to distribute it in future by lot.

In the Western Synagogue of London (established by the Jews of Westminster and its neighbourhood in the middle of the eighteenth century), the Simhat Torah revels must have become a little too riotous at one period, and steps were taken to keep them within moderate limits. Here (we read in the regulations drawn up at the period of the Napoleonic wars) the evening circuits were discontinued 'for the sake of decorum,' and it was expressly laid down that no liveried servants (persons in *livery-malbushim*, is the original phrase!) might participate. Here, too, it was customary to escort the Hatanim home with a torchlight procession. Fortunately the majority of the members lived hard by, in and about Denmark Court; otherwise, the young sparks of the West End might have had a reasonable pretext for hilarity. The torches, it may be mentioned, cost the congregation half-a-crown!

MORE REGIONAL VARIATIONS[2]

There is, indeed, no end to the variety in local rites and usages as far as Simhat Torah is concerned. Half the communities in Italy published their own Rite of Service for the Circuits on the Rejoicing of the Law; five for Ferrara alone lie before me as I write. The great Hayim Joseph David Azulai – eighteenth-century Jerusalem-born traveller, Cabbalist and Bibliophile – laid down detailed mystical prescriptions for the occasion [a copy of which Cecil Roth possessed at the time of writing]. The communities of Cochin, on the Malabar Coast in India, evolved, during their long centuries of isolation from the rest of their brethren, their own characteristic rite for the afternoon service, unlike anything to be found elsewhere and winding up with a special form of *Kaddish*, of unique interest, which stretches over four closely printed pages.

In Avignon and the Comtat Venaissin, a selection of scriptural readings, with their Aramaic paraphrase, was prescribed for recitation in the home on the previous evening, before *Kiddush* – similar in its way to the Passover Haggadah, and indeed sometimes found in the same manuscripts as that better-known work. Hymns recited on the following day are to be found in no other rite.

Not all of the Simhat Torah rites of former days were jolly. The scriptural lesson of the day tells the story of the passing of Moses, and this could not fail to leave its traces in the liturgy. One or two of our Ashkenazi *piyyutim*[3] bear reference to this event. None, however, is so touching as one in the Italian rite:

Jochebed went entreating Egypt
'Egypt, Egypt, have you seen my son Moses?'
'By thy life, Jochebed, we have not seen him
Since the day he slew all my firstborn'...

In some parts they were not content with giving literary expression to their grief, and the ceremonial of the day assumed a definitely melancholy tinge. From a Responsum of the famous Hai Gaon,[4] it appears that in Mesopotamia in the eleventh century it was customary for the congregation to remove the Scroll of the Law from its case on Simhat Torah, in token of grief for the passing of Moses. In the south of France, among the honours of the day were the two *Mekonenim*, or mourners, whose function it was to stand on the reading desk and weep at the death of the great Prophet; and in the liturgy, certain hymns marked 'dirges' are set aside for them to recite.

Nowadays, alas, the Simhat Torah celebration is showing a growing tendency to be restricted to the reading desk. What was once a popular feast tends to become more and more a purely religious celebration. Surely, we have lost more than we have gained. The House of God, is, after all, the House of His children.

'The world subsists only upon the babble of school children's mouths,' says the Talmud. When the school children's babble ceases to be heard in our Synagogues, the world may continue; but our world will have come to its end.

First published in the *Jewish Chronicle*, London, 28 September 1934.

NOTES

1. Salonica-born apostate and missionary (1612–83).
2. And see next chapter.
3. Poetic additions to the liturgy.
4. Scholar of wide culture and authority in his time (939–1038).

12 The Jews who Prayed for the Pope

To collectors of Jewish historical curiosities, there is hardly anything with quite the same appeal as the stories of the romantic Jewries of Avignon and the Comtat Venaissin. The story is one to which I have often referred before. When the Jews were expelled from France in the Middle Ages, they were allowed to remain only in this tiny area in the south of the country, which had come under the rule of the Pope.

The Roman Catholic Church was loath to encourage the Jews, sometimes persecuted them, but never resorted to the last expedient of expelling them. Accordingly, the Jewish community of Avignon, like that of Rome itself, was able to protract its existence undisturbed throughout the Middle Ages. It was here that the glorious traditions of medieval French Jewry, of Rashi and of Levi ben Gershom, were, albeit faintly, perpetuated, cut off almost entirely from the rest of the Jewish world. Thus the region produced its own distinctive Jewish culture, with its own *patois*, its own style of synagogue architecture, its own fashion of pronouncing Hebrew, its own traditions, its own folk lore, its own style of calligraphy, and above all, its own rite of prayers.

This rite continued for many long centuries to be copied by hand, simply by reason of the paucity in numbers of those who followed it. It was published only in the eighteenth century, but the printed copies are now even more rare than those in manuscript.

These Four Holy Communities, as they were called (of Avignon, Carpentras, Cavaillon, and Lisle), survived the persecution of ages until, at last, they succumbed to the toleration of the nineteenth century. Nowadays a shadowy congregation still exists in the first-named city, the rest are dead beyond the hope of recall. Yet I am personally romantic enough, on the occasion of the Jewish festivals, to take up my copy of the liturgy which they once practised, and to glance at the prayers and hymns composed by their local poets, redolent with memories of the ancient City of the Popes.

The hymns and other special prayers of this rite are quite unique, to be found nowhere else in the world. On festival days, for instance, before the scrolls of the law were put back into the Ark, an extremely elaborate form of prayer was recited on behalf of the governing civil power. Inasmuch as this region was under the rule of the Popes down to the period of the French Revolution (that, indeed, is why the Jews were allowed to remain there), one amazingly finds in the old prayer-books a special and extraordinarily elaborate *haNoten Teshua* which was recited enthusiastically by the Congregational Reader on behalf of His Holiness, the Pope:

> May He who gives salvation unto Kings ... in His mercy exalt, raise, and uplift higher and higher our Lord the Pope ... May the Living God magnify his throne, that they may say in every land and city: 'May our Lord, Pope ... live for ever!'

At Passover, my attention is attracted above all by one feature which is to be found in no other branch of the Jewish liturgy – special formulas and poems to be recited on the *Yom haHasger* – 'The Day of Shutting In'.

The significance of this is a little difficult to trace, if one confines oneself to the allied Hebrew sources. A glance at the prevailing conditions, on the other hand, provides the clue. It very frequently happens that Passover coincides almost exactly with Easter.

In former times this was, for the Jew, a period of horror. It was the season of the Crucifixion, when every Christian hooligan considered it his duty to avenge the Passion of Jesus upon the arch-unbeliever. In the Middle Ages, throughout Europe – in places as far afield as Beziers in south France and the island of Corfu in the Adriatic – it was the practice for the populace, or even of Government officials, to stone the Jews publicly in the streets. At Toulouse, when the Count left the Cathedral after service on Good Friday, the oldest or most respected member of the Jewish community had to present himself before him and submit to the indignity of receiving a box on the ear – a formality which on one occasion at least, in 1018, ended fatally.

Ultimately, the practice grew up of accentuating the Jew's inferiority by forbidding him to be seen outside his own quarter during the Easter period, when the popular passions were at their height. The regulations of the Jews in Venice, as late as 1777, specify this in unequivocal terms:

> §74. *The whole of Holy Thursday, from sunrise, up to the service of Nones on Holy Saturday, the Jews shall be compelled to remain closed up in their Ghetto...*

The same regulations applied elsewhere in the Catholic world. But nowhere were they enforced more severely than in the Papal possessions, particularly in Avignon and the Comtat Venaissin.

The occasion thus became deeply embedded in their consciousness. They called it the *Yom HaHasger* – the Day of Shutting In – and, when (as so often) it corresponded with Passover, they recited special hymns in the synagogue, composed by local poets in allusion to the occasion. Thus, for the morning service on the second day of Passover, we find an alternative hymn for Nishmat, for 'The Day of Shutting In':

> *The soul of him who is suppressed and repressed, shalt Thou heal with Thy word.*
> *On the day when he hides from fear of the people who betrays His secret,*
> *'Stoning him with stones, and covering him with dust.'*
> *The soul of him who moans in his captivity, awaiting his freedom, shalt Thou heal with Thy word.*
> *On the day when justice is distant from His holy ones,*
> *'When any who ventures from the door of his house, his blood is on his head'...*

On the following day, when the period of incarceration ended, a similar hymn was interpolated (to be found printed in the morning service for the Intermediate Sabbath), similarly referring to conditions which prevailed upon that day:

The soul *of those pressed and persecuted, who have come forth to call upon Thy name*, will glorify Thee.

> *For the honour of Thy name were they set in dungeon,*
> *'And concealed in a prison house.'*
> *The soul of the troubled remnant who could not raise their head*, will praise Thee.
> *This day they have come forth to plead for their soul,*
> *'From the holes wherein they were concealed.'*

The most interesting of all these compositions is one which is printed as an alternative hymn for 'The Day of Shutting In,' in the morning service on the second day of Passover. Psychologically, it is an extraordinary production.

Their neighbors shut the Jews up in their ghetto at this period as a sign of contumely and disgrace. The latter regarded it, instead, as a high distinction! I have endeavoured to render the hymn in which this conception is expressed, in verse:

Like a Princess set away
In her Palace on this day,
Hidden like a lovely maid,
Thus her prayer 'fore God she laid
(He Whose spirit, wondrous wise,
All that Liveth vivifies):
'Rouse Thee, at this spring-tide feast,
Till our servitude hath ceased!'

First published in the *Jewish Chronicle*, London, 3 April 1936, p. 32.

13 Old Time Hanukkah

The Feast of Hanukkah is perhaps the only minor celebration of the Jewish year which has maintained, or even enhanced, its position in the last two or three generations. The reason for this lies partly in its martial appeal (which nineteenth-century jingoism found so sympathetic), but to an even greater extent in its calendrical position, which so closely approximates to Christmas. It has accordingly tended to take on something of the complexion of the latter, with Hanukkah presents and Hanukkah trees and Hanukkah puddings and even (in a few ultra-British households) an evanescent but generous appearance of Old Father Hanukkah.

A witty German cartoonist, indeed, once showed the gradual evolution from an eight-branched Hanukkah lamp to an equally multi-branched Christmas Tree!

In the old days, however, Hanukkah had its own independent importance and its own essentially Jewish celebrations. It is worth while gathering together a few of these, before they are altogether lost under the dust of years.

The traditional Hanukkah possessed none of the careless license of Purim, which, closely approximating as it did to the Catholic Carnival, took on a good many of its characteristics. The diversions indulged in tended to be more intellectual (an aspect ruled out of court on Purim itself by the reason of the low degree of sobriety which that day imposed). Hence it was only on Hanukkah and the middle days of the Festivals, that the sterner rabbis of the Middle Ages permitted gambling and card playing – and even so only on condition that there were no money stakes. Not, of course, that this latter condition was complied with implicitly. Card parties on Hanukkah seem to have been one of the features of the Italian Ghetto; and that prodigal prodigy, Leone Da Modena,[1] recounts how he started his ruinous gambling career on the Hanukkah of 1594 by losing one hundred ducats.

Women were prohibited from sewing or doing any other

household work while the Hanukkah lights were burning; and it was plainly necessary to find them some other way of occupying their minds – if only to forestall Satan. Hanukkah was, moreover, the traditional occasion for parlor games. The best known, of course, was the Hanukkah *Trendel*. This is in fact none other than the Jewish grandmother of 'Put and Take' (which Herr Hitler should therefore banish from German homes). The *Trendel* itself (from the German *dreden*) is a little top, with four sides, each bearing the initials of the Hebrew N.G.H.S.

For the purpose of the game, they are read as Yiddish – *nichts* (nothing), *ganz* (all), *halb* (half), and *stell* (put); and the players are expected to act accordingly.

While the children were playing with their *Trendel*, the parents would amuse themselves in a staider fashion. Hanukkah was especially associated with riddles and enigmas – many of them in the form of acrostics turning on the name of the feast. Very frequently, these (the so called *Hanukkah Ketowaus*) were arithmetical in character, and assisted in giving the Jew that mathematical mind which was afterwards to be turned to such good account on the Stock Exchange. Very large numbers of these have survived, in printed or manuscript form.

Some of the most ingenious were written by Rabbi Abraham ibn Ezra,[2] that wandering, restless, versatile genius. We can picture him, if we please, in Joseph de Mandeville's house in the Old Jewry in London, in the winter of 1168, composing one after the other of these for the diversion of his host's family. And can it have been in London that he wrote his rollicking Hanukkah tablesong, with its still more rollicking tune?:

> Your chattels and your lands,
> Go and pledge, go and sell!
> Put money in your hands,
> To feast Hanukkah well.
> > (This version is by the late Dr Israel Abrahams.)

One completely forgotten characteristic of the feast is associated with the Scroll of Antiochus. The medieval Jew was a little distressed at the fact that, since Hanukkah is a post-Biblical celebration (post Old Testament, that is; it is of course mentioned in John x. 22), there was nothing Scriptural to recite upon it. Accordingly, an extremely apocryphal work upon the origins of the feast, based upon I Maccabees and other ancient sources, was widely read upon the day.

It is obviously written upon the model of the Scroll of Esther, beginning with an exaggerated account of the grandeur and atrocities of Antiochus, and it was therefore called 'The Scroll of Antiochus'. In the Middle Ages it was elevated almost to semi-canonicity. It was sometimes written in Megillah form; it was included in various liturgical manuscripts; it was recited publicly upon the feast, with the statutory benedictions before and after.

In the Spanish Bibles printed at Amsterdam for the benefit of the Marranos, who always desired Scriptural authority for every practice, the Scroll of Antiochus sometimes figures by way of appendix. As a matter of fact, though mentioned with deference by Saadiah and other eminent authorities, it is obviously a late compilation of no historical value. There is no need to bewail the fact that (though still to be found in a few antiquated editions of the prayer book) it has now passed into oblivion.

The central feature of the Hanukkah celebration was, of course, the kindling of the lights in their special lamp. This constitutes one of the favourite categories of Jewish ritual art. They are to be seen in all materials. In the Middle Ages, the very poor used egg-shells for the purpose, just as the later Polish *yeshiva-bachur*[3] would use potatoes.

An eight-wicked earthenware lamp, which may or may not have been made for this feast, has been found in the course of excavations at Jerusalem. Excepting for this, perhaps the oldest known is that in the Musée de Cluny in Paris, which was discovered in Lyons and is attributed to the twelfth century. There is, of course, no limit as to materials. They are to be found in soapstone, wood, copper, brass, silver, perhaps even gold. Some splendid examples were made in pewter. Perhaps the finest of these is one formerly in the Howitt Collection, in which the lights are laid in a trough ingeniously drained into two hanging buckets through the mouths of dolphins. One of the treasures of the A.E. Franklin collection is one adapted from a reliquary which is said to have belonged to Queen Elizabeth the First. This is of imposing dimensions, though not quite so imposing as the magnificent five-foot candelabrum from the Hambro Synagogue, of early eighteenth century English workmanship, which now adorns the Jewish Museum, London.

At the other end of the scale, the Jewish Museum possesses one bijou Dutch specimen in silver, obviously made by some fond father for his daughter's dolls-house.

The motifs for the decoration were extremely catholic. Lions and eagles and mythical beasts and Aaron the Priest all figure promiscuously. Very frequently, the wicks were made to come out of lions' mouths. A few specimens exist (the present writer has seen more than one, so the phenomena cannot be accidental) in which the main decoration of the back piece is constituted by the coat-of-arms of a sixteenth-century cardinal, complete with broadrimmed hat! On another sequence, there is somewhat mysteriously a group depicting the angels' visit to the Patriarch Abraham, announcing the birth of Isaac.

The examples given above are sufficient to make it plain that in spite of traditional prejudices, there was no reluctance to adorn the Hanukkah Lamp with representations of the human figure.

In addition to the eight burners, of course, there was an additional provision for the shamash or master light, from which the others were kindled. This, however, was not absolutely requisite, and is often missing from Oriental specimens. In compensation, many Eastern European examples (manufactured according to Hasidic prescriptions) secure symmetry by having two of these, one on either side.

The traditional Hanukkah dishes – unlike those of other festivities – were not peculiarly exciting. It was customary in many places, however, to eat milk and cheese foods. This was in memory of the triumph of Judith, who used this diet to make Holophernes doze when she visited his tent. For, without historical authority, Judith and her achievement were traditionally connected with Hanukkah; and she figures in the decoration of many ancient Hanukkah lamps, exultantly bearing the head of her enemy. It was because of the legendary association of this heroine with the feast that women were so closely associated with its celebration, being empowered to kindle the lights on behalf of absent husbands or in any case, obliged to witness the ceremony.

In some strict households, every member of the family had his own lamp for the occasion. It was supposed to be placed in such a manner as to be visible from without, in order to render the celebration as public as possible. One may imagine what a blaze of light and glory the old *Judengasse* presented towards the close of the feast, when the illuminations were reaching their maximum!

There was one other characteristic feature of the celebrations in the Ghetto. Hanukkah fell in mid-winter when the icy winds were beginning to find thin patches in the clothing of the lower classes. Accordingly, one day of the festival (in Italy, at least) was set apart for collecting clothing on behalf of the poor children (and poor teachers, too!) in the Congregational schools. The Rabbi delivered a special sermon – several specimens are to be found in the old homiletical collections – and the faithful were expected to do the rest. The Synagogue on these occasions must have presented a curious spectacle, for it was festooned all around the walls with the boots and clothing which the charitably inclined had brought as their contribution. Hardly as decorative, perhaps as the Harvest Home, yet in its way more beautiful by far.

First published in the *Jewish Chronicle*, London, 22 December 1933.

NOTES

1. Venetian-born (1531–1648) Hebrew scholar, poet, gambler, and prominent personality in the Venetian ghetto music academy.
2. Spanish-born (1093–1167) Hebrew grammarian, poet, biblical commentator, traveller, and a recognised authority on Arabic as well as Jewish culture.
3. Talmudic college student.

14 The New Year for Trees

'There are four New Years,' asserts the Mishnah, in a passage the more familiar since it was so often used for beginners to cut their wisdom teeth. It goes on to enumerate them.

On the first of *Nisan*, kings began their regnal years, and from that date, the festivals were computed. On the first of *Ellul*, animal tithes began to be reckoned. The first of *Tishri*, marked (as it still marks) the beginning of the religious year, and on the fifteenth of *Shevat* (the first of that month, according to the School of Shammai) was the New Year for Trees. It does not appear that when they made this last statement the Rabbis had anything particularly romantic in mind. All that they probably meant was that this date was fixed for settling the tithes of fruits, everything before that day being included in the previous year.

But the Jew has a remarkable faculty for infusing the most arid legal detail with the breath of poetry, and in the course of time, imaginative detail began to cluster round the occasion. Now, it was imagined, the sap first began to stir in the boughs after the long winter pause, so that in very truth, it was the trees' New Year.

When Israel was divorced from his land, and indeed from every other, there was little opportunity to appreciate the beauties of nature and of the observances bound up with it. In the sixteenth century, however, a new spirit was engendered among the Cabbalists who had made their home in the Holy City of Safed, and it soon swept the four corners of the Jewish world. In some respects, there can be little doubt that this all-pervading mystical tendency was distinctly harmful, yet even now it is sufficiently appreciated how the Sages of Safed reimbued many arid aspects of Jewish life and observance with a new poetry. The New Year for Trees seemed to them an admirable opportunity for insisting upon the especial significance of the traditional fruits of Palestine – fig, grape, pomegranate, date, and olive. In honour of this day, it was enjoined, all these varieties, at the least, should be eaten with the appropriate blessings, and various readings were specified to be recited between one species and another.

Thus, in the course of time a whole elaborate ritual became evolved, which the curious may find in a little pamphlet entitled *Peri Ez Hadar* of 'The Fruit of a Goodly Tree' (first published in Venice in 1762). First came selections from the Pentateuch and prophets and psalms, referring to the marvels of nature; then readings from the mystical classic, the Zohar; and finally, prayers specially written for the occasion. After this, course after course of fruit was eaten (seventeen in all), each with the appropriate benediction and reading.

Thus a new and highly picturesque minor festival was added to the Jewish calendar, and the murky Ghetto synagogues were reminded once again, as on Pentecost and Tabernacles, of the beauties of the world as God created it.

This ritual has continued to be observed to our own days, in many parts of the Orient. At the very least, every householder would make a special effort to obtain the Five Fruits of Palestine, the eating of which would be preceded by the *Shehecheyanu* benediction recited on special occasions. The schools, too, would be granted a holiday, and there would be trifling changes in the liturgy. In western Europe, on the other hand, the usual uniformalizing process which has robbed Jewish life of so much that was picturesque, on the ground that it is superfluous, was followed, and the Jewish schoolboy knew of the New Year for Trees only as an additional date to be remembered in the Jewish calendar, memorable only for the fact that a doleful passage was omitted in its honour from the morning service.

Without discussing the merits and demerits of Zionism (and it is rumoured that it has its supply of both), it may be asserted without fear of contradiction that the new generation in Palestine has shown a remarkable faculty for revitalizing old observances. Hanukkah, under its aegis, has become once more a really national feast. The reputation of the Purim Carnival at Tel-Aviv is now worldwide.

It could not be expected that a generation which has once more come into contact with the soil should have neglected the potentialities of that one traditional observance that is more associated with nature than any other. Accordingly, the New Year for Trees has taken on, in Jewish Palestine, a completely new aspect. There is evidence that even in Talmudic times the day was observed as one for the plantation of new trees. We find Rabbi Judah the Prince planting a 'plant of joy' at this season of the year, though not indeed on this particular day, and it is known that it was formerly customary to plant a cedar tree for every new-born male and a cypress for every girl, the boughs being used to support the nuptial canopy on the occasion of their wedding. It is this side of the *Rosh haShanah leIlanot* (New Year for Trees) which has been seized upon and developed. Is not the greatest curse of Palestine its treelessness, due to the wanton destruction and progressive neglect under Romans, Byzantines, Arabs and finally Turks? And is not one of the greatest benefits which Jewish effort has conferred upon the country the work of reafforestation – for the benefit not of one section of the population only, but of the land as a whole?

What more natural, then, to associate this work preeminently with the New Year for Trees, apparently bound up with something similar in remotest times, and one of the occasions of the Jewish year which, in the long nightmare of the *Galut*, served to keep alive in the Jew the recollection of his ancestral home and of nature?

Accordingly, a new era in the observance of *Rosh haShanah leIlanot* has dawned in Palestine. On this day it is that the great works of afforestation are commenced, whenever possible. Moreover, every Jewish inhabitant (especially, of course, the Jewish child) considers it to be his duty to plant on that day at least one tree with his own hands, and all over the country it is possible to see processions and groups and individuals performing this sacred yet beloved duty.

Not all, perhaps, will live to see the saplings they have planted grow to maturity, yet like the old man in the Talmudic legend, they are happy to know that their posterity will enjoy the fruit of their hands. Benjamin Disraeli seems to have grasped the essence of the question. 'The vineyards of Israel have ceased to exist,' he wrote, 'but the eternal Law enjoins the Children of Israel still to celebrate the vintage. *A race that persists to celebrate their vintage, although they have no fruits to gather, will regain their vineyards.*' (*Tancred*, 1847.)

First published in *American Hebrew*, New York, 18 January 1935.

15 How Jews Once Commemorated Purim

THE LORD OF MISRULE

In medieval Europe, it was formerly the custom that every year at Christmastide, the master of every house, from the royal palace downwards, should abdicate for a brief space. His place was taken by one of his own servants – generally, the one with the shrewdest wit and greatest love of pranks – who, for a time was (within certain limits) the master of the household. He had the power to do whatever he pleased. The Christmas revels were completely in his hands, and the more daring his sallies, the greater the roars of laughter which greeted them. Even his lord and master had to do exactly as he bade. Only when the festive period was over, and all had returned to its normal state, might the knave be called to account for any over-hazardous remarks and sent to think over them in the solitude of the castle's deepest dungeon. This, in brief outline, is the story of the institution of the Lord (sometimes called the Abbot, or else the Master) of Misrule, of which those interested may find fuller accounts in all the standard histories of social life in the Middle Ages.

Jewish romantics, reading these picturesque accounts of the European scene seven centuries ago, sigh at their own drabber heritage and regret that Jewish life lacked this colour. But they are wrong. The reason why this impression has got about, to our deep loss, is that short-sighted reformers of a previous generation deliberately – on the grounds that it was 'indecorous' or 'foreign' – shed much of that which in Jewish life was most colourful. The institution of the Lord of Misrule was, as a matter of fact, as well-known in Jewish life as in secular life, in the Middle Ages and after. The only difference was that, whereas the general population associated the institution with Christmas, the Jews (as was natural), observed it in connection with their own great season of merrymaking – Purim.

THE PURIM KING

This institution, in Jewish life, went by the name of the Purim King, and it appears to have flourished especially in Provence, with a weak reflection in Italy. A good part of the information which we have concerning it comes from the daring parody of a Talmudic treatise, known as the *Megillat Setarim*. This was compiled as a Purim diversion by that profound philosopher and daring exegete, Rabbi Levi ben Gershom,[1] whose perfected astrolabe was not without its importance for the discoveries of Christopher Columbus. Every city wherein ten Jewish households were to be found, we are gravely informed by this erudite humorist, had incumbent upon it the obligation to appoint a Purim King. On the first day of Adar (a fortnight, that is, before the great anniversary) he summoned all his fellow citizens together for a feast. At its close, he handed over his staff of authority to another, who had to arrange a second feast as soon as possible. This continued until the sixteenth day of Adar, when all re-assembled in the Purim King's house for a farewell celebration.

Another satirical source, the *Massekhet Purim*, informs us that every Jewish community elected its Purim King a month before the feast and invested him with plenary power over the lives and property of his temporary subjects – precisely in the same manner as the Christmas Lord of Misrule. Elsewhere we learn that the temporary potentate had to entertain his fellow-citizens with music, and to provide them with ample liquor, during his period of office. Uproariously funny is a contemporary series of Rules and Regulations (*Haskamot*) relating to the institution. This opens with the solemn declaration that the Purim King, as ruler of the Vineyard, was to be regarded as the supreme potentate of potentates. It goes on to stipulate that he should administer a solemn oath to all lesser dignitaries than himself to observe the laws of the Prophet Bakbuk (bottle!). Other sections deal with the various fines and assessments imposed on the community for the King's maintenance.

The institution of the Purim took on a slightly different form from that in Provence and Italy. Learning, here, was more highly respected than temporal authority, and the Purim Ruler therefore supplanted those who had authority by reason of scholarship, rather than of might. This had its non-Jewish counterpart. We know, in Northern Europe, of the Boy Bishop – one of the choristers who was elected each year on the Feast of St. Nicholas (or Santa Claus, December 6th). Dressed in Bishop's robes, he exercised mock jurisdiction for three weeks, until Holy Innocents' Day (December 28th), holding plenary authority in school and choir and cloister.

In the medieval German-Jewish communities, this institution was copied almost exactly. We read, for example, in the Customary (Minhagbuch) of Worms, written by the egregious Juspa the Shamash, how on Friday evening after Purim all the students went to a house some distance from the Synagogue where they dressed up in mock state. Thence they returned to the Synagogue in procession, headed by the Treasurers of the Community, each bearing a painted wand. In front of them pranced a youth who went by the name of *Knell the Gabbai*, wearing the clothes of a jester, pirouetting about in the approved fashion and generally 'playing the fool' (in the original sense of that term). In the Synagogue, they stormed the reading desk, dispossessed those who usually had their seats there, and generally took charge of the proceedings. In the course of the Service they left their seats, circumambulated the building, and stormed the women's gallery on the pretext of receiving the blessing of the Rabbi's spouse.

DRINKING AND MERRIMENT

During the Morning Service on the following day, the students once again assumed control. They monopolised, willy nilly, all the *mitzvot*, which they distributed among themselves, and any householder who for some reason particularly desired to be summoned to the Reading of the Law had to pay them a fine – generally in measures of wine, arbitrarily assessed in accordance with the victim's reputed means. On the following days, special banquets were arranged for the students by well-to-do members of the Community, and the accumulation of wine was drunk. It was customary, we are informed, for the students to sew a cockade on their hats on the occasion of the feast, and not to remove it so long as any wine remained in the common store. The foregoing account is based upon the official Usages of the Community. One can only imagine what gloriously riotous excesses sometimes took place in practice.

This custom, formerly, no doubt observed with local modifications all over Germany, was allowed in Poland down to the present day. Here, in the Talmudical schools (Yeshivot), where throughout the year the sacred folios are studied a little too unremittingly, Purim sees a reaction. The students chose a Purim Rabbi among themselves and it became his special function to mimic the teachers – even the venerated Rosh Yeshiva, or Head of the Academy, himself. [This, then, is my suggestion to those romantics who deplore the disappearance from contemporary life of picturesque detail, such as the institution of the Boy Bishop. Go to the Yeshivot of Poland, and there, year by year at the Purim feast, you will see his functions reproduced much as in medieval Europe, though whether you will think it quite so picturesque when you see it is another question.]

First published in the *Jewish Chronicle*, London, 15 March 1935.

NOTE

1. Known as Gersonides (1288–1344). Provence-born polymath.

16 Down With Haman!

NOISY ENTHUSIASM OF YEARS AGO

When men attend Synagogue every day, or even every week, they have the right to be boisterous in the place of worship once or twice a year. So, at least, our fathers thought. Hence, the vocal and even terpsichorean jubilation which once marked the Rejoicing the Law; hence, too, the noisy disapproval of the villain of the piece which once marked the reading of the *Megillah* on Purim. At every mention of Haman or of his family (and there are many in that miniature masterpiece), desks were banged, feet were stamped, rattles were whirled, and the general atmosphere became rather like that of a particularly boisterous gallery-crowd at the close of a singularly unfortunate First Night.

Many centuries ago, an attempt was made to rationalise, and hence by inference palliate, this practice. In thirteenth-century France and Provence, we are informed, it was customary for the children on Purim eve to take smooth stones and write the name of Haman on them. When the execrated name was mentioned in the *Megillah*, they would bang them together and obliterate the writing, fulfilling thus the injunction to 'blot out' the name of Amalek (the ancestor of Haman, as all the world knows). As time went on, the formality was modified but the banging still continued. Leone da Modena, describing seventeenth-century Venice, informs us that 'while this book is being read, there are some that, as often as they hear Haman named, they beat the ground and make a great murmuring noise in token of cursing him and execrating his memory.' In Eastern Europe, where such matters were taken seriously, the cacophony was organised and special rattles like those formerly used by watchmen (named *gregars*) were manufactured for the purpose of producing the maximum of noise with the minimum of effort.

But the original idea still prevailed in some circles. Thus, in the Levant it was customary to write the name of Haman in chalk on the soles of the shoes and to obliterate it scientifically, by stamping at the prescribed intervals on the floor. Others, more decorously, would scribble the name every now and again on a scrap of paper and rub it out with an indiarubber when the time arrived, or else wash it out with water on returning home. A picture of the Amsterdam Synagogue, published in 1731, would lead one to imagine that the primitive method of systematically pounding an inscribed stone still prevailed there so late. But an examination of the other details serves to indicate that the artist had probably never attended a Purim Service, and his drawing is the product of a lively imagination fed by misguided study.

DECORUM INTERVENES

The reader is earnestly entreated not to imagine that this account is a mere antiquarian diversion. 'Haman-klapping' sometimes attained a considerable importance in communal politics, leading to quarrelling, schisms and even secessions. As the Synagogue became more Westernised, it was thought desirable to make the standard of conduct approximate, even on exceptional occasions such as Purim, to what the environment expected of a place of worship. Hence, at intervals all over Europe the communal magnates passed regulations forbidding the traditional practice. One day, about the year of Waterloo, the Shammas of the Hambro' Synagogue in London was instructed to make a proclamation to that effect. What the result was, history fails to record. But in other places it led to more turmoil than it prevented. In Bordeaux, for example, during the reign of Louis Phillipe (1830–48) it was found necessary to appeal to the gendarmerie to assist in carrying out the new regulations.

But London cannot afford to sneer at this, for there was no other place where the consequences were quite so serious. In March, 1783, the *Mahamad* of the Spanish and Portuguese community issued strict orders enjoining the observance of the most complete decorum during the reading of the *Megillah* on the forthcoming Purim. When the night came, a vociferous minority persisted in carrying out the time-honoured (or dishonoured) custom. The gentlemen of the Mahamad would not be thwarted, and next morning a couple of constables were present who removed the delinquents, upon some of whom a pecuniary fine was subsequently inflicted.

There was one pillar of misplaced orthodoxy, however, who refused to pay. This was Mr. Isaac Mendes Furtado, who not only declined to appear before the *Mahamad*, but sent them a scurrilous letter upbraiding them soundly for their recent action. He had been disturbed in his devotions, he said, by the entry into the Synagogue of the constables, who (and not the rioters) had outraged his feelings. He could not countenance a step tending towards the disruption of the time-honoured traditions of Judaism, and he would no longer be associated with so irreligious a body. Accordingly, he withdrew from the Congregation. Some time after, he had his children baptised, and in memory of this grotesque episode he erected in Mile End Road a terrace of houses which he called 'Purim Place,' and which until recently survived under the same name, to remind the world of the misguided zeal of the hero of this most extravagant Purimspiel.

First published in the *Jewish Chronicle*, London, 19 February 1937.

17 A Purim Habdala

Purim had always formed a welcome interlude in the somewhat solemn round of Jewish life, and amid the constant cares and fears of the Ghetto, this season of joy was appreciated to an extent which we can now hardly realize. But the reaction was not, as so many would have us believe, in the direction of physical indulgence only; the intellectual world no less enjoyed a relaxation from the serious studies of all the year round. And so a whole literature of parodies came into being, written with a rich humour, though at times with a freedom which seems to us excessive.

Nothing was held too sacred for travesty. The Talmud itself was made to yield a new tractate, *Massechet Purim*, all complete with the *Rashi* and *Tosafot* commentaries, in which Rabbinic dialectic was mimicked with a skill possible only for men who had serious acquaintance with the original. Thus it was shown that Noah alone, out of all the Patriarchs, was chosen for mention in the Megillah (see Esther ix., 17, Hebrew text!) and his convivial habits are suggested as the reason for this high privilege. The Passover Haggadah was followed, paragraph by paragraph, by another for Purim, which commences with the solemn rubric, 'Here pour out the ninth glass.'

Even the liturgical poetry of the Synagogue did not escape. In one parody, one hardly realizes that the selection being read is not one of the authentic evening hymns for the Passover until one notices, almost with a start, that the refrain is not *Lel Shimmurim*, Night of Watching, but *Lel Shikkurim*, Night of Drinking.

The translation that follows is of a parody of the well-known *Hammavdil* for the termination of the Sabbath. In line 2 of the second verse, reference should be made to Genesis xxxii, 5.

May He, who Purim set away
For joy from Kippur's solemn day,
Smile on us roysterers so gay
    Who raise our cries at night-time.

I've gazed on wine when it was red,
And from the white turn not my head,
And look on Pussyfoots with dread,
   E'en as the stars of night-time.

Tears from my eyes have never cased
Since I saw water at the feast.
Bring twenty flagons, at the least!
   Perchance they'll last this night-time.

O, how we'd bless your name, dear friend,
If wines to fill the cup you send,
And flowing goblets without end.
   I may be drunk this night-time.

A Hallowing prepare to hear:
Ye sage of heart, incline your ear.
All water from your houses clear.
   It has no place this night-time.

Be strong, wise sirs, to play your part
For Noah's sake, the pure of heart.
Who first did viticulture start,
   And drank day and night-time.

First published in the *Jewish Guardian*, London, 18 March 1921.

18 An Avignoese Purim

It was the pious custom of our fathers to perpetuate the recollection of any especially noteworthy episode in their history by introducing a fresh commemoration into their religious calendar. Many of these, perforce, were fasts, intended to keep alive the memory of some outstanding disaster – usually a massacre or some such sinister event. Yet even persecution sometimes had its compensations and so there was frequently cause to institute a special local feast – a minor Purim, as it would generally be called – in gratitude for some deliverance. Almost all of the more important of the ancient Jewish communities had more than one such annual celebration, sometimes with its own *Megillah*, read solemnly upon the anniversary, like the original Scroll of Esther. Lists of these local Purims have been published, but their number is in fact so great that even the most detailed of these accounts is woefully defective.

One of the branches of the House of Israel which tended to indulge most of all in this practice was the exiguous remnant (of the tribe of Benjamin, as it boasted) which continued a truncated existence till our own days in the Papal possessions in the south of France. Here, on these festive occasions, not only were special hymns by the local poetasters recited, but it was customary actually to interpolate a passage of thanksgiving into the *Amidah* itself and to read an apposite section out of the scroll of the Law.

Even in little Cavaillon, where a beautiful old synagogue is all that now remains to show the sometime existence of a congregation, two such celebrations existed. On Iyyar 25, they annually recalled, with gratitude, their deliverance from the plague by having made a timely exodus from the city in 5391 (May 27, 1631), and on Sivan 29 they feasted the anniversary of an accusation of ritual murder which had providentially failed its purpose in 5473 (May 31, 1713).

Carpentras, its greater neighbour, was naturally more prolific of memories which had intertwined themselves in its religious life. No less than three times each year (including the seventh day of

Passover, traditional anniversary of the overthrow of Pharaoh in the Red Sea), they jubilantly celebrated the failure of popular *emeutes* directed against their fathers.

All of these strange local Purims are recorded in the local liturgies, with full directions for their observance. But the most curious commemoration of all, which can assuredly have no parallel elsewhere, was one which took place year by year at Avignon, the principal city of the region.

Late on a night in February, 1757 (Shevat 28, 5517), a certain person – a Gentile – happened to be making his way through the narrow courts of the *carriere* of the city (it was thus that the Ghetto was locally called). It was a dark night, for the New Moon was approaching, but nevertheless, he had neglected to provide himself with a lantern, and the Jews were no more advanced in their ideas of street illumination than their fellow townsfolk.

Near the synagogue was a deep well, watched as we know with great anxiety at any period of flood, and this unfortunate individual apparently tripped over the coping and was precipitated into it. According to the account which he afterwards gave, he fell head first, but before he reached the bottom he somehow recovered his equilibrium! In any case, just as he arrived at the narrowest point, he had the presence of mind to throw out his legs, so that his fall was arrested. Hearing his cries, the Jews of the vicinity rushed out of their houses and in the nick of time discovered what was the matter. They would not trust to the strength of the cord which served for the bucket. Instead they knotted together a couple of ropes, which they let down the well. By this means, the person was extricated, little the worse for his adventure.

On that day, the Jews of Avignon declared a public feast, to be celebrated year by year throughout their generations. All shops in the *carriere* were to be closed, and no business whatsoever was to be transacted, just as on a major holiday. And in the synagogal service, they inserted a prayer of thanksgiving, specially composed for the occasion, which was subsequently printed in the curious local liturgy, the *Seder haTamid*. Their celebration was confirmed in the *Statutes of the Jews of Avignon*, which received the sanction of the Papal representative in 1779. It continued in force, as is to be imagined, at least until the French Revolution brought the local communities freedom after so many centuries of oppression, and probably for some time after.

At first glance, it is difficult to understand why such commotion should have been caused by so simple an affair. The person in question was obviously of no great consequence – it was not considered worth while even to record his name. The celebration, however, was not for *his* deliverance, but for that of the community. For – argued the unhappy Jews – had this clumsy Gentile perished and his corpse been found so near our Synagogue, we would inevitably have been accused of doing him to death and would assuredly have suffered for the crime. His providential escape possibly saved us all from massacre!

There is perhaps no other document in the whole of Jewish literature, historical or otherwise, which is so eloquent of the constant fear in which the people of the Ghetto lived. It seems an exaggerated fulfillment of even the terrible prophecy of Moses: 'And the sound of a driven leaf shall chase them.' Amongst all of these old-time local festivities, there is none which should make a stronger appeal to our own generation. We, ourselves, may well feel thankful on the 28th Shevat each year, not at the escape of this anonymous Avignonese but at the fact that we are no longer living in an age when an accident similar to his might well have brought about the destruction of a whole community.

First published in the *Jewish Guardian*, London, 1 February 1933.

NOTE

1. The author refers to the Jewish New Moon, whose onset coincides with the first visible appearance of the newborn moon, and not to the secular New Moon, which begins when the moon in its monthly cycle enters upon its non-visible stage. Thus, during the secular New Moon the nights would be dark when the New Moon had just begun, but not while it was still approaching.

19 The Madonna of the Scroll

When you visit Sienna, you will of course inspect the synagogue. It lies in the very center of the town, just behind the magnificent old Palazzo Pubblico, in a narrow medieval street. Not much imagination is needed to see in this street the ancient Ghetto, and indeed it is not long since these courts, now almost abandoned, were throbbing with an intense Jewish life. Around this well – adorned with a statue until certain Polish pietists raised objections to this breach of the second commandment – the women sat and gossiped while the men prayed and studied and worked and quarrelled, and sometimes, according to that semi-illiterate seventeenth-century huckster-historian, Guiseppa da Modena – who, since he was foremost in every row that took place in the Ghetto, should know – came to blows.

The Synagogue itself, you will be told by experts, dates back almost to the foundation of the community, to the fourteenth century. But it was restored about 1770, when all the poetasters in Italy combined in a volume of hymns that were recited on the occasion of its rededication. The interior is a trifle ornate, though not without a certain dignity.

But your eyes will be drawn by the Ark of the Law, with its heavily ornamented bronze doors. For the slender veneer of gilt with which the bronze is overlaid cannot hide the dents and gashes which cover their whole surface – the marks of axes once used to break into the sanctuary. Used so ruthlessly that perfect restoration has become impossible; indeed, the eye of credulity can even see a few bullet-holes among the ancient scars. Your cicerone, if he likes you, will tell you how the doors came by these scars, and it may be that he will add the tale of the Madonna of the Scroll.

The progress of the French Revolution was hailed by the Jewish communities in Italy with a not unnatural joy. Up to the close of the eighteenth century, they had been treated throughout the peninsula with a more than medieval intolerance, from which the French armies of the Revolution, as they poured over the Alps in the brilliant campaign of 1796–97, brought instantaneous deliverance. In every place to which they penetrated, the Rights of Man were proclaimed, the gates of the Ghetto were broken down, and the inmates were summoned forth at last to enjoy the free air of the outer world. Small wonder, then, that the Jews enthusiastically espoused the principles of the Revolution and became among the most zealous supporters of the new regime. They entered eagerly into the new civic life. They enrolled themselves in the Revolutionary Guard.

But the Generals whom Citizen Bonaparte left in charge, during his absence in Egypt, were unable to make headway against the coalition which was formed against them. In the spring of 1799, the French armies were driven back towards the Alps and the Cisalpine Republic was overthrown. Everywhere, counter-revolutionary principles triumphed. And when the reaction came, Jewry suffered anew.

In the Romagna, the communities were terrorized, and though Pesaro and Urbino had occasion to institute local Purims to celebrate their deliverance, a veritable pogrom took place at Senigalia, where thirteen persons perished, the rest of the community taking refuge in Ancona. On the other side of the Apenines, the reverses of the French encouraged the fervently Catholic and reactionary city of Arezzo to rise and expel their garrison. Emboldened by this success, they set out in the name of the Church and political absolutism to free the rest of the province from the new ideas introduced by the French oppressor. That the Jews were, in a special measure, their bugbear, goes without saying. At Arezzo itself, there was only the merest handful, and they escaped without great hurt. In Pitigliano one Jew was killed in a popular outbreak on June 16, while eighteen more were thrown into gaol. Further outbreaks took place at Florence and at Leghorn. The community of the little township of Monte San Savino, whose houses were sacked, anticipated further danger by abandoning their homes. They took refuge in the neighboring city of Sienna, and never again properly re-established themselves in Monte San Savino. Among the refugees was Salamone Fiorentino, the famous poet, whose admirers compared him to Petrarch himself. The choice of a refuge was not a wise one, for at Sienna, itself, excesses took place which have left an indelible impression in the minds of the people of Tuscany and of the Jews of all Italy.

The relief experienced by the community of Sienna, during the brief period of French domination, had been so great that the Ghetto had been impregnated by its principles. The Jews had taken a prominent share in setting up the inevitable 'Tree of Liberty', on which, it was said, they had the intention of hanging all loyal Christians. Domestically, the spiritual and lay heads of the Jewish community were for a time actually designated as the 'Citizen' Rabbi and the 'Citizen' wardens. There was, accordingly, all the more pretext for identifying Jewry with all that was objectionable in the Revolutionary regime. Moreover, the anti-religious campaign in which the French had indulged invested the reaction with something of the nature of a crusade. And in any crusade, those who had persistently refused the Cross were inevitably marked out for attack.

It was on the morning of Friday, June 28, 1799, that the Aretine detachments entered Sienna, having forced the French garrison to capitulate. A considerable detachment of the invaders, joined by some of the worst elements among the population of the city, made its way to the Ghetto.

Houses were broken into and sacked, and whatever could be found was carried off. Account books and notes of hand were destroyed indiscriminately by prudent debtors. For the zeal of the people had not been entirely political or religious in origin. 'Burn those damned books,' called one involved patrician who had become indebted to the Jews, as he joined the mob. Several persons were killed, and many others wounded. The experience of the Gallichi family was terrible, but it was more fortunate than that of the generality. 'They broke down the door of our house,' one of them wrote, 'and forced their way in with the intention of killing us: and they carried off six hundred ducats' worth of silver and linen, as well as three watches, one of which was of gold. Five times did they return, always with their weapons girt on and cudgels raised, and pistols pointed at our chests. It is impossible to describe how we felt, for we were reduced to the end of our lives. The said [the word here used is untranscribable] tried to break into our shop, but, praised be God, we were miraculously saved...'

Not all, however, were so lucky. More than one person was murdered in his own house. Michael Valech, on entering his home, was killed in the sight of his young wife, already six months advanced in pregnancy. She threw herself sobbing across his corpse, her body wracked with premature labor, and shared his fate. To the day of his death, the person responsible for this double crime (a servant in a monastery near Lucignano) was known as 'The Beast.' It was popularly believed – and not by the Jews alone – that every one of these responsible for those outrages perished miserably.

The butchery continued throughout the city. Two Jews caught abroad were hounded to death in the Piazza. Another, who had taken refuge in a church, was chased out by the verger and barbarously put to death on the threshold. Meanwhile, the Tree of Liberty in front of the Palazzo Publico had been torn down and burned. Drunk with passion, the mob rushed into the neighbouring Ghetto and returned dragging the bodies of several Jews, which they threw into the flames. Some were not quite dead, and made terrible efforts to escape their agony. Those who succeeded in getting clear of the flames were ruthlessly cast back with pitchforks amid the stench of the burning bodies. In all, thirteen persons were killed, including four of the refugees from the Monte San Savino and a couple of women. Of the number of those wounded, no record was kept.

A few of the priests, more humane than the rest, begged the Archbishop to do the duty of a Christian and to bear the Sacrament into the Ghetto in order to check the crimes which were being perpetrated in the name of Jesus. '*Furor Populi, furor Dei,*' replied the Prince of the Church, coldly. Only when the worst was over did he allow himself to be persuaded to go out and address the mob, at some little distance from the actual scene of the outrage. On the other hand, an Abbe, Carlo Bellanti, who had sheltered one of the Jews in his house until the riots were over, was long remembered with gratitude.

Meanwhile, the Synagogue was crowded with fugitives, trusting in solidarity or in the sanctity of the building, and praying for a miracle to save them. But the miracle did not come. The infuriated mob broke into the synagogue. Four persons were killed and many more wounded, and the floor of the building ran with human blood...

At the far end of the building, the Ark of the Law, austere and mysterious, attracted the attention of the invaders. Assuredly, they thought, this was where the Jews kept their treasures. The doors were massive and new, but they did not long withstand the axes. The interior, when the doors were at last forced open, was disappointing. There was nothing within but a row of Scrolls. The silver bells and ornaments upon them soon disappeared (as the charity boxes at the entrance had done earlier). As for the Scrolls themselves, their sanctity was recognized sufficiently for them to be made the object of special insult. The parchments were ripped of their embroidered covers and thrown to the floor. One was pulled open, dragged into the street, and rolled about in the mire amid the jeers of the mob.

At this point (so legend reports) a most curious thing occurred. There happened to be in Sienna that day a *Shadar*, an 'Emissary of the Merciful' from Palestine, collecting money on behalf of the Four Holy Jewish Communities of the Promised Land. With him was his daughter, a young girl of unusual beauty, brought up in the fullest traditions of a Rabbinical house. With horror, she saw the holy Scroll of the Law – given by God on Sinai – thrown to the ground with the probability of worse desecration to come. Suddenly, from where they knew not, the barbaric invaders saw a beautiful unknown girl, clad in a strange oriental robe, white and flowing, spring into their midst and gather up the yellow parchment from the ground. Too much taken aback to move, they then saw her disappear as suddenly and as mysteriously as she had come. To the superstitious mob, only one explanation offered itself. 'Assuredly,' they said, 'it is the Madonna, come down from Heaven to save the Bible.'...

Late that evening, the Sabbath brought some measure of peace. Guards were stationed at the Ghetto gates and, though it was unsafe for the Jews to stir abroad for another week or ten days, the worst was over. Captain Karl Schneider, Commandant of the counter-revolutionary forces in Tuscany and the Romagna, entered the city on June 30th. Besides retaining such of the property stolen from the Ghetto as was brought to his headquarters, he imposed an extraordinary levy of fifty thousand lire on the Jewish community, to be paid within two hours under the penalty of setting fire to the Ghetto. To meet this, it was found necessary to sell the few objects of silver which had 'miraculously' escaped the sack of a couple of days earlier. This did not, however, save the community from another similar imposition payable within one hour, a week later, and another eight days after that. As a result, the once prosperous community was reduced to petition all of its neighbours for assistance in the maintenance of the widows and orphans with whom it was now burdened. Three weeks after the riot, having discovered where the miserable remains of the victims of the massacre had been dragged from the Piazza and were still lying – the majority in a pit in the Old Market, others hard by covered merely with a sprinkling of earth – they obtained permission from the government to give them proper burial. On this same day, they had to make a special 'honorific' contribution for the equipment of the new Civic Guard, from which they were excluded.[1]

The following week, provision was made for the repair of the doors of the Ark. Rightly they should have been replaced. But the expense at such a moment would have been too great, and the community contented itself with crude repairing which perpetuated, rather than concealed, the traces of the outrage. And in perennial recollection of the event, the whole congregation bound itself by solemn vow to celebrate a general fast each year upon the anniversary of the massacre, Sivan 25th. This every individual – man, woman and child – was to observe. The synagogue, centre of some of the worst scenes, was to be kept open all night, as well as by day, and a special order of service was laid down to be recited.

Human memory is short, however. It was not long before the French armies again swept Tuscany. The second reaction which followed the downfall of Napoleon was mild by comparison with the first, and soon old events lost their appeal. Moreover, their unhappy experience had so terrified some of the wealthiest and most influential members of the community that they had thought it prudent to remove elsewhere, thus accelerating the natural flow to the larger towns. Thus the community was sadly reduced in numbers, and those left were beginning to suffer from apathy. Whatever the reason, no later than 1825 (barely a quarter of a century after the event), the community came to the conclusion that their vow had been 'too great for the general observance.' With the permission of the Rabbi of the neighbouring community of Florence, who was called in as a disinterested party, it was therefore abrogated, upon condition that ten poor men should make the fast and recite the statutory prayers each year in lieu of the whole congregation – in return, naturally, for some slight monetary consideration.

From that period the decadence of the community of Sienna continued apace. Today [1928] the ancient synagogue is opened for service only occasionally, and it is doubtful whether the statutory ten poor Hebrews can be mustered in the whole city. So the observance of the fast of commemoration has fallen into complete desuetude. Nevertheless, the memory of the events of June 28, 1799, is still vivid among the Jews throughout Tuscany. And among the superstitious gentile populace of Sienna, one may still hear how, on the day of the incursion of the Aretines, the Madonna herself came down from heaven to save the Bible.

First published in the *Menorah Journal*, New York, Vol. 15, 1928.

NOTE

1. See also *History of the Jews in Italy*, by Cecil Roth (1946), where on p. 437 he states that the Jews returned: 'The grand duke, however, first suspended and then cancelled this imposition and in the end even reimbursed what had been extorted – a unique happening perhaps in Jewish history.'

20 The Purim of Buda

August 20th, 1934, marks the two hundred and fiftieth anniversary of a famous event in Italian Jewish history, which continued until our own time, to be commemorated by the community of Padua, year by year, under the title 'The Purim of Buda'. Though the annual celebration has now fallen into more or less complete oblivion, it is hardly right to permit the anniversary of an event which so deeply impressed contemporary minds to be passed over in utter silence.

In 1683, the Turks, little realizing that their once redoubtable empire was on the brink of decay, made a final, superhuman military effort and advanced to the siege of Vienna. The whole of Europe watched the progress of operations with bated breath, wondering whether the crescent was to sweep triumphant across the plains of Germany and the muezzin was to summon the faithful to prayer from the towers of Nuremberg and Munich. The city was on the point of capitulation when the besieged saw on the surrounding hills the beacon fires of John Sobieski, the heroic king of Poland. In a brilliant action, he inflicted a decisive defeat on the enemy. Vienna was saved!

Throughout Christendom a spontaneous sigh of relief went up, in which the Jews dutifully joined; and throughout Italy the houses of the Ghettos were illuminated, and bonfires were kindled in the narrow streets.

In the following year, a 'Holy League' was formed against the Sultan by the Holy Roman Emperor, in conjunction with Poland and Venice. In all the synagogues of the Venetian territory, and no doubt elsewhere as well, special services were held for the victory of the allied arms. In the war which followed, however – as in all wars – the Jews suffered disproportionately. Thus in 1685, when an allied fleet under Francesco Morosini sacked the city of Coron on the Dalmatian coast, a score of Jews were brought back as prisoners and sold into slavery at Malta, while as many more were sent to row in the galleys. The Fraternity for Redemption of the Captives at Venice, which watched over the pious duty of redeeming captive brethren, was hard put to it to find the means of ransoming all these captives, the more so since the synagogue had been sacked as well, and a large number of Scrolls of the Law, with their trappings, had to be saved in addition to the human victims.

In the previous year (1684) the allied forces had laid siege to Buda – the older portion of the capital of Hungary, better known today as Budapest. The Turks had held this city since 1541, and they defended it in a manner worthy of their old military reputation. Feeling in Italy ran high. Since there were no Moslems at hand on whom the popular spleen could be vented, the Jews, as usual, had to serve as scapegoats.

It is true that some of their Jewish coreligionists were in the besieged Hungarian Christian city, who performed their duty manfully against the assailants but the reports which spread abroad far outstripped the facts. It was alleged that their numbers exceeded 30,000 (and all of phenomenal wealth), that they were mainly responsible for stimulating the defence, and that they perpetrated unheard of atrocities against any Christian who was so unfortunate as to fall into their hands.

The Jews of Italy were made to suffer for the various misdemeanours of this supposed troop of fanatics. At Rome, feeling against the Jews ran so high that they were unable to venture into the streets without an escort. In Monselice, Montagnana, Castelfranco and Citadella, little places in the Venetian territories, conditions were much the same. But it was at Padua that the wave of anti-Semitism reached its climax. This was partly in consequence of economic causes, as is so often the case.

The purblind policy of the Venetian government (oblivious of the fact that all commerce and industry enriched the state and created employment, whatever the religious beliefs of the entrepreneur) endeavoured to exclude the Jews completely from all activities other than money-lending and dealing in old clothes. Nevertheless, a few of those in Padua were interested in the woolen industry. In the previous year, there had been a dispute about this, which led to a house to house perquisition in the Ghetto. A case had been brought before the authorities, and on August 16th, 1684, a judgment unfavourable to the Gentile manufacturers had been delivered at Venice. Almost contemporaneously, the Jews observed with the traditional ceremonies the fast of the Ninth of Ab – the date of the destruction of the Temple in Jerusalem on two occasions, and the anniversary of many other mournful events in Jewish life.

A rumour circulated about the city that this sad service was in consequence of the threatening state of affairs in Hungary, and that the Jews were praying to their God that Buda would not fall into the hands of the triumphant Christian host.

It may be imagined how this absurd fable was greeted in the city. An ugly spirit spread abroad. It was dangerous for a Jew to be seen in the streets. Twice the leaders of the community waited upon the governor, or Podesta, begging him to take action in order to safeguard them, while others approached lesser dignitaries. The authorities, however, were powerless, for the city had been stripped of its garrison because of the war, and however favourably inclined they may have felt, they had no force at their disposal to back their decisions. All that was done, accordingly, was to announce once more, to the sound of the trumpet, an old proclamation of the Doge, dating back to 1671, forbidding the Jews to be molested. Meanwhile, feeling ran higher and higher.

On Sunday, August 20th, a rumuor spread through the city that Buda had fallen. The popular delight knew no bounds. Crowds collected and surged through the streets. The few Jews who were about in the city took to their heels and sought refuge in the comparative security of their own quarter, the gates of which were immediately closed and barred. The mob soon made its way after them. An enormous crowd collected outside the gate of San Casinano, the main entrance to the Ghetto, notwithstanding the propinquity of the Palace of the Podesta. Smaller bodies besieged the other three gates. Volleys of stones, some of which fell inside the Ghetto, followed the preliminary shoutings. A half-hearted attempt of the civic police to disperse the crown proved quite ineffectual. The terror-stricken Jews within heard voices shouting for fire to be applied to burn down the gate, when they would all be caught like rats in a trap. The *gastaldi*, or leaders of the community, could think of nothing better than to convey food and money to the mob, in the hope of assuaging their rage. In the event, it only served to whet their appetites.

Meanwhile, with every minute that passed, the crowd was increasing, some of them now being armed with iron bars. The Podesta had a proclamation read ordering all who heard it to disperse peaceably to their homes. The mob momentarily recoiled but soon returned again, more threatening than ever. Ultimately, the other gates were deserted, and the whole attack was concentrated at that of San Urbano. The few civic officers who tried to pacify the storm were saluted with volleys of stones, while those of the better-class citizens who counselled more peaceful procedure were accused of having been bought over by the Jews.

Ultimately, taking advantage of the fact that the gate was opened for a moment to let a messenger slip out, the mob forced an entrance, rushed inside, and began to sack the Ghetto systematically. The Jews barricaded themselves into their houses and awaited their fate. Some of the poorer lost all that they possessed. A crowd collected in the courtyard of the Ashkenazi synagogue, where a large number of persons had taken refuge, and attempted to smash in the doorway. It seemed a miracle from heaven that they did not succeed.

Not a moment too soon, a regiment of the cuirassiers which happened to be in the city on the point of departure for the front, was ordered out. The troopers clattered down the cobbled streets with drawn swords, just in time to prevent bloodshed, and the Ghetto was momentarily freed from its invaders. Nevertheless, the mob continued to rage, and soon reassembled in the street outside in a temper even uglier than before. War had been proclaimed, they said, on the Turk yet a beginning had been made in Padua by shedding Christian blood in defence of a rabble of Jews.

Fuel was added to the flames by a woman of questionable reputation who came forward with the old, old story which has caused the Jews such immeasurable suffering. She had lost her son, and not being able to find him on a first search, she accused the Jews of having kidnapped and murdered him. Such now was the fury of the mob that the cuirassiers themselves had great difficulty in returning to their quarters, losing one man in the process.

The Jews, notwithstanding all assurances to the contrary, were left to their fate. The gate of San Urbano, through which entrance had been forced on the previous occasion, was hastily fortified from within, and it was now assaulted with increased fury.

The fall of night enhanced the horrors of the situation. Within the ghetto, despair reigned. The uproar of the mob, the sound of the sledgehammers beating upon the gate, and the glare of the fire which was kindled in the hopes of burning it down, all added to the terrors of the trapped inmates. For the first time within living memory, the regular sequence of services in the synagogues was interrupted. A few persons improvised ladders and escaped with their wives and children to Christian residences abutting on the Ghetto, where they were generously allowed to take refuge. Others hid in the eaves, or else foregathered in the houses of relatives, hoping for safety in numbers. Even invalids rose from their sickbeds to seek shelter. Some of the merchants removed their goods from their warehouses to lofts; but the majority were too preoccupied to think of such mundane matters.

Suddenly, with a crash, the gate gave way. For a moment, those within could see the figures of the assailants silhouetted against the flames. Then the mob poured in and the sack began.

Isaac Cohen Cantarini, poet, rabbi, author, and physician (to whose literary genius our knowledge of these events is largely due), was standing at the door of his house when he heard the mob rushing down the street. He immediately entered and was about to bar the door, when he heard a voice outside imploring help.

It was one David Ghirondi, who was being pursued by a band of hooligans but got inside just in time. Anxious for the welfare of his family, he made his way to the house-top and jumped from room to roof until he reached his own house.

Matters were at their worst when the Podesta, hitherto almost apathetic, at last realized the gravity of the situation. He took a step unprecedented hitherto in case of internal turmoil, calling out the bombardiers, who could have dispersed an unarmed mob in a few moments by firing a few shots. Several of this body, indeed, were among the assailants, whose ranks presumably they were now forced to abandon.

In order to make certain that his order was obeyed, the Podesta, attended by torch bearers, came in person to the scene of the disorder. Simultaneously, a yet further proclamation was made, threatening with death any person who molested the Jews. The mob, intimidated by this display, began to disperse. Its ardour was further dampened by the sudden disappearance of one of the ringleaders. Ultimately he was discovered in a cesspool, into which he had fallen while creeping stealthily, with flint and tinder, with the obvious intention of setting the ghetto on fire at some unfrequented spot. Thus, at length, after an anxious interval, the ghetto was freed from its assailants once more. A detachment of fifty bombardiers was left to maintain order.

All that night, however, the Jews waited up in fear and trembling for what the morrow might bring.

It happened by a very fortunate coincidence that one of the most important members of the community, Simon Lustro (whose shop had been sacked during the course of the previous disorders), was then in Venice on business. A little time before, when the unrest began, a special messenger had been dispatched to inform him to do whatever seemed desirable under the circumstances. He had immediately gone to the Doges' Palace and begged that immediate steps be taken to protect his coreligionists. His intervention had an immediate effect. At dawn on the following day (August 21st) there arrived in Padua a special messenger bearing instructions from the Doge that *any person who insulted or molested the Jews should be put to death*. This was immediately proclaimed by the criers throughout the city; the unruly populace, who knew how sharp Venetian justice could sometimes be, was cowed.

When a little later the peasants streamed in from the surrounding countryside to join in the sack, they found each of the entrances to the ghetto guarded by a squadron of bombardiers and their associates in the city in no mood to risk their necks. Meanwhile, for the first time for some days, the fishermen and market-gardeners brought their wares into the ghetto for sale. All the synagogues were crowded with men and women returning thanks for their deliverance, and praying that the menace would finally pass.

Thus, gradually, quiet was restored, though it was not until the Friday, after a reign of terror which had lasted for six days, that the Jews began to creep about the city once more, timidly, on their business. Ill-feeling, on the other hand, continued to last for some time after. It flared up again when excited reports arrived from the Christian camp before Buda, indicating that the city had not yet fallen, that the Jews were encouraging the protraction of the defence, and that eighty of them had been found in a mine dug by the besieged under the Christian camp.

When finally there came official news of the fall of Buda (accompanied by the inevitable butchery of the few Jews actually found in the city) the community of Padua thought it desirable to contribute liberally to the expenses of the civic illuminations. Nevertheless, the authorities expected another outbreak. Fortunately, on that very night, October 26th–27th, all the rivers and streams overflowed with a terrific downpour of rain, heavy enough to dampen any ardour.

However, feelings were allayed only when letters arrived from Fra

Marco d'Avianoa (an immensely popular preacher, who had been with the Emperor in the camp before Buda) utterly contradicting the report that the Jews had been serving with the Turkish forces or had been maltreating the Christians. With this influential and authoritative intervention, the danger finally came to an end.

These events created an indelible impression on the popular mind. No less than three contemporary writers who participated in the events wrote detailed descriptions of them. The most important was Rabbi Isaac Cantarini, who published in Amsterdam, in the following year, his famous '*Pahad Isaac*', giving a detailed account of all that had happened in a vivacious, though involved, Hebrew.

Solomon Eleazar Ghirondi (plainly a relative of the David Ghirondi mentioned above) wrote a second Hebrew account under the title *Maaseh Nissim* ('The Miracle'), never published, but preserved in manuscript in the Library of Jews' College, London (in the printed catalogue of which it is wrongly described).

Another account, in Italian doggerel, was written by one Sema Cuzzeri, parts of it being printed in Ciscato's '*Storia degli ebrei in Padova.*'

But the happy event was celebrated also in another fashion. The community of Padua, full of gratitude at its escape, instituted an annual celebration in honour of its deliverance, to be kept each year on the tenth of Ellul, the anniversary of the frustrated attack. This, under the name of the Purim of Buda, continued to be observed; and it is of this that the two hundred and fiftieth anniversary was observed.

First published in Italian in *Israel*, 9 and 16 August 1934 and in English in the *American Hebrew*, New York, 10 August 1934.

21 A Passover Deliverance

Some persons use prayer-books exclusively for prayer. However, a *Siddur* or *Machzor* is (or should be) far more than a synagogal handbook. It contains (or should contain) some great literature that may be appreciated aesthetically as well as spiritually – if, indeed, the two can ever be completely divided. It may be a monument of typography, a pearl of great price, a bibliophile's treasure. It may be the product of a rare press, a delight to the eyes and a drain to the pocket. The fly-leaves may contain historical and family records of considerable significance. And the contents often reflect the history and the miseries and the vicissitudes of the community for whose use the edition was printed.

The liturgy of the isolated Communities of the Comtat Venaissin, in Southern France, is in particular an almost inexhaustible mine for the inquiring historian, as the tradition of Jewish life in these parts was continuous. Even when the Jews were expelled from the rest of the country, they were suffered to continue here, under the aegis of the Pope, whose name is mentioned with magniloquent veneration in the prayer-book of the local Communities. Theirs was the satisfaction of the French sage who, when asked what he did during the Terror in 1799, responded simply, 'I kept alive.' These Communities, during the terror of the Middle Ages and after, when hardly a single Jewish settlement in the West of Europe continued its existence, had the satisfaction that they survived; and this, if the truth be told, was their greatest title to fame, other than that of having produced Adolphe Cremieux in the last generation but one, Armand Lunel, and Darius Milhaud in our own.[1]

THE CARPENTRAS MACHZOR

But the fact that they survived did not imply that they were consistently well treated. Indeed the reverse; and their chronicles and their records, and even their liturgy, bear ample testimony to the persecutions and petty annoyances that they underwent from time to time. On one occasion, persecution and deliverance happened to fall on the anniversary of a greater deliverance, many many centuries before, to the ancestors of the entire Jewish people. That is why, in the exceedingly rare *Mahzor* of the Rite of Carpentras for the Three Festivals (printed at Amsterdam in 1759), you will find in the service for the seventh day of Passover certain poems and prayers and hymns of thanks that are elsewhere entirely unknown.

It was in the spring of the year 1651. The Bishop of Carpentras at that time was the Cardinal Bicchi, the Recteur of the Comtat (representing the Pope at Carpentras and serving as Vice-Legate at Avignon) was Monsieur Jean. As so often happened, and so often with terrible results, Passover coincided that year, nearly enough, with Eastertide, the first day of the feast falling on Holy Thursday, April 6th. Throughout Good Friday and down to late on the Saturday, the Jews remained shut up in their ghetto (which was known as the *carriere*), their presence in the streets of the city at such a season being reckoned an insult to Christianity. Characteristically, they turned the tables by thinking of themselves as the elect, kept away from contamination, and in their liturgy they actually introduced special hymns for this occasion, the Yom haHasger or 'Day of Shutting In.'

ATTACK BY AN ARMY OF BEGGARS

Good Friday, however, passed peaceably, and Holy Saturday and Easter Sunday itself, and the unfortunate Jews began to imagine that they had nothing more to fear for the moment. On the following Wednesday night they began to observe the last solemn days of the Holiday. But unfortunately, it was a time of peculiarly great economic distress. The city was filled with penniless, starving beggars, who imagined that in the ghetto they could find relief and food. Late that night, they made an assault upon the *carriere*, and, whether by treachery or by stealth, they managed to open the gate that led to the Synagogue – already ancient, but still standing and declared an historical monument not long since.

Terror spread within. The assailants surged through the streets and began to assault the houses. The Jews, terror-stricken, sought concealment in the attics and cellars, and could anticipate nothing but imminent massacre almost to the last man, with dishonour for their womenfolk and enforced apostasy, worse than dishonour or even death, for their children. The first objective of the attackers was, of course, the Synagogue, where they knew that they could find the sacred ornaments and appurtenances of precious metal. For once, the Jews found that the repressive Papal code that governed their lives was useful, for everything was done by the Government to prevent them from making their synagogue appear similar in the slightest degree to a Christian place of worship. Hence there was no monumental entrance, such as might have been expected and imagined, and in consequence – it is almost comic – the assailants could not find their way in!

Foiled here, the mob turned their attention to the shops, which were broken into and systematically sacked, one after the other. Nothing could be done to stop them. However, the martial spirit (which was subsequently to present to France more than one distinguished soldier of the Valabregue and other families) was not entirely dead in the Carpentras Jewry, and some of the hardier spirits climbed up to the roofs and prepared to sell their lives dearly, using stones as their only weapon and munition.

HELP FROM THE CARDINAL ARCHBISHOP

The *carriere*, as it happens, was provided with two gates, one at either end. While the mob was streaming in at the one, the leaders of the Community slipped out of the other and made their way to the palace of the Cardinal Archbishop. The latter, compassionate Churchman, took immediate action and ordered the Governor and town council to proceed against the rioters. By this time, the rioters were too unruly. When they were summoned to desist, they turned against the Governor himself and pelted him with stones, and he thought himself lucky to be able to come back to the Archbishop's palace alive. Yet – it seemed miraculous to the Jews – his intervention had the desired effect. The rioters began to get afraid of the consequences, and the crowd melted away as if by magic. Before long the *carriere* was quiet again. Only the Jewish young men remained on guard, together with a sprinkling of soldiers sent to assist them to make sure there was no recurrence. Next morning, before dawn, the troops occupied all the strategic points in the city, and vigorous action was taken. Many of the ringleaders fled; others were arrested, put on trial, and severely punished. The Jews breathed securely once again.

It was already a holy day, the seventh day of Passover, the anniversary of the overthrow of Pharaoh and his host in the Red Sea. But to the miserable Jew of Carpentras, the deliverance that he had experienced was hardly less than that vouchsafed to his ancestors. The Rabbis of the community accordingly ordered that day to be observed for all time as an extraordinary feast-day. *Yom va Yoshaa*, they called it, the day of 'And He saved', with obvious reference to the Scriptural portion of the day (Exodus xiv, 30). Special prayers were introduced into the Synagogue service, night and morning, and a hymn of praise recounting the details of the deliverance was composed by a local poet, Joseph ben Abraham de Montel, and inserted in the liturgy. And so long as there were Jews in Carpentras and public worship was regularly held (at the time of writing there were barely sufficient local residents to constitute a *Minyan* in that lovely Synagogue, even if all attended), this special observance was regularly held.

It seems a little elementary to us, perhaps, and one might have wondered at the naivety of the Jews, in terming this escape of theirs a 'miracle'. But one wonders no longer. In how many cities of Central Europe to-day can one be sure that the authorities – even though they might be princes of the Church – would intervene to protect the unhappy Jews?

First published in the *Jewish Guardian*, London, 19 April 1920.

NOTE

1. Cremieux was a nineteenth-century French lawyer and statesman and Jewish emancipationist and philanthropist; Lunel was a French novelist who wrote the librettos of the operas *Esther of Carpentras* (1925) and *David* (1954), by Milhaud, a French composer who became music professor in California and Paris.

22 The Miracle of the Bomb

The name of Fossano is familiar to all students of Jewish literature. It is not that the little North-Italian city ever harboured a community of peculiar numerical importance, or that it gave birth to any personage of especial distinction in the annals of Hebrew life and letters. It was never even the scene of a massacre or persecution of extraordinary virulence, to place it in the record of Jewish martyrdom. Far from it. The history of the community was a humdrum one, so much so that it has not as yet been deemed worthy even of fossilary preservation in a learned monograph. It is not the vicissitudes, but the origin, of the community which provide its especial interest.

Fossano is situated in Piedmont, on a little hill at the foot of the Alps, at the very gateway to Italy. Standing in its citadel, one may see close at hand on the one side the bleak snow-capped peaks which separate the country from France, and in sharp contrast to it, on the other, the typical monotonous landscape of the Piedmontese plain, flat as a marsh and verdant with intensive cultivation. And standing there, the history of the Jews in the place becomes clear.

When, in the fourteenth century, there took place the great expulsions from France, the majority of the refugees made their way overland to Germany or Spain, or took ship for the greater freedom of southern Europe and the Levant. Some bands, however, crossed the Alps and settled down with a sigh of relief in the very first spot to which they came. One of the places in question was Fossano – the first city of the Piedmontese plain. Others were the neighboring towns of Asti and Moncalvo. In these three havens of refuge, the French fugitives long preserved something of their ancestral type and traditions, and even of their names. (At Fossano, one family of especial prominence was named Colon, which name was Italicised as Colombo and Latinised, on occasion, as Columbus. Who knows?)

But above all, they clung with pathetic tenacity to the French rite of prayers which their fathers had followed in the old country –

different from both the Italian ritual employed by the original inhabitants, and from the German or Ashkenazi rite introduced by some recent immigrants, though not altogether dissimilar from the latter. Their numbers never justified the printing of a prayer-book, but it was industriously copied by hand by the experienced local scribes, and so preserved, even to our own day. Scholars speak of this as the rite of APaM (really AFaM), after the initials of the three towns where it was formerly followed. When, in 1918, Galician prisoners who were interned in the fortress of Fossano borrowed the congregational prayer-books for the High Festivals, they noticed with suspicion and disdain the textual differences from the formula to which they had been accustomed, and wondered to what outlandish country they had come.

Now the same mountain passes which had brought the Jews over the Alps lay open to other migrants whose objects were less pacific. Nearly every community of Piedmont preserves, in mural inscriptions in its synagogue or in certain annual celebrations, the memory of some providential deliverance at the time of a siege by invaders from the north. Fossano, occupying an immensely important strategic position, was no exception in this respect. Thus it came about that in the spring of the year 1796, the city was summoned to surrender by the armies of the French Revolution, under the French general with the curiously Italian name of Bonaparte. The natural position of the city was strong, and the inhabitants none too sympathetic to revolutionary ideas. The French, therefore, settled down to a formal siege, and bringing up their artillery, began a destructive bombardment.

In time of trouble, even in the eighteenth century, an almost universal popular expedient was to assault the Jews. They were disliked, they were defenceless, and what was more, they were reputed to be wealthy. Moreover, in the present case they were suspected (not without reason) of a cordial sympathy with the invader. This was by no means remarkable. The Jews of Piedmont had been kept cooped up in their Ghettos under conditions of more than mediaeval degradation, but they knew full well that Jewish equality had been the rule in France for some time, and that emancipation had been carried by the Revolutionary armies to every city of Italy to which they had penetrated. For the community of Fossano not to feel, and perhaps to express, some sympathy with the invader would have been almost superhuman. (There is, in the possession of the writer, a local ritual, the fly-leaves of which are adorned with crude sketches of the tree and cap of liberty with the tell-tale date 1789!) It may be imagined that they were inspired especially by that worthy enthusiast, Abraham Sinigaglia, to save whose life at a subsequent period of reaction a worthy patrician sacrificed a wig; but that is quite another story.

Easter had passed, with its reminder of the Passion. The perilous Passover season had arrived, and in the midst of the siege, the Jews had the audacity to celebrate the festival of freedom with their ancestral rites – assuredly a manifest token of sympathy with the enemy. On the fourth night of the siege (Monday, 26th April, 1796), when the enemy opened his usual bombardment – apparently with more deadly effects than the ordinary – the rabble of the city could bear it no longer. Snatching up any arms they could find, they made their way to the Jewish quarter, confident there, at least, of a signal victory.

The Ghetto at Fossano (now the Via dell' Orfantrofi) is a long narrow street close to the city wall – this itself perhaps an additional cause to nourish a suspicion of treachery. Against this the mob rushed. They gained access without opposition. Once entered, they did as they pleased, hacking down the doors with their axes, breaking into the shops and houses, and pillaging the contents.

The Jews were entirely in their power. They were absolutely shut off from the rest of the town. Here, moreover, the soldiers of the garrison were otherwise engaged. The more moderate elements in the population, alarmed by the bombardment which had just been opened, remained cooped up in their houses with no thought left for incidental matters such as the welfare of the Jews. Thus all appeals for assistance remained unanswered. All night long, until the dawn, the sack continued. Meanwhile the Jews sought refuge in the diminutive synagogue, centre of their religious and social life, the sanctity of which they trusted would protect them.

The sacred edifice stood (in accordance with a fairly common architectural convention of the period) on an upper story at the far end of the street, access being gained by a narrow staircase which led into a little vestibule. From the far end of this, there opened out the synagogue itself – a small but picturesque structure which still preserved its original form in spite of a restoration in 1812. The sanctity of the place proved, however, no deterrent for the rabble. Here there was assuredly the best of all chances of pillage. No doubt jewellery of untold value hung around the necks of the fair Jewesses. Moreover, the massive silver lamps which burned perpetually before the Ark, and the other adornments used in divine service, were famous. Athirst for spoil and blood, the ruffians followed. The Jews were huddled together in the little synagogue, weeping, praying, and waiting for the end. A massacre such as those which took place a little later under almost identical circumstances at Sienna or Senigallia seemed inevitable. Meanwhile the flash of the bombardment made the fading night almost as light as day, while the shriek of the shells, followed by the confused reverberation of the explosions and of the falling masonry, added to the terror of the scene.

The mob pressed up the stairs with wild cries and threats, and entered into the vestibule. Massacre seemed unavoidable unless a miracle intervened.

According to local legend, that is precisely what happened. Just as the first members of the crowd arrived at the top of the staircase, an enemy cannon fired, almost at a venture. The shell burst through the wall of the vestibule, midway between the surging mob and their cowering victims. As it happens, it did no great material damage. But the attackers, terror-stricken, took to their heels and fled, throwing away as they ran a great part of their spoil. The community was saved. Very shortly afterwards, the French entered the city and the Jews were at last out of danger.

This marvellous escape seemed a direct act of God. Searching of conscience and internal repentance seemed to be a poor way of commemorating so signal a deliverance. Accordingly, the anniversary of that date, the fourth night and day of Passover, was declared by the leaders of the community a special holiday, to be observed by the Holy Congregation of Fossano in every generation for all time until the Messianic redemption. The Rabbi of the community, a certain Abraham, celebrated the event in a turgid memorial poem to be recited year by year both night and morning, which was vilely printed in pamphlet form on (apparently) war-time paper – probably in the neighbouring city of Turin. Of this, unknown to bibliographers, a solitary copy is in the collection of the present writer. It is hence, and from local legend auricularly collected on the spot, that the above account has been compiled.

But the event was commemorated, also, in a manner less commonplace by far. The aperture through which the providential shell burst its way into the synagogue building has never been repaired. It survived the reconstruction of sixteen years later and is still to be seen today, by any person who takes the trouble to make the pilgrimage (for the aboriginal community is virtually dead). It now serves a useful purpose as a window to throw much-needed light upon the internal obscurity. Around it is written, in Hebrew, in letters of would-be gold, the simple phrase: *The Miracle of the Bomb*.

Who, even in our incredulous age, shall say it nay?

First published in the *American Hebrew*, New York, 7 April 1933.

23 My Grandmother's Seder Tray

AN AUTHORITY ON RITUAL PRACTICES DISCOURSES
INFORMATIVELY ON SOME PASSOVER CEREMONIALS

There is no occasion of the Jewish year so redolent of domestic memories as the Passover, no service-book so generally familiar as the Haggadah, no ritual so beloved as the Seder. It is small wonder, then that our fathers, in accordance with their practise of beautifying every religious ceremony (it was thus that they interpreted the verse in the Song of Moses: *'This is my God, and I will glorify Him'*) devoted particular attention to this night of nights.

The central object on the Seder table is, of course, the dish or platter which contains the *Matzoth*. Nowadays one uses an enamel tray, a basket, or what-not, but in former times no household which could afford it failed to have a special receptacle for the purpose. These are extant in two forms. In Italy, (particularly on the East coast, about Faenza) they were generally made of majolica.

The plate's centre invariably bears an inscription comprising the catch-words of the Passover service, or perhaps the *Kiddush*, while round the rim are little cartouches showing the ritual in progress. Many of these plates are signed on the reverse side by the craftsman. It seems that one single family – that of Azulai – was engaged in the manufacture at Padua and Pesaro for some two hundred years, from the sixteenth century to the eighteenth.

Majolica, unfortunately, is brittle, and probably a majority of the articles just described have long since been consigned to the limbo of broken crockery. In Northern Europe, however, a more durable material was used. Plutocrats, of course, could afford precious metal, but the ordinary householder had to be content with pewter – the poor man's silver. Nowadays, when pewter is so eagerly sought after by dilettanti, no collection is complete without an example of these Paschal dishes.

The most valuable assortment ever brought together was

probably that owned formerly by Mr. Arthur Howitt of Richmond, Surrey, which was dispersed at Christie's in May 1932. Fortunately, some of the finest specimens were acquired by the Jewish Museum, London. The most noteworthy of all is a magnificent, deep platter, 22 inches in diameter, which was purchased for the Museum by the National Arts-Collection Fund (this fact, in itself, is an endorsement of the importance of the piece in question). This happens to be signed by the manufacturer, or engraver – Baruch Schtecher of Furth. The design includes prominently a pair of hands outspread in benediction, in allusion to the fact that the owner was a certain Jacob Cohen.

These plates are generally decorated either with representations of the various Paschal symbols (the lamb, unleavened bread, etc.) or with a geometrical design, supplemented in either case by Hebrew inscriptions. In exceptional cases (an example in the collection of the present writer is a case in point), the engraved design shows the Seder Service in progress. One word of warning is perhaps desirable. The reader is implored to beware of embossed designs, which are invariably modern imitations. The ingenious three-tiered dishes found sometimes on the Continent are, to the best of my knowledge, a modern German innovation.

The main object of the platter is, of course, to hold the three Matzot. These had to be covered, and, accordingly the Matzot-cover, embroidered by the housewife during the long winter nights, was another category of Jewish paschal art. There was, however, no tradition with regard to this, every needlewoman suiting her own fancy. In the Levant, special cloths were used also as table-centres, or to cover the bitter herbs and other condiments. The Haroset, too, had its special receptacle – the writer can recall one in the form of a wheelbarrow propelled by a man-at-arms! In some parts, elaborately decorated cushions were used, upon which the celebrant reclined as he conducted the service. I myself have a specially embroidered towel for the ritual washing of the hands, but it is not very old – 1932, to be precise – and I know quite intimately the lady responsible for its manufacture!

Next to the Matzot in importance came the wine. Special receptacles and beakers were often used for the Seder ceremony. Sometimes the octagonal *kiddush*-cups made at Nuremberg and Augsburg in the eighteenth century were engraved with special Passover-tide inscriptions, or else great goblets were adorned with representations of the Exodus, or of the Four Sons whose conversational variations are recorded in the Haggadah.

For the Cup of Elijah, a double barrel-shaped cup, with the two halves fitting into one another, (otherwise associated in Jewish ceremonial only with Elijah's other gala-day, the B'rith Milah) was often employed. One half was used by the Celebrant; the other was set aside for the invisible guest. This usage must go back for a very long time, for among the relics of 'St.' Simon, victim of an alleged ritual murder in 1475, there is preserved at Trent in North Italy a cup of this sort, which the Jews are said to have used on the occasion of their Seder Service in that fatal year. Sometimes the wine beakers were made in sets, every member of the household being provided with one.

Lionel de Rothschild had one very exquisite service, in silver, dating back to the sixteenth century. They are to be found also, in exceptional cases, in glass, every piece being suitably engraved with Paschal scenes and inscriptions. Other objects encountered now and again in silver (though it was in fact a needless extravagance to specially provision for this occasion), were the ewer and basin for laving the hands.

Every member of the household, of course, needed his own platter for use during the ritual. Sometimes whole sets were made expressly for this purpose, suitably inscribed in Hebrew characters. I recall having seen one such set, from a distance, on the solitary occasion when I had the pleasure of visiting Israel Solomons – that devoted collector of all things Jewish. If I am not mistaken, he informed me that they were made by Wedgewood, but I took no special note at the time and the plates are now gone from England, beyond recall. These were not, however, quite so curious in their way as a set owned by the late Sir Moses Montefiore, and employed by him in a very special way.

It would be an insult to the reader were I to inform him in detail of the old custom whereby the names of the Ten Plagues are recited, each person present dipping his finger in his goblet and sprinkling or spilling a few drops of wine. (This was no doubt intended originally to attenuate the rejoicing at the Egyptians' disaster). Sir Moses went so far as to have a special set of plates upon which this ritual could be performed without a prejudice to his table-cloth. But he had a tidy mind, and an eye which was offended at the sight of the besprinkled receptacles lying on the table after their immediate utility was concluded. Accordingly, when he pronounced the last of the series, 'The Slaying of the First-Born,' it was his custom to ring the bell. When the butler appeared, the venerable Baronet made a gesture towards the desolation. 'Remove the Plagues,' he ordered. And the service could proceed.

First published in *American Hebrew*, New York, 12 April 1935, p. 441.

24 The Omer Days in History

Some eighteen centuries ago, according to Jewish legend, plague broke out in Palestine. Shortly after Passover, the first victim was mourned at B'ne B'rak in the school of Rabbi Akiba, among whose pupils the mortality continued until the eighteenth day of Iyyar. Ever since that time, these Omer days have been considered a period of semi-mourning in Jewish lore and life, with a break only on the Thirty-Third Day of the Omer, the Scholars' Festival.

This legend seems to have been emphasised in order to explain the sad tinge with which this period of the year was imbued in the ancient Jewish folk-lore of all countries. In the Middle Ages, however, the course of Jewish history was such that current events were enough, in themselves, to provide the emphasis. It must be remembered that the Spring was the obvious period for the movement of armies and the opening of campaigns after the inactivity of winter, and that it was now, therefore, that the Crusading forces would begin their march through the densely-packed Jewish settlements, leaving a trail of blood and rapine behind them. Moreover it was now, year by year, that preachers in the pulpit, repeating the story of the Crucifixion in connection with Eastertide, re-aroused primitive passions against the innocent descendants of those who were inaccurately alleged to have perpetrated it. Hence, it is precisely this period of the *Omer*-days between Passover and Pentecost, which is associated in Jewish history with the most appalling of the medieval massacres.

The tradition was set at the time of the First Crusade of 1096, which opened a fresh chapter in Jewish history, written in blood and fire – the chapter of medieval persecution and suffering. It was on May 3 of that year, the third Sabbath after Passover, that the unruly horde of soldiers of the Cross arrived at Spires in the Rhineland and surrounded the Synagogue with the intention of putting the worshippers to the sword. Those within defended themselves manfully, and for the moment only a few of them lost their lives. The next time, the assailants were better prepared. A fortnight later they arrived at Worms, where the community was martyred in two successive attacks, on May 18 and 25. The next city in their path was Mainz, where the Archbishop invited the Jews to take refuge in his own palace. But even this did not save them; the archbishop's guards refused to do their duty and the Jews were put to death almost to a man, on May 27. In Cologne the synagogue was surrounded on May 30 – the first day of the Feast of Pentecost – by a mob of Crusaders under the command of William the Carpenter; and though, owing to timely precautions, there were not many casualties on that day, most of the survivors were tracked down and pitilessly massacred on June 1.

Similar scenes were enacted in those bloody weeks at place after place along the Rhine, where we only know of the existence of Jewish communities at this period because of the tragic report of these events. The coincidence with the Feast of Pentecost – the feast of the Giving of the Law – did not escape the attention of contemporary writers and poets. 'On the day that the Torah was given,' writes one of them, 'on that same day it returned to Heaven in flames, together with its case and container, those who studied it and knew it.'

It was this series of massacres, as has been indicated, that marks the beginning of what had been considered, until a few days ago, the darkest period of Jewish history; and it is especially with the *Omer* days that these tragic events are associated. It is impossible – it would take too long, and it would be too harrowing – to list even a selection of the most memorable. One may, however, mention that long sequence of disasters throughout the Jewish year, from the Blood Accusation at Mainz in 1283 to the outbreak of the disorders in Palestine in 1936, which make their date, April 19, run through Jewish history like a crimson cord; that it was on April 28, 1881, that the wave of Russian Pogroms began at Elizabethgrad; that it was on May 15, 1882, that the infamous May Laws were issued by the Government of the Czar.

The sad tinge of this period in Jewish life is due to the record of the Middle Ages, but the tradition has continued, alas, to our own day. Small wonder, then, that it has found its echoes in religious practise. As is well known, it is customary for weddings not to be solemnised during most of this period. The *Lecha Dodi* hymn on Friday night is recited to a special mournful tune. The heartrending prayer for martyrs, *Av haRachamim*, written with special reference to the Rhineland massacres, is recited in the morning before the Scrolls of the Law are put back into the Ark. Our fathers, moreover, added to the Liturgy at this period several elegies on these events. In the old-fashioned prayer-books, for example, there can be seen a special hymn by Isaac ben Shalom for the Sabbath after Passover on the massacre at Wurzburg on 20 Nisan, 1147; and on the Sabbath before the Pentecost, a heartrending threnody on the Rhineland Massacres of 1096.

Our Rabbis realised, however, with characteristic common-sense, that too long a period of unmitigated mourning was undesirable, and a break was therefore introduced into it on the 18 Iyyar, being the Thirty-Third day of the Omer ('Lag BeOmer'). It was on this occasion, they said, that the plague among the pupils of Rabbi Akiba ceased; it was therefore a time for rejoicing above all on the part of the students and scholars. Moreover Lag BeOmer was, according to legend, the day when Rabbi Simeon ben Yohai, the author of the great mystical classic, the *Zohar*, revealed its secrets to his pupils before being gathered to his last rest; and this added to its claims as a day of rejoicing in the eyes of the Jewish mystics. Besides, it was generally believed that the Manna first came down from Heaven on this day. Hence Lag beOmer became a semi-holyday – and for school-children, a whole holiday. Little changes were introduced into the liturgy, prayers with a specially mournful tinge being omitted. The period of sadness was suspended. Weddings were held. The barber was visited. The old pietists held a special watch-night service from dark to dawn, studying the *Zohar* in honour of its author. Children were given bows and arrows to play with, and staged mock-battles – for, according to tradition, the rainbow did not appear during Rabbi Simeon's life. In the south of France the school-children elected a Captain of Youth (*Capitaine de la Jeunesse*), with his lieutenant and treasurer, and was given full authority over his compeers.

It must have been a jolly time for students, young and old, in the medieval Ghetto. Like so much else that was colourful and delightful in the traditional scheme, it tended to be discarded in the nineteenth century, and little remained but a pale liturgical reminiscence. But – again like so much else – the new Palestine has revived it and given it a fresh lease of life. It was long customary for the Cabbalists to meet at the tomb of Rabbi Simeon ben Yohai, at Meron, where a bonfire was kindled in his honour and they danced with mystic devotion round the flames. Of late years this has become one of the great annual celebrations in Palestine, and people have come from all over the country to be present.

But why should the jollity be confined, after all, to Meron in Upper Galilee? Others who could not get there would appreciate the opportunity as well. Accordingly, it has become customary for bonfires to be kindled all over the country, in every Jewish settlement, on every vacant plot; children compete among themselves for the finest *medurah*, and when their own has burned out they go round the neighbourhood looking for others, private or public, to dance round; and their elders continue to do so long after the children have gone to bed. It is a sort of Guy Fawkes day, but with a tradition of two thousand instead of three hundred years behind it, and with a religious inspiration in the last instance.

Next day, the pious men of Jerusalem visit the sepulchre of Simeon the Righteous, the famous High Priest of Hellenistic times who is said to have encountered and appeased Alexander the Great. A jolly fair is held in an adjacent open place (appreciated to the full by the Arabs, who profit not a little from it), with donkeys and swings and roundabouts. Thus the New Palestine has already begun to fulfil its function of revivifying Jewish religious life, and showing how the time-honoured customs have lost nothing of their relevance and their appeal.

First published by the Jewish Education Committee, London, 1943.

25 A Pentecostal Rite

We are all familiar with the idea of the symbolical marriage of the *Torah* as it is associated with the Rejoicing of the Law, with its *Hatan Torah* and *Hatan Bereshit*. Few realise, on the other hand, that a somewhat similar idea, carried to a more daring conclusion, was formerly associated (and indeed, is still in many parts) with the Pentecost.

The main conception is that this feast commemorates the espousal of Israel and the *Torah* at the foot of Mount Sinai. This quaint but lovely idea can be traced back in Jewish literature for a long way, owing its origin, perhaps, to the betrothal of Israel of which the prophet Hosea speaks. In the course of the Middle Ages, it took on a wider development. The Zohar refers to the period of the Omer, between Passover and Pentecost as the days of courting between Israel and the Torah, his bride. In the eleventh century, the liturgical poet, Isaac ben Reuben, interpolated into the synagogue service, in the introduction to his *Azharot*, a sort of parody of the actual Marriage Contract, in which the conditions of this espousal were not only enumerated but stipulated. After his day there was a large number of literary imitations, both in verse and in prose, culminating in a characteristic production of that marvellously gifted Levantine singer of the sixteenth century, Israel Najara, author of the hymn *Lecha Dodi*, whose sublimations of the erotic are among the masterpieces of Hebrew literature. In many editions of the Sefardi liturgy – especially those printed for Oriental usage – there are contained examples of this, both in Hebrew and in the vernacular, sometimes with alternates, for both the first and the second day of the Holy-day.

All this is not new to those who are interested in the byways of the prayer-book, or who have studied Professor Israel Davidson's classical work on *Parody in Jewish Literature*. Few, however, know the practical application of these literary exercises, which explains their existence and gives them so much more point. The account which follows is based on personal observation at Gibraltar during an unforgettable, exquisitely enjoyable Pentecost in 1929. The neighbouring communities of North Africa, of course, follow the same practice, and it is to be traced, also, further East in the Mediterranean world. Among the Marrano communities of Northern Europe, however (London, Amsterdam, Hamburg, etc.), it either never obtained, or else fell into desuetude at an early date.

In these communities, then, one of the features of Pentecost is the actual solemn celebration – not merely a symbolic recounting – of the espousals of Israel with the *Torah*. The parallel is carried out as exactly as possible. In front of the Ark burn bridal torches, surrounded with bouquets. The Scrolls of the Law are decked in white vestments, like a bride. When the Ark is opened, special hymns are sung. And then comes the climax. The Reader unrolls a parchment, illuminated in colour as all *Ketubot* should be, and from it he reads, in the characteristic chant reserved for such occasions, the Contract of Marriage. Its form is exactly the same as that which serves on all similar occasions – though with a few poetic embellishments.

> On Friday...the sixth day of the month of Sivan, on the day when the Lord came from Sinai and shone forth from Seir...in the year two thousand four hundred and forty-eight from the creation of the world, according to the reckoning which we here reckon in gladness and song, in this lovely and glorious land, the great and awesome wilderness, there came before us the prince of princes and noble of nobles who is named Israel...and said to the dear and pleasant child of many qualities, the perfect Law of God...be unto me as wife, thou who art lovely as the moon, and I will betroth thee unto me forever...By the bidding and with the help of Heaven I will cherish and honour thee all the days, for ever and for ever. I will give unto thee, moreover, as the price of thy maidenhood, an ear that hears and an eye that sees, which may have abundant fruit. And this bride, the holy Torah, was willing, and became his wife, engraven on the tablet of his heart; and he placed the crown of sovereignty on her head...

There is a good deal more, in the same hyperbolic language. When the recital is finished, the Scrolls are taken up to the reading

1. Cecil with Dorion Liebgott, the curator, at Beth Tzedek Synagogue Museum, probably taken at the formal opening of Cecil's collection at the museum. (Courtesy of *The Telegram*, Toronto.)

2. Irene and Cecil, taken at Cecil's final American appearance in April 1970 at Brandeis University.

3. Cecil Roth by Claude Marks, New York 1968.

4. Cecil Roth by Salon.

5. The Cecil Roth Medal.

6. Cecil's bookplate, a woodcut probably by
H. Fuchenback.

desk, preceded by a boy bearing a bouquet of flowers. The greatest *Mitzvah* of the day is that of holding the mantle during the procession – accompanying the bride, as it were, to the espousals. Meanwhile, the usual Psalm is sung to the melody generally reserved for the Marriage Hymn.

In our northern climes, nothing of this picturesque ceremonial remains – any more than of the one-time induction of boys to their studies of the Pentecost to the accompaniment of charming, picturesque formalities. There are still some pietists who sit up studying the whole of the first night of the feast, in honour of the Torah which was given to mankind on the following day. In Gibraltar, indeed, open house is kept by some hospitable souls on this occasion; nowhere else has the present writer made a social call for the first time at 2.30 a.m.

The kitchen, too, paid homage to the feast. There is a universal custom of eating dairy-foods and cheese-cakes in honour of the Law, likened in the Midrash to honey and milk. Indeed, according to some of the standard authorities, the statutory interval between meat and milk is abrogated on this occasion. In Italy, cone-shaped cakes known as *Monte Sinai* were baked, to represent the sacred mountain. (This custom is alluded to in the *Eben Bohan* by Calonymus ben Calonymus, in the fourteenth century, and survived at Avignon and Carpentras to a period within living memory.)

The Provençal Jews imitated the Lenten custom of their neighbours, preparing cakes in the shape of a seven-branched ladder. This presumably was intended to symbolize the bridge between earth and heaven by suggesting the seven heavenly spheres that had to be reached before the Torah could be brought down to earth. Subsequently it was ingeniously pointed out that the Hebrew word for ladder (mem, lamud, mem) had the same numerical value as that for Sinai (samech, yad, nun, yad).

In all this, however, there is nothing to recall the Oriental marriage rite. But do we not perhaps still retain, in our Synagogues, a faint reminiscence of the idea? It is an almost universal custom – especially among the Ashkenazim – to decorate the Synagogue with flowers on Pentecost. The earliest trace of this is said to be found in the practice of Jacob ben Moses Molin ('Maharil', d. 1427), who recommended the custom of scattering roses and other odorous blossoms on the floors of the houses of prayer on this feast, as an expression of joy. In some parts of Italy, rose-leaves are scattered also in the path of the Scroll on its way from the Ark, and on the table at mealtime.

Many reasons are given for this practice. It is said that it commemorated the harvest festival of former days, or the Day of Judgement for fruit trees, which is associated in a well-known passage of the *Mishnah* with Pentecost; while the greenery reminds us of the verdure on the Mount of Sinai. Yet in view of the practices described above, another explanation appears more likely. It is a natural custom to adorn the Synagogue with flowers on the occasion of a wedding. When was such decoration more in place, then, than on the Pentecost, when Israel himself celebrated his union with his mystic bride, the Torah?

First published in the *Jewish Chronicle*, London, 18 May 1934.

26 A Forgotten Shavuoth Ceremony

It is the morning of the first day of Pentecost in some mediaeval English or French or German Jewry, any time during the twelfth or the thirteenth century. The community was astir betimes, though perhaps not quite so early as on other holy days, for many of the householders have spent the whole of the previous night in study, retiring only after daybreak.

For little Joseph, as for one or two other children of his own age (he is a little more than three years old), it is an occasion of special excitement, for to-day he is to make his first conscious public appearance. It is the occasion when he is to be taken officially to the Synagogue for the first time, to be initiated in the study of the Torah, in honour of the anniversary of its promulgation to mankind at Mount Sinai.

There as a foretaste of this, indeed, long ago, shortly after his initiation into the Covenant of Abraham. A *Minyan* of adults had gathered in his father's house after the morning service in the Synagogue, on the Sabbath when his mother appeared in public for the first time after his birth. The child, dressed in all his dainty finery, was taken from her arms by the godmother and placed in his cradle. Meanwhile the godfather stood at the side holding a Bible, open at the Ten Commandments. The Chazan then placed his hand alternately on the child's head and on the open book, and chanted: 'May *this* one prove worthy of what is written in *this*; may *this* one study what is written in *this*; may this one learn what is written in this; may this one fulfil what is written in *this*.' Afterwards, they had recited verses of good augury from the Bible, and pronounced a special benediction. In addition, they had placed a quill-pen in his tiny hand to symbolise their hope that he would grow up to be a ready scribe in the Law of God.

Of all this, of course, little Joseph knows nothing, though perhaps they remind him of it this morning as they are dressing him in his new *Yom-Tov* clothes. He is then wrapped in a cloak, to prevent his eyes from resting on anything of evil augury on his path, and taken to Synagogue – not by his father, but by some renowned scholar who (to Joseph's surprise) makes a point of passing through the adjacent schoolhouse on his way.

When he arrives in the place of worship, a great surprise awaits him. The building is all festooned about with flowers, and sweet herbs are strewn about the floor, in honour of the feast. Instead of taking his place at his father's side, as usual, he is put up on the *Almemar* for all the congregation to see. Here he remains while the Scroll of the Law is taken out and the chapter which describes the giving of the Torah is read. He then receives the privilege of *Gelilah*, or redecking the sacred scroll, using for the purpose a specially-embroidered binder (*wimpel*) made years before by his mother, which was swathed about him when he was circumcised. This bore an inscription which was always in the following stereotyped form (the name and date are, of course, imaginary):

> (Joseph) son of (Moses): born for good fortune on (26 of Ellul 5307). May the Holy One, Blessed be He, cause him to grow up to study His law, and to enter beneath the marriage canopy, and to perform good deeds. Amen!

In recent years, the presentation of a child's wimpel to the synagogue has not been associated with any specific day. Originally, however, there can be little doubt that they were presented by the child whose name they bore, on the occasion of the Pentecost Feast when he was taken officially for the first time to Synagogue to pay homage to the Torah.

But greater excitement still is in store. When the service is over, his father receives congratulations and everyone pinches Joseph's cheek. Then, either in the Synagogue or in the adjacent schoolroom, he is given his first lesson. But what a lesson! On the previous day, some of the letters of the Hebrew alphabet had been written on a slate, together with verses such as 'Moses commanded us the Law.' This slate is now brought in, and each letter smeared over with honey. Joseph watches with wide-open eyes, wondering what can be the reason for all these preparations. He has not long to wait. When everything is ready, the venerable Rabbi or teacher takes him in his lap and holds up the slate before his eyes.

'*Aleph*,' he says, pointing.

As soon as Joseph repeats the name of the letter, he is allowed to lick off the honey which covers it. It is not likely that he will readily forget what an *Aleph* looks like! This continues until the child has licked the slate quite clean, and the Torah has literally become sweet in his mouth.

There is more still to come. Three cakes of flour and honey, on which were inscribed various texts, were baked by a young maiden yesterday for his special benefit. In addition, the preparations include a hard-boiled egg with its shell removed, and the white similarly decorated (a lost culinary art, apparently). The Rabbi reads these verses, word by word, and little Joseph lisps them after him. As each text is finished, he is allowed to have the 'cookie' and to eat it. He is then handed back into the arms of his mother, who has been a delighted spectator of the whole charming scene.

On the day following the feast, little Joseph will be taken to school to begin his studies in the ordinary way. No doubt he will be disappointed to find that there will be no sweetmeats on this or on subsequent occasions. Nevertheless, the charming formality is enough to give the study of the Torah an abiding pleasantness in his mind. He is now embarked on the path of study. It will not be many years before he is immersed in the mysteries of the Talmud. Perhaps later on he will go to Worms or to Troyes or to Norwich, to study in the *Yeshiva* at the feet of some famous Rabbi. In the end he may, himself, turn out to be a scholar of repute. But throughout life, he will never be able to forget that delightful Pentecostal ceremony which symbolises the sweetness which the Torah had for the Jew at all times. It does not seem too much to suggest that this Jewish practice, imitated uncritically in the Gentile world, gave rise to the old German custom, which still prevails, of mitigating the horrors of a child's first day at school by giving him a bag of candy. (Herr Hitler may perhaps care to devote his reforming enthusiasm, when he has the leisure, to eradicating this Semitic excrescence.) Nowadays all this is not only superseded, but completely forgotten.

First published in the *American Hebrew*, New York, 11 May 1934.

27 England and the Ninth of Ab[1]

One of the lesser mysteries of Anglo-Jewish history relates to the crowning tragedy of the medieval period – the expulsion of the Jews from England in 1290. Curiously enough, the text of the edict which brought this about has been lost. Its wording is unknown. Even its precise date is uncertain. In consequence, there was a rare degree of wrangling on the subject on the part of scholars and jurists of past generations. Lord Coke, the great 17th-century lawyer, denied that any formal banishment of the Jews ever took place, putting forward as an alternative the ingenious theory that their connection with England ended as the result of a voluntary exodus. Some authorities, like the learned, malevolent, earless William Prynne, considered that it was by Act of Parliament. Others, with greater plausibility, considered it to be the result of the exercise of the royal prerogative, this being the view officially taken at the time of the Whitehall Conference in 1655. An obscure Latin document, the so-called *Statutum de Judeis exeundis Regnum Angliae*, was at one time considered to preserve the actual text involved. Unfortunately this happens to be dated subsequent to the event, and there can be little doubt that it is in fact nothing more than a royal letter justifying the drastic step that had been taken. Modern historical criticism, though it has simplified the problem, has not succeeded in solving it.

However, certain Hebrew documents do furnish the clue to the solution of one of the questions involved —- that of the exact date of the measure. Rabbi Isaac Hayyim Cantarini, of Padua, recounting in his *Pahad Yitzhak* (Amsterdam, 1685) the tribulations of his own community at the time of the wars with Turkey, calls attention to the manifold catastrophes which had befallen the Jewish people on the Fast of the Ninth Day of Ab:

> Woe, woe to this day: this it is that troubleth Israel. Indeed, the anger of the Lord is kindled against this day, for He hath desired it to be a day of rebuking and off – casting from times

of yore, a day of final destruction and of dreadful curse. Upon it He was enangered against the generation of the Wilderness; upon it was the First Temple destroyed; upon it did He pour forth His anger through the minions of Nero, and wreak havoc in the ranks of Israel; upon it was the Second Temple torn asunder; upon it was the community of Alexandria laid waste; *upon it was Israel expelled from the kingdom of Inghilterra*; upon it was the exile from France in the year 5155 (1395); thereon in the year 5224 (1464) did the Evil begin (in Germany); thereon were they expelled from Spain in the year 5252 (1492), without pity; thereon, in the year 5315 (1555), Pope Paul IV made them drink of the cup of staggering, with a noise as of sickness; thereon was the commencement of oppression and trouble in Mantua (in 1632); and in the month of Ab, as we have heard, was the expulsion from Vienna. Such and such things have occurred to us upon this sorry day.

The date of this statement is so late that, without corroboration, it would be difficult to put credence in every detail. The first part of the passage, however, plainly goes back to an earlier authority, nearly two hundred years nearer the events which he describes. Don Isaac Abrabanel, the great scholar-statesman who witnessed with his own eyes the expulsion from Spain, gives, in his commentary on Jeremiah 2.24 (*in her Month shall they find her*), a precisely similar sequence of disasters which took place on the Ninth of Ab. To prove that Cantarini derived his information from this source, it is sufficient to point out that the error regarding the date of the expulsion from France (1395 instead of 1394) occurs in both passages. Abrabanel's statement, too, is worth quoting in full:

In that month was decreed the decree upon the Generation of the Wilderness, that they should die there; and it was the night of the ninth of Ab. On that day was the First Temple destroyed. On that day was the Second Temple destroyed. On that day was destroyed Alexandria, with the great congregation of Jews that was there. *On that day was wrought the expulsion of the island that is the End of the Earth, which is called Ingla-terra.* On that day was wrought the expulsion from France in the year 5155. Many other destructions and expulsions were similarly wrought in that month for Israel.

And what shall I add? For behold, when the king of Spain decreed banishment for all the Jews that were in all his dominions, that they should go forth within three months, the time ended and the day of departure fell on the Ninth of Ab. Yet he knew nothing of this, as though he were set upon his way by Heaven to determine the limit thus, in order to fulfil the word of the Prophet.

It may be mentioned that this passage returned ultimately to England, being cited by Haham David Nieto in his Spanish work on Divine Providence, published in London in 1715 in order to vindicate him from the charge of being a Spinozist.

What, however, was Abrabanel's authority? It is necessary to enquire into this point before deciding what credence is to be placed in his statement, which is corroborated by no other early writer. He had access, however, when he dealt with English matters, to a source which, to posterity's loss, is no longer extant. He refers to this in his work on the Messiah, *The Salvation of his Anointed*, in a very important passage:

> ... But an expulsion that the kings of the land and its authorities should expel the Jews from their land, saying: 'Arise, go forth from the midst of my people: ye shall dwell no longer in our land' – it is not known that this was done in all the land whence they were exiled, until the year 5020 of the Creation (i.e. 5050 = 1290); and its commencement was in France where it was not general, but in single cities. But a general expulsion in a whole kingdom was first made in the island which is called the Corner of the Earth, that is Ingla-terra, in the aforementioned year: there being here several great communities, and especially the great city which is called Londres, where there were of the children of Israel two thousand householders ... And the king of this island made, in the same year which I have mentioned, a general expulsion of all the Jewish communities of his realm ... as you shall see all this in the work *Record of the Persecutions of Israel after the Destruction*, composed and collected by the author of the *Ephod*.

The similarity of language and other considerations make it virtually certain that it was from this same work that Abrabanel derived his information regarding the date of the expulsion from England – the Ninth of Ab. The author to whom he refers is, of course, the famous satirist and philosopher, Profiat Duran, whose lost historical work (now, alas! gone beyond hope of recovery) was used by other chroniclers of the 16th century such as Solomon Usque and Judah ibn Verga. Duran was born in the second half of the 14th century in the south of France, and died not long after the year 1400. He flourished, accordingly, less than a century after the actual expulsion from England, and his information regarding this event must therefore be treated with deference.

It must be confessed, nevertheless, that generic statements of the sort quoted above from Isaac Cantarini and Isaac Abrabanel, are always open to suspicion, and on some occasions can actually be proved inaccurate. It was not, indeed, unnatural to enhance the significance of the anniversary by exaggerating its terrible record through further, slightly subjective, approximations.

Thus, for example, the expulsion from Spain, which all Jewish authorities assert to have culminated on the Ninth of Ab (which in 1492 fell on August 2) actually took place two days earlier, on July 31. Modern historians, in order to reconcile the two accounts, assume that a slight extension of time was accorded to the unhappy exiles; but this does not find any corroboration in the official documents. The fact of the matter is, no doubt, that the exiles were so impressed by the approximation of their disaster with the great national day of mourning, that they overlooked the slight difference; or that isolated groups here and there managed to delay their departure for another couple of days. Some of the other events given in the old lists, on the other hand, are purely legendary or even fictitious.

However, before dismissing the statement regarding the expulsion from England into this category, it is advisable to examine the circumstances more closely. On doing this, a remarkable result appears. The Ninth of Ab, in the year 1290, coincided with the 18th day of July. This, as it happens, is *the actual date of the still-extant royal writs to the sheriffs of the various English counties, intimating that a decree had been issued for the expulsion of the Jews.* That these writs should have been sent out on the actual day on which the edict of expulsion was published is not by any means to be taken for granted. But on the other hand, there is no reason whatsoever why this should not have been the case. Jewish historians of the 14th and

15th and 16th centuries knew nothing of sheriffs' writs and charters, and musty English records. They had nothing to go upon but oral tradition or Hebrew martyrologies, which may or may not have been correct. In this particular case, however, the information which they give is borne out in a striking manner by actual English records which came to light long after.

We may say that the edict for the expulsion of the Jews from England was issued, then, on July 18, 1290, on the same day that the proposed measure was communicated for enforcement to the sheriffs of the counties (of course it did not come into effect until much later, on November 1). On the same day, no doubt, it became known to the community of London. It happened to be the Ninth of Ab. The coincidence inevitably impressed the imagination of the Jewish people, becoming part of its legendary recollection, handed down from generation to generation.

First published in the *Jewish Chronicle*, July supplement, 1933.

NOTE

1.   'Ab' and 'Av' are used interchangeably in this volume.

28 The Ninth of Av in History

Haham David Nieto, Rabbi of the Sefardi Community of London at the beginning of the eighteenth century, refers in one of his philosophical treatises to the extraordinary series of disasters which has overtaken the Jewish people on the Ninth of Av, as a proof of the immanence and activity of Divine Providence in human affairs. Indeed, the sequence of major tragedies associated in Jewish history with this date is so protracted and so intense, that it hardly seems sufficient to ascribe it simply to the long arm of coincidence.

Of course, there are certainly legendary associations with the day which are Midrashic. Thus, for example, Rabbinic lore asserted that is was upon the Ninth of Av that the Divine decree went out against their forefathers in the wilderness of Sinai, that all should die without seeing the promised Land. Similarly, at a later date, certain rough-and-ready approximations enhanced artificially the tragic memories of the day. Nevertheless, no degree of minimisation can prevent the list from being long and impressive; a scarlet thread running throughout the whole course of Jewish history from primitive times down almost to our own day.

586 BCE – DESTRUCTION OF THE FIRST TEMPLE

The date of Av 10 (the tenth day of the fifth month) is given in Jeremiah lii., 12–13, for the destruction of the first Temple by the Babylonians: 'Now, in the fifth month, in the tenth day of the month...came Nebuzaradan, captain of the guard, which served the king of Babylon, into Jerusalem, and burned the house of the Lord and the king's house; and all the houses of Jerusalem, and all the houses of the great men, burned he with fire.' From Zechariah vii., 5, and viii., 19, it appears that a fast in commemoration of this disaster was kept by the Jews as early as the time of the Babylonian exile.

70 CE – THE SECOND TEMPLE DESTROYED BY THE ROMANS

Fire was set to the gates on Av 9; the conflagration consumed the building itself on the following day. (Parts of the city, on the other hand, held out for another month.) The coincidence of date impressed even so callous an observer as Josephus who wrote: 'God had doomed the Temple to the fire, according to the destiny of the ages, on that same fatal day, the tenth of the month of Lous, on which it was formerly burned by the King of Babylon.' In view of this, some authorities of the following generations were of the opinion that the fast should rightly have been fixed on Av 10th, not 9th. This, in point of fact, is the date observed by the Karaites.

117 CE – MASSACRE OF THE JEWS OF ALEXANDRIA

During the reign of the Emperor Trajan, the Egyptian Jews participated in a world-wide revolt against the Roman rule. At first they gained some advantages. In a battle outside the gates of Alexandria, the Imperial troops were worsted and retired into the city; but here they gained the upper hand and massacred the Jewish inhabitants. According to the Rabbinic reports, this took place on the Ninth of Av. It was from the time of this disaster that the community in Egypt, once so flourishing and so important, dated its downfall.

135 CE – FALL OF BETAR

With the fall of Betar and the collapse of the great Jewish revolt under Bar Cochba, ended the last hopes for the revival of Jewish independence in Palestine in the Classical period. The massacres accompanying this disaster were, moreover, so ghastly and so widespread that it is to this, rather than to the great revolt of sixty years previous, that the depopulation of Judea is to be traced. It was probably this disaster which finally established the ninth, rather than the tenth, of Av as the great national fast.

136 CE – THE SITE OF JERUSALEM PLOUGHED

The coincidence on this occasion was probably not accidental, but deliberately fixed by the Romans. It was carried out at the order of the Emperor Trajan as a token of the final obliteration of the ancient Jewish capital, the site of which was henceforth to be occupied by a Roman colony bearing an entirely different name, into which no Jew was allowed to enter. This is reckoned in the Mishnah (Taanit iv. 4) as the fifth of the great national disasters that occurred upon this anniversary (the first being the edict of extermination against the Generation of the Wilderness).

1290 CE – EXPULSION FROM ENGLAND

The writs to the Sheriffs of the various English counties, intimating that a decree had been issued for the expulsion of the Jews, were sent out on July 18. This, as it happens, was the Ninth of Av. Medieval Jewish historians counted this as one of the manifold national disasters which had occurred on that day; and rightly so, for it was the first of the series of wholesale expulsions from various lands which marked the tragic course of the Jewish Middle Ages. Upwards of three months were allowed for the unfortunate exiles to leave the country, the final limit being fixed for November 1.

1306 CE – ARREST OF THE JEWS IN FRANCE

The arrest of the Jews in France by Philip the Fair was preparatory to their expulsion. In prison they were informed that, for some unspecified sin, they had been condemned to exile and would have to leave the country within one month. With them they were allowed to take only the clothes they wore and a miserably small sum of money. This disaster marked the end of the glories of the French Jewry of the Middle Ages. The arrest took place on July 22 – the tenth of Av.

1492 CE – JEWS LEAVE SPAIN

The decree of expulsion had been issued by Ferdinand and Isabella on March 31, four months being given for it to be carried into effect. This brought the date down to July 31 – two days before the Ninth of Av. The great Don Isaac Abrabanel, however, who himself was among the victims, explicitly states that the day of departure fell on the Ninth of Av 'as though he (the king) were set upon his way by Heaven to determine the limit thus, in order to fulfil the word of the Prophet'. There can be no doubt, accordingly, that some at least of the exiles, if not the main body, left the land upon this fatal day.

1555 CE – GHETTO ESTABLISHED AT ROME

Italy had once been a halcyon land for the Jews, but the Catholic Reaction in the middle of the sixteenth century reversed this. It was Pope Paul IV's Bull, Cumnimis absurdum, of July 12, 1555, which gave the new spirit its expression. In accordance with this, on July 26 of that year, all the Jews of the Papal capital were herded into a malodorous district near the Tiber, peculiarly subject to inundations and disease, subsequently to be known as the Ghetto. This day marked the inception of the long martyrdom of Roman Jewry, which lasted until 1870, as well as the beginning of the darkest chapter in the history of Italy as a whole. It coincided exactly – probably through the intentional malevolence of those responsible – with the Ninth of Av.

1571 CE – GHETTO SYSTEM INTRODUCED INTO FLORENCE

In order to obtain, from the Pope, official recognition of his elevation to the dignity of Grand Duke, Cosimo de Medici sacrificed his principles and his Jewish subjects. On July 31, 1571, there was published an edict introducing into his dominions the Ghetto system in all its severity, including the wearing of the distinctive Jewish hat. The date coincided with the Ninth of Av.

1579 CE – DEATH OF JOSEPH NASI

Marrano Prince, virutal ruler of the Turkish Empire, courted by all the monarchs and statesmen of Europe, staunch friend and champion of his own people, pioneer of the Jewish settlement in the Holy Land, Joseph Nasi occupied a position in the eyes of the world and of his people equalled by no other Jew in recent centuries. His death in 1579 was a national disaster. It is small wonder that contemporaries called attention to the fact that it took place upon the anniversary of the great national catastrophe – the Ninth of Av.

1626 CE – BIRTH OF SABBETAI ZEVI

Sabbetai Zevi, the arch false messiah of the Jews, who beguiled hundreds of thousands to his cause before abandoning them and publicly embracing Islam, was born in Smyrna in 1626, on the Ninth of Av.

1630 CE – EXPULSION FROM MANUS

On the extinction of the line of Gonzaga, the Duchy was contested by Charles of Rethel, the French nominee, and the Holy Roman Emperor, Ferdinand II. The former, the legitimate heir, entered into enjoyment of his inheritance, but the city was besieged by a combined army of Germans and Spaniards. When in 1630 the city was betrayed to the enemy, the Jews (who had eagerly espoused Duke Charles' claim) were driven out mercilessly, without the slightest pretext, from the city in which their ancestors had so long resided. It was one of the worst tragedies of the sort that seventeenth-century Jewish life witnessed; and it took place, as succeeding generations continued to remember with superstitious awe, on Thursday, July 18 – the Ninth of Av.

1670 CE – EXPULSION FROM VIENNA

Leopold I's marriage in 1660, to a Spanish princess, had brought his natural fanaticism to a head, and it hardly needed the pretext that the Jews were rumoured to be in treasonable correspondence with the Swedes for him to give expression to this. Accordingly, there was issued on February 27, 1670, and solemnly proclaimed on March 1, an order for all the Jews to leave Upper and Lower Austria, including the capital. This had to enter into effect on August 1; but it was on July 28 that the Jews left the city, the last day that they passed in it undisturbed being the fast of the Ninth of Av. It was to this event, incidentally, that many of the important German Jewish communities, including that of Berlin itself, owed their origin.

1684 CE – ATTACK ON JEWS OF PADUA

It happened that on this day – August 4 – news reached Padua that the Christian forces had captured Budapest from the Turk. The report, as a matter of fact, was false, but the joy of the people knew no bounds. Only the Jews failed to show their jubilance in public, for it was the anniversary of their great national fast and they were holding the usual mournful services in their Synagogues. The populace took this as proof of Jewish sympathy with the Turk, the enemy of Christendom. Thus began the series of attacks which came to a head on August 20, when the Community experienced so narrow an escape that it is commemorated, year by year, down to the present day.

1929 CE – ARAB RIOTS IN PALESTINE

There was indeed, in this case, no question of accidental coincidence, since the trouble centered about the fact that the Arabs questioned the right of the Jews to pray, as they had done from time immemorial, at the fragmentary Western Wall, all that was left of the bygone Temple glories, on this solemn anniversary. In consequence of this, a wave of massacres swept through the country, reaching their climax at Hebron, where the entire Community was either butchered or else driven into flight. It was the most tragic episode by far in the recent history of Palestine. But the reactions were very different from what might have been expected. Instead of giving itself up to panic, the Yishuv set its teeth and dedicated itself with renewed intensity to the sacred task of rebuilding the ancestral land. This, plainly, is the lesson which the Ninth of Av should have for us today – not one of mourning for the past, but of triumph in survival and hope in the future. '*Thus saith the Lord of Hosts: the fast of the fourth month, and the fast of the fifth, and the fast of the seventh, and the fast of the tenth, shall be to the house of Judah joy and gladness and cheerful feasts...*'

First published in the *Jewish Chronicle*, London, 2 August 1935.

29 The Historical Elegies of the Ninth of Ab

The Jewish liturgy is full of historical reminiscences, not only those relating to the remote period of the genesis of the Hebrew people and their faith, but more recent features, added little by little in the course of the Middle Ages and after. The great savant, Leopold Zunz, father of scientific Jewish scholarship in the modern sense, devoted a famous chapter in one of his works to a description of Jewish persecutions in Europe and their liturgical echoes, especially in the synagogal poetry, and even in his day the tale was not ended. It is fascinating, though sad, to turn over the pages of the prayer-books published for the use of remote and now defunct Jewish communities, and to read the features which were included in them in commemoration of some tragic local event, of which they may sometimes be the only memorial. These were generally written for recital at some annual fast which was observed locally. In the German ritual, moreover, you may find them interspersed in the special hymns which used to be recited (and still are in some congregations) during the Sabbath Morning services between Passover and Pentecost, when the worst of the Rhineland massacres took place at the time of the Crusades. (The *Zulath* for the first week after Passover, and for the week before Pentecost, are especially memorable.)

The Ninth of Ab, the great day of national mourning, was, however, regarded as especially fitting for the interposition of material of this sort, suitable equally well as the actual anniversaries of the events in question. In many local liturgies, therefore, you will find historic elegies prescribed for recital on this occasion in order, as it were, to renew the bitterness of the recollection. In the Sephardi rite as it is followed in England, for example, there are two – one by Judah ibn Jahia, sung to a particularly beautiful melody, which commemorates the disaster which overtook Spanish Jewry in 1391, another on the general expulsion from Spain in 1492, which as is well known, coincided with the Ninth of Ab. Similar features are to be found, too, in the Ashkenazi ritual. It is well that when we hear them, we should know something about the events to which they refer.

Jewish martyrdom in Europe began with the First Crusade, in 1096, when the soldiers of the Cross, confident that the death of an unbeliever would secure them eternal felicity, tried to secure it on easy terms by attacking the Jews even before they left home. The first attack took place on May 3 at Speyer, where the synagogue was surrounded and attacked, though the casualties were kept low through the protection of the Bishop, true to the nobler traditions of the Church. A fortnight afterwards, on May 18, there was an onslaught at Worms; here the whole Jewish community was butchered, almost to a man, the names of no fewer than 350 martyrs being recorded in the Memorial Books of the local communities. From Worms the Crusaders made their way to Mainz, where similar carnage ensued on May 27 – immediately before Pentecost, on which day there was a similar massacre at Cologne. It was the season of the giving of the Law, as the Jews did not fail to note; on the day of its giving, they said, it now returned on high in flames.

There are heartrending accounts of this series of massacres in the various chronicles of the time, with which the tradition of mediaeval Jewish historiography begins. Many elegies were written on the victims by contemporary poets. That which has entered into the Ninth of Ab liturgy, Mi Yitten Roshi Mayim, is by Kalonymus ben Judah of Spiers, who was probably a boy at the time of the attack:

> Would that my head were of water, and my eyes the fount of my tears! Then would I weep all my days and nights for my slain ones – my children and my babes, and the old men of my congregations. And answer ye with all manner of cries of woe, and weep ye with a great lamentation *for the house of Israel, and the people of the Lord, for they are fallen by the sword.*
>
> Mine eyes weep bitterly, and I go to the field of weeping, and I weep with those that are bitter of heart and distraught, for the beauteous maidens and tender children who, enwrapped in their scrolls, were dragged to the slaughter. More ruddy in body than rubies[1] – like sapphires or carbuncles – they are trampled and cast forth like the mire of the streets. 'Depart ye! unclean!' men cry,[2] that none should approach *the house of Israel, and the people of the Lord, for they are fallen by the sword.*

Mine eyes flow with tears and I shriek and mourn, and I call for weeping and the girding on of sackcloth in lament. More precious than fine gold! More worth than treasure! Greater her honour than any precious thing! I have seen her rent – bereft and solitary; the Law and the Scriptures! The Mishna and Gemara! Wail ye and mourn ye, to make this known. Where is the Law? Where the pupil that studied it? Is not the place desolate, that none dwelleth therein, *of the house of Israel and the people of the Lord, for they are fallen by the sword.*

Mine eyelids drip with water and flow with tears, and I mourn bitterly for those who were slain at Spiers; in the second month, on the eighth day, on the precious day of rest,[3] they were turned from repose to storm in destruction. The precious youths and goodly old men were gathered up together, and gave up their souls in awe, for the unity of the One God, and gloriously testified to the Unity. Mighty in steadfastness, and speedy to do His will, there died of my priests and my young men, ten in all. In the bitterness of my anguish and my sorrow, I join in wailing, as I call to mind this day – the martyrdom of the holy congregations.

The community of Worms, tested and chosen, the mighty ones of the earth, perfect in purity – twice did they, in awe, sanctify the One Name. On the twenty-third of Ziv (Iyyar) in purity, and on the third month at the chanting of the Hallel,[4] did they render up their souls, united in love. (Crowned were they, with a chaplet upon their heads, as an adornment) I shall moan for them, pouring forth my wails in tears, and for the mighty ones of the congregation of Mayence, the beautiful. Swifter than eagles and more valiant than lions, they gave up their souls for the Unity of the great Name. For them shall I lament with a cry of destruction, and for the laying waste of my lesser temples[5] and houses of study of the Law.

On the third day of the third month was added more care and bane, and the month was changed to trouble and stress. Upon the day of the Giving of the Law had I hoped to be strengthened; but on the day of its giving, then did it return. It mounted up on high to the place of its dwelling, together with those who held it and contained it,[6] who studied it and expounded it who learned it and taught it at midnight as in day. Take this to your hearts, and gird on a bitter mourning, for worthy is their slaughter that one mourn and roll in the dust, even for the burning of the House of our God, the Palace and the City. Yet since we may not add a fresh season of mourning for destruction and burning, and since we may lament only after the anniversary, and not before it,[7] therefore this day do I arouse my plaint, and I mourn and wail and weep with bitter soul, and my groans are heavy from morning unto eve, *for the house of Israel and the people of the Lord, for they are fallen by the sword.*

The famous elegy Shaali Serufah – 'Ask, is it well, O thou consumed in fire' – is by Rabbi Meir of Rothenburg, one of the most famous German Talmudists of the thirteenth century. In 1242 he was in Paris as a student, and there witnessed what the Jews of that day considered to be the greatest of the tragedies that had overwhelmed them even in that tragic time. Two years before, an apostate from Judaism named Nicholas Donin had denounced the Talmud to the Pope as being pernicious and filled with blasphemies against Christianity. In consequence, orders were issued for the seizure of all copies of the much-decried work and an investigation into its contents. In France the order was implicitly obeyed, all Hebrew literature that could be found (not the Talmud alone) being seized throughout he country on March 3, 1240, while the Jews were at service in their Synagogues. On June 12, an enquiry into its merits and demerits was opened in Paris, in the presence of members of the royal court. The Jewish case was presented by Rabbi Jehiel of Paris, perhaps the most famous teacher of the day. The 'verdict' was, of course, certain: Donin was adjudged to have proved his case, and the work he had denounced was finally condemned to the flames.

On Friday, June 17, 1242, twenty-four cartloads of priceless Hebrew manuscripts were publicly burned in Paris – the prelude to many other similar holocausts, culminating in those which have taken place in our own day in Germany. The disaster was mourned by the Jews – and rightly – hardly less than the physical martyrdom of their brethren. That the elegy by Meir of Rothenburg was included in the Ninth of Ab liturgy is in itself eloquent testimony to this. The beautiful translation that follows is from the pen of the late Nina Salaman, one of the most gifted and charming of English Jewesses of our day:

Ask, is it well, O thou consumed of fire,
      With those that mourn for thee,
That yearn to tread thy courts, that sore desire
      Thy sanctuary;

That panting for thy land's sweet dust, are grieved,
      And sorrow in their souls,
And by the flames of wasting fire bereaved,
      Mourn for thy scrolls;

That grope in shadow of unbroken night,
      Waiting the day to see,
Which o'er them yet shall cast a radiance bright,
      And over thee?

Ask of the welfare of the man of woe,
      With breaking heart, in vain
Lamenting ever for thine overthrow,
      And for thy pain;

Of him that crieth, as the jackals cry,
      As owls their moaning make,
Proclaiming bitter wailing far and nigh;
      Yea, for thy sake.

And thou, revealed amid a heavenly fire,
      By earthly fire consume,
Say how the foe, unscorched, escaped the pyre,
      Thy flames illumed!

How long shalt thou, that art at ease, abide
      In peace, unknown to woe,
While o'er my flowers, humbled from their pride,
      Thy nettles grow?

Thou sittest high exalted, lofty foe,
      To judge the sons of God;
And with thy judgments stern, dost bring them low
      Beneath thy rod.

Yea, more, to burn the Law durst decree
    God's word to banish hence;
Then blest be he who shall award to thee
    Thy recompense!

E'en as thy rock hath sore afflicted thee,
    He will assuage thy woe:
Will turn again the tribes' captivity,
    And raise the low.

Yet shalt thou wear thy scarlet raiment choice,
    And sound the timbrels high,
And yet amid the dancers shalt rejoice
    With gladdened cry.

My heart shall be uplifted on the day
    Thy Rock shall be thy light,
When He shall make thy gloom to pass away,
    Thy darkness bright.

While speaking of the historical elegies of the Ninth of Ab, it is necessary, at least, to mention Arze Ha Lebanon – 'The Cedars of Lebanon, mighty in the Law.' The reading of this elegy is generally assigned to the Rabbi, for it commemorates the *Assarah Haruge Malchuth*, or Ten Martyrs of the (Roman) State, Rabbi Akiba and the rest. (There is a similar elegy in the Sephardi Ninth of Ab liturgy, and yet another is included in our Afternoon Service for the Day of Atonement.) These poems are all relatively late, being written many hundreds of years after the event which they describe, and they have therefore no historic value. In fact, the list of the Ten Martyrs is variously made up in the different accounts that have come down to us, and is obviously artificial; indeed, all of those mentioned were not contemporary, some dying at the time of the Fall of Jerusalem in 70 and some over sixty years later, during the Bar Cochba revolt. Probably there was a well-founded tradition that on a certain occasion, whether in the year 70 or in 135, ten famous scholars (including some of those named in the elegies) were martyred together, and later on the popular fantasy tried to make up the number by including martyrs of that age, not paying as much attention as they should to the niceties of chronology.

There is one other famous Ninth of Ab poem which has a touching historical association. I am referring to that most famous of Judah ha Levi's compositions, Zion Halo Tish'ali. It was the great poet's finest expression of his yearning for the land of his dreams. Not long after he wrote it, he went to Palestine at last. When he arrived within sight of Jerusalem, it is recounted, he prostrated himself on the earth. A passing Arab horseman spurred over his body, and he sobbed out his life to the immortal cadences of his great ode:

> Zion, wilt thou not ask if Peace's wing
>   Shadows the captives that ensue thy peace,
> Left lonely from thine ancient shepherding?

First published in *Aspects of Jewish Life and Education*, London, 1945.

NOTES

1. Lamentations iv, 7. (CR)
2. Ibid., iv, 15. (CR)
3. That is, on the Sabbath, the eighth of Iyyar. (CR)
4. That is, the New Moon of sivan. (CR)
5. According to the idea that prayer now replaces sacrifice, the Synagogue is the 'lesser temple'. (CR)
6. Literally, 'its casing and casket'. It was hoped that upon the day when the Law was given, the Pentecost, its merit would come to the aid of those who had received it, but, instead it returned to Heaven in the flames. (CR)
7. Thus, if the Ninth of Ab falls upon the Sabbath, the commemoration is postponed till the next day, and never anticipated. (CR)

30 May Jews Return to Spain?

There is a very widespread impression among Jews that at the time of the Jewish Expulsion from Spain, the Rabbis of that generation placed a *Cherem* on the country, imposing a formal ban on any person who should return there. This idea is widely prevalent, and I have come across it in all parts of the world, though curiously enough, more perhaps among Ashkenazim than among Sephardim. In making enquiry in a class of future Jewish ministers, whose answers on other occasions tended regrettably to be at variance in points of fact, I found that three-quarters of those present had heard of it.

A rabbi once told me that, travelling in the South of France, he approached the Spanish border and looked longingly over on the forbidden soil, but did not set foot on it because of the Cherem! I recall that the then president of the Board of Deputies of British Jews, at the height of the Nazi persecutions, stated in a public speech that the Jews should impose a Cherem on resettling in Germany or entering the country, as their fathers had done four and a half centuries earlier in connection with Spain. And among less-informed persons in all parts of the world, I have found a similar unanimity of opinion on this historical episode.

Always this tale presented certain difficulties to me, when I heard of it, and for two main reasons. First, that I could not understand why such a Cherem should have been imposed in the case of Spain and not of other countries. To be sure, it was a horrible episode in our history, ended a brilliant age and caused a great amount of suffering – but not more (save in scale) than in the case of the expulsions from, say, England in 1290 and from France in 1306 etc., in connection with which we are not told anything of this nature. Nor do we hear anything analogous in connection with the various cities and provinces of Germany, in which the Jews were massacred and persecuted in the Middle Ages with a ferocity unknown in any other land. If there were a Cherem on the resettlement of the Jews in

Spain, surely there should have been a similar one against, let us say, the resettlement of the Jews in places such as Nuremberg. But nothing of the sort is known.

And there was another difficulty, too, which made the report suspect. In point of fact, it is not true that Jews have been entirely absent from Spain in the centuries after the Expulsion. All manner of sources – Inquisitional reports, governmental regulations, and so on – make it clear that there was, in the seventeenth and eighteenth centuries, a constant trickle of visitors – most of them from North Africa, or later on, merchants from the British stronghold of Gibraltar. Indeed, their presence was so notorious that at intervals the Spanish government issued instructions that they should wear a hat of distinguishing colour so that they could be recognized.

The Inquisition objected to their presence, protested against it, sometimes took steps for their surveillance and even ejection, but otherwise it was powerless against born Jews who had never professed, nor pretended to profess, Christianity. The numbers involved were, indeed, very small. One can only adduce a score or so of cases spread over a period of centuries; but nevertheless, this is sufficient to demonstrate that the exclusion was not complete. Yet if it be true that the Cherem against the entry of Jews into Spain was in force, how was it possible that these persons should have overlooked it? In many cases they were probably poor and ignorant, but this was not so in all.

One of the Jewish bibliographical treasures which I possess is the Spanish edition of Moses Almosnino's remarkable work on Turkish history, published in Madrid in 1638 by Jacob Cansino, member of a most erudite Moroccan family and an interpreter in the Spanish service, who had lived in the Spanish capital, it seems, for half a dozen years previously. There is a more outstanding case in the person of the learned and pious Rabbi Sasportas, later Haham in London and then in Amsterdam, who was for a long time the diplomatic representative of the Sultan of Morocco at the Spanish Court. That such a man, one of the great scholars of the age, would have flouted the alleged Cherem, had it existed, is inconceivable; and surely, if he were specifically and formally exempted from it, there would certainly have been some record of the fact.

Seeking some positive evidence when I was last in Jerusalem, I consulted some of the persons whose vast knowledge of the sources might be of assistance in such an inquiry. One of them was Professor

Yitzhak Baer, the eminent authority on Spanish Jewish history, whose great work on the Jews in Christian Spain is one of the historical classics of our age. He replied that he too had long been searching for the evidence, but without result. I then repeated the inquiry in the house of my venerated friend, Haham Yitzchak Nissim, Chief Rabbi of the Sephardi Jewish communities of Israel, whose knowledge of the Responsa Literature, Sh'eyloth U'teshuvoth, especially of the Sephardi Rabbis, is unrivalled.

The Haham knew of nothing bearing on the subject, though his erudite son, Meir Benayahu, a great authority on the history of the Oriental Jewish communities, called my attention to an interesting *teshuvah*[1] of Rabbi Moses Trami, the great Safed scholar of the sixteenth century, in which he expressed his confidence that no Jew would return to Spain because the regathering of Jewish people to Palestine was imminent. (It seems that he wrote under the dramatic impact of Don Joseph Nasi's attempt to colonize Tiberias.) This, however, is a long way removed from a Cherem. Indeed, the conception could not be more different. So my search still continued.

We have, therefore, no positive evidence for the existence of the Cherem, but there is definite proof that scholars of the seventeenth century did not know of it; yet, at the same time, there is a persistent and widespread legend which cannot be overlooked. How are these evidences to be reconciled?

I am confident that at last I have found the solution to the mystery. Such a Cherem did in fact exist – but it was not in the form, and did not have the implications, generally believed.

There was a recurrent problem which troubled the Sephardi Jewish communities of Northern Europe of Marrano origin. It was the conduct of some of their members who, after escaping from Spain or Portugal and formally embracing the Jewish faith in public, and joining the Jewish communities in their new places of residence, went back to the Peninsula for longer or shorter periods for business purposes, or sometimes even for social visits. They hoped that none there would know how they had acted during their absence, and therefore pretended that they were still (and had always remained) Catholics. Sometimes, indeed, the Inquisition found out about them, proceedings were taken against them, and there would be a tragic conclusion at an auto-da-fe.

On the other hand, such visits presented serious problems for the Jewish communities as well. It was intolerable that those who had declared their allegiance to Judaism, and had become members of the synagogue, should throw it all up temporarily, travel voluntarily to countries where they would not be able to practise the Jewish religion and there be compelled to conform again to Christianity, then return and expect to be received in the Synagogue on the same terms as before. Obviously this created an intolerable situation, which could not be passed over casually.

On one occasion, as I seem to recall having read in an eighteenth-century document, great scandal was caused at Bayonne when, on the ninth of Av, a member of the community returned to the town after a long business trip over the border of Spain, and a severe punishment was imposed on him. Similarly, the regulations of the famous Society for Dowering the Brides (*Hebra da cazar Orjas*) at Leghorn, as drawn up in 1727, excluded from membership and benefits of the body any person who should pay a protracted visit to Spain or Portugal, as a logical corollary to the exclusion of any convert to Christianity. And in London, the congregation Sahar Asamaim put the matter on the most formal footing in its 'Ascamoth' or Regulations. I translate from the printed edition of 1785:

> Any person of our Nation who has come from Spain or Portugal to this or any other land where Judaism is tolerated, and there professed our Holy Law, and who afterwards returns to either of the said countries or to any other where he is obliged to live as a Christian, shall be excluded from being a *Yahid*. Moreover, if he returns to dwell in this land he shall not be admitted to our Congregation, nor to any other convenience which he could enjoy as a Jew, unless he goes upon the Teba on the day when the entire Mahamad shall appoint, at the time of prayer, and shall ask pardon in a loud voice for his crime from God and the *Kahal*, and shall submit himself moreover to the penitence which the Senhor *Haham* . . . shall impose . . .

There is more to the same effect, elaborating the circumstances and defining the penalties which are, in effect, equivalent to a *Cherem*. I do not know precisely when this regulation was passed – it does not figure in the original communal regulations of the seventeenth century – but it certainly went back well before 1784. Moreover, most of the London *Hascamot* are based on those of the

Sephardi community of Amsterdam, which was in turn strongly influenced by that of the so-called 'Nazione Ponentina' of Venice. And I have no doubt that the same attitude prevailed, and similar penalties were enforced, in those communities, whether or not they were formally enunciated (which indeed in the Catholic atmosphere of Venice might have been somewhat dangerous).

It appears to me, then, that we have now reached the end of our enquiry and solved the mystery that has been puzzling us. There was, in fact, no religious objection to the resettlement of Jews in Spain, still less to a temporary visit. But there was a very proper and deep-rooted objection to the return to Spain on the part of members of the Spanish and Portuguese communities in circumstances in which they would have been compelled to dissemble their faith; and the penalties laid down virtually converted this into something hardly distinguishable from a Cherem. In conversation with their Ashkenazi neighbors, Sephardim would state, not inaccurately, that a ban was imposed by their religious authorities on a visit to Spain. Taken out of its context, this was reinterpreted into something far more sweeping, more comprehensive, and more dramatic. But there is not (and never has been) any Cherem on the resettlement of Jews in Spain.

First published in *Orthodox Jewish Life*, New York, February 1957.

NOTE

1. Rabbinic response to question on Jewish law in practice.

31 The Last Days of Jewish Salonica

The fate of the Jews of Salonica at the hands of the Nazis is an episode of recent history that for some reason or other has been relatively overlooked. Yet even in recent history, there are few stories more terrible.

On the eve of World War II, Salonica, Greece's third largest city, had a Jewish population of some 50,000 in a total of 240,000; compared to the past, this represented a sharp decline for what was traditionally a Jewish city. The ancient intellectual preeminence had also waned somewhat. But Salonica was still the greatest centre of Sephardi Jewry in the world, with its synagogues and academies, its rabbis and its teachers, its newspapers and its printing presses, and some scholars of distinction among the sixty rabbis and communal functionaries. Moreover, the city was still a happy hunting ground for Spanish philologists and scholars, anxious to trace, in the speech of the descendants of the exiles of 1492, the authentic accent and folklore of 15th-century Castile; and the old folk still paraded along the quayside on a Sabbath afternoon in medieval Spanish costume.

Economically, the Jewish community was well balanced. Certainly, there was here no excessive proportion of professional men. (Indeed, the number was so low that the community officially employed non-Jewish physicians.) There were now no great fortunes. There were many petty shopkeepers; but the bulk of the community were, as their ancestors had been, peddlers, craftsmen, and manual labourers. Whatever bogey of Jewish 'influence' and 'infiltration' could be erected by German anti-Semitism elsewhere in Europe, it had no relevance whatsoever in the case of Salonica's old-established, picturesque, hard-working Jewish masses. Yet this fact did not save them.

The account that follows – the first detailed report in the English language, I believe – is based in part on reports received by the writer in the course of a visit to Greece not long after liberation, in part on the invaluable material assembled by Michael Molho, the sole surviving spiritual leader of Salonican Jewry, in a touching work, *In Memoriam*, which he has devoted to this subject.

When Paul of Tarsus visited Salonica, in the year 50 CE, he found there a strong Jewish community, with its synagogue, in which we are informed he preached for three Sabbaths in succession. The community's history may already have gone back some generations; afterwards, certainly, it was uninterrupted down to modern times.

The Turks were soldiers and peasants, uninterested in trade and inexpert in handicrafts. The Jews were merchants and craftsmen, long excluded from the land and inexpert in war. Hence the two peoples were in a sense complementary; and when the Jews were expelled from Spain in 1492 the Sultan tolerantly opened the gates of his empire to them. Most of them settled naturally in the seaports, and above all in Salonica, which from this time onwards was one of Europe's greatest Jewish communities – for a time, indeed, the greatest. It was a microcosm of the Jewish world. There were refugees from France, Italy, Germany, Hungary, Calabria, Apulia, Sicily, and every province and city of Spain, each group maintaining its own synagogue and congregation.

For a while, the Jews were probably a majority of the population. They not only controlled trade and industry, but also provided the artisans, the fishermen, the stevedores, and the harbour workers. (Almost down to our own day, no ship could unload in the port on Sabbath.) The fashions, the habits, the dishes, the languages, the costumes, and even the lullabies of Toledo and Seville, as they had existed in the age of Ferdinand and Isabella, were incongruously perpetuated, generation after generation. Indeed, it has been said that could Columbus have returned to this earth four centuries after his momentous voyage, he would have found himself more at home in Salonica than in Palos. Every synagogue had its academy attached to it, and for many generations the city was one of the world's centres of rabbinic learning.

Down to the beginning of the 20th century, the picture remained almost unchanged. The community had suffered great material losses, indeed, in periodic conflagrations, and even greater spiritual disillusionment in the 17th century when it pinned over-great hopes on the false messiah of Smyrna, Sabbatai Zevi (whose secret votaries, the Donmeh, posing as Moslems, were still numerous and influential in Salonica until a few years ago). But Salonica remained largely a Jewish city, having in 1912, at the close of the period of

Turkish rule, a Jewish population of over 80,000 (excluding the Donmeh) out of a total of 173,000. The great fire of 1917, during World War I, destroyed their ancient quarter and left 50,000 of them homeless; economic instability, inflation, anti-Semitic agitation in the following years caused a considerable emigration, mostly to France, Palestine, and Latin America; the exchanges of population between Greece and Turkey brought about a rapid artificial expansion of the Greek population (hitherto a minority), and a forced process of Hellenization. But life remained at least tolerable when it was not actually pleasant.

On April 9, 1941, at about nine o'clock in the morning, the first German armed columns entered Salonica. Two days later, the *Messagero* – the sole surviving Judeo-Spanish daily paper – was suppressed, and a number of houses and public buildings were requisitioned for military needs, including the Jewish hospital founded by Baron de Hirsch and bearing his name. On April 15, the communal council was arrested and its offices raided. In the course of the following week, placards forbidding entrance to Jews began to make their appearance in the cafés, and later on all Jews were ordered to give up their radios.

Meanwhile, a new quisling newspaper had begun to make its appearance, the 'New Europe' (*Nea Evropi*), which devoted a great deal of its space to anti-Semitic propaganda in the full Goebbels style. But clearly, everything was going to be done in an orderly fashion. The Germans even nominated a new president of the community to transmit their orders; and when the *soi-disant* Prime Minister, General Tsolacoglou, visited the city, he gave comforting reassurances to a Jewish deputation which waited on him.

For over a year, no specific anti-Jewish regulations were applied. There were occasional cases of assault, Jews were arrested or even executed on other charges (e.g., of Communism, after the invasion of Russia), and there was terrible economic distress. But nothing was done against the Jewish community as such. A false sense of security had begun to spread.

The beginning of the persecution was in a disguised form, as was often the Nazi practice. It came in the summer of 1942 on Saturday, July 11, when orders were issued for all adult male Jews between the ages of eighteen and forty-five to present themselves to be enrolled for forced labour at Liberty Square, where in 1908 the Young Turks had proclaimed the new regime for all the peoples of the Ottoman

Empire. Here they were kept, packed together under the broiling sun until the afternoon, surrounded by companies of soldiers armed with machine guns, the slightest movement being savagely punished. Many were sent off immediately to malaria-stricken areas, where they worked in the sun ten hours a day with inadequate rations. Within ten weeks, 12 per cent of those taken had died.

Ultimately, after prolonged negotiations, the Germans agreed to exempt the Jews from forced labour in return for a ransom of two and a half billion drachmae, equivalent to about 40,000 US gold dollars. The bulk of the sum was raised, with enormous difficulty. It seemed that the community was saved.

However, there were in the following months more and more expropriations and seizures of Jewish businesses, warehouses, and property. This culminated in December 1942, in the expropriation of the ancient cemetery, containing nearly half a million graves and dating back certainly to the 15th century. It became a quarry for the entire city. Tombstones of inestimable historic value, as well as those erected by persons still alive, were removed regardless of age or associations, and can still be seen all over the city, used as paving stones or even to line latrines.

Throughout Europe, the Nazi authorities showed a somewhat paradoxical interest in Jewish libraries, intellectual treasures, and ritual objects, partly because what was valuable could be sold (even if it first had to be melted down), partly because they were engaged in building up at Frankfurt, for anti-Semitic purposes, what was rapidly becoming the world's greatest Jewish research library. The ancient fame of Salonica attracted special attention, and not long after the German occupation a section of the Kommando Rosenberg, which supervised this important matter, installed itself in the former American consulate, its work being under the direction of a not incompetent scholar, Dr. J. Pohl, director of the Hebrew section of the Frankfurt Institute. All the libraries and synagogues of Salonica were now raided and their treasures seized, packed, and dispatched northward by these perverted collectors. (It is even said that they included in their number expert forgers, who introduced material for anti-Jewish libels in their booty whenever it was possible.)

It was noticed that some of these 'experts' looked at everything from the point of view of German history. They were making frenzied inquiries into the exact position of the ghetto that they assumed had once existed in Salonica, and seemed disappointed when they discovered that in this quasi-Jewish city, which had formed part of the tolerant Turkish Empire, there had never been (and indeed could not have been) anything of the sort. Why this exaggerated antiquarian interest? The reason was very soon to become apparent.

At this stage, the puppet-president of the community, whom the Germans had nominated when they first arrived, was removed from office and replaced by the rabbi, Dr. Koretz. It is necessary to devote a few lines to this unhappy figure. He was not a Salonican in origin. The community, feeling the need for a rabbi of Western education, one who could better represent them vis-a-vis their fellow citizens and government, had appointed this Eastern European Ashkenazi, trained in a German rabbinical seminary, to the post which he had filled, not without dignity, for a number of years. Regarding Germany with the fundamental deference that was once universal among Eastern European Jews, brought up in that country and imbued with veneration for its intellectual achievement, speaking German and thus able to enter into personal contact with the occupying authorities – he was unable to believe the worst of them and had tended from the first to temporise. He became convinced that by unquestioning compliance, the Nazis' resentment (he did not realize that it was in fact an implacable hatred) might be mollified. Now, in his double capacity both as rabbi and as president, he not only carried out every German instruction but also urged his community to obey implicitly.

It is on this policy of appeasement and compliance that the few surviving Salonican Jews put the blame for the fact that the disaster which burst upon them was so overwhelming and universal, and that so few escaped. Some of them go so far in their bitterness as to accuse Koretz of having been, in effect, a German agent. It certainly seems that he displayed not only a deplorable weakness, but also a degree of compliance that in the circumstances verged upon treachery. In due course, his work was seconded by a local Jew of the lowest origin, named Vital Hasson. About the latter's function there was no doubt; he was a traitor and quisling, interested only in the satisfaction of his own greed and vices.

By the beginning of 1943, the mechanism had been prepared and all the preliminaries finished. The time had now arrived for the acceleration of the persecution. In the course of six months, between February and August of that year, Salonican Jewry met its doom.

On February 6, a German commission headed by Dieter Wisliceny and Alois Brunner arrived in Salonica to put the racial laws into operation. The same day, an order was drawn up (it was issued two days later) imposing the supreme indignities that had already become the rule elsewhere in Nazi-dominated Europe. All Jews were henceforth to wear a special distinguishing badge of yellow colour, in the shape of the Star of David – their shops and offices also had to be similarly marked. A special ghetto quarter was to be set up in which all Jews were to be concentrated. Within a few days further regulations were issued, elaborating these instructions and indicating, in the spirit of the Nuremberg Laws, precisely what was necessary in order to qualify a person as a Jew and subject him to these restrictions. One hundred thousand yellow badges were manufactured at top speed, so that all Jews of either sex, from the age of five upwards, could have one on their overcoats as well as on their ordinary clothing. Each bore a distinctive number which corresponded with that on his special registration card. Within a few days, the Salonican Jews were marked off like pariahs.

No single Jewish quarter was set up (that was impossible in view of the circumstances), but a number of areas were marked off in those districts which were largely inhabited by Jews. The space assigned was nevertheless hopelessly inadequate, four or six families often being crowded together in accommodations suited only for one. Any Jew who changed his residence without permission was treated as a deserter and shot outright. No Jew was allowed in the public streets after nightfall; no Jew was allowed to use the telephone; no Jew could ride on the tramway or any other sort of conveyance.

Camouflaging their intent, the authorities maintained the pretext that the new system would facilitate the reorganization of the Jewish community on quasi-autonomous lines, independent of the city as such. There was to be a Jewish mayor and Jewish chamber of commerce, and a Jewish police force was organized in order to maintain order. But the real object of the new provisions (which Rabbi Koretz had obediently proclaimed to his flock, from the pulpit of the Synagogue) gradually emerged. If the Jews were isolated they could be despoiled with greater ease, and having been despoiled, they could be exterminated. Simultaneously with the creation of the ghettos, a detailed inquiry was ordered into all the property of every sort in Jewish hands, including even domestic animals and household furniture. The reason soon became clear.

On March 13, a proclamation was issued placing upon the Jewish community the duty of administering all Jewish property, except household goods and other articles of the most simple description. Everything possible was to be transformed with all speed into cash, which was to be deposited in the banks in a collective credit; and upwards of one hundred communal notables were designated as hostages to insure that these and all the other instructions were punctually obeyed. This, in effect, signified utter spoliation under a mildly euphemistic title.

One of the finest villas in Salonica, in Velissariou Street, had already been taken over as the headquarters of the Commission for Jewish Affairs; and this, its floors strewn with priceless stolen carpets and its cellars filled with accumulated stolen treasures, became the scene of sadistic tortures by day and bacchanalian revelries by night. Hitherto, Jews had been restricted to the ghetto areas only by night. They were now forbidden to leave them even by day. There was no longer any question of these districts being autonomous units; they were obviously intended only as prisons, or as condemned cells pending the execution of sentence.

Some half-century before, the charitable Baron de Hirsch had paid for the construction near the railway station of a number of little houses, to give shelter to Jewish refugees from the Russian pogroms. This Hirsch quarter was to be the scene of the final tragedy. While the ghetto legislation was being perfected and enforced, this district, which had a population of something less than 2,500 souls massed together in 593 rooms, was being divided off from the rest of the city – not by the usual barbed wire, but by a fence of high planks. There were three entrances, each surmounted by a trilingual inscription in German, Greek, and Ladino; and outside, searchlights and machine guns were installed. It was thus a ghetto in a fuller sense than the other newly-designated Jewish quarters. But its function was to be even more sinister than this; it was to serve as the corral where the human cattle were to be rounded up at the last, before being taken to the slaughter. Three hundred empty railway wagons were known to be lined up on the sidings, awaiting the victims.

On the morning of Sunday, March 14, the inhabitants of the Hirsch quarter were instructed to assemble in the local synagogue where they were informed by Rabbi Koretz that they were to be deported to Poland. With what was, at the most charitable interpretation, an unbelievable naivety, he informed them that they would find a new home there among their own people; the great Jewish community of Cracow (could he have been unaware that Cracow Jewry had already been destroyed?) would receive them as brothers, and each man would find employment in accordance with his aptitude and experience. To give some verisimilitude to the farce, some Polish paper money was made available to the victims; they were of course forbidden to take with them any gold or silver or anything else of value, or more than twenty kilograms of personal property done up in bundles (valises were not allowed).

The next morning, the inhabitants of the quarter were assembled and marched to the station. There they were driven into the waiting railroad cars, which were soon overladen to twice their capacity, closed, and then sealed. Soon the cargo of human misery began its journey to the Polish slaughterhouse. Four hundred and fifty-one years before, their ancestors had been the victims of one of the greatest tragedies in the history of medieval Europe when they had been driven out of Spain, hoping in vain for a miracle that would save them at the last moment. Now, an age had come when miracles were no longer even hoped for.

The Hirsch quarter was now clear and ready to receive a new convoy. A few hours later, the ghetto in the Aghia Paraskevi district was suddenly surrounded and its inhabitants were ordered to be ready to leave in twenty minutes. They were then marched – aged, children, invalids, cripples – to the Hirsch quarter, where they were joined on the next day by the Jews of the district near the smaller station. On Wednesday, March 17, another convoy left for the north, under much the same conditions as before (though, to do him justice, the Rabbi secured some slight alleviation). Day by day, thenceforth, these scenes repeated themselves, group after group being dispatched to the Hirsch quarter, and convoy after convoy, each of some 2,800 persons, being sent off.

There was a brief interlude in the middle of March, when military requirements necessitated the recruitment of forced labour. But this did not last for long; moreover, the treatment of the labourers was so appalling that most persons preferred the alternative of deportation, many still pathetically believing the tale that they were being sent to start a new life in a distant region. Indeed, such are the unfathomable resources of human optimism that there was a veritable epidemic of marriages at this time, even in the Hirsch quarter itself. On the eve of deportation, as many as a hundred young couples would be married on a single day, here or in the other ghettos, with the pathetically incongruous traditional formula in which praise is offered to the God who created man in his own image, who makes the bridegroom to rejoice in his bride, and who will speedily cause the streets of Jerusalem to resound to the happy voice of youths and maidens newly joined in wedlock.

Few details are known as to what happened to the deportees in the course of their tragic journey northwards. But their fate was in all cases the same. The talk of sending them to start a fresh life in Poland was nothing but mockery; by this time no Jew survived in Cracow, which was supposed to be their destination. The trains were directed one after the other to the great annihilation camps of Oswiecim (Auschwitz) and the adjacent Brzezinka (Birkenau) in Poland, where more than 1,750,000 Jews from various countries were murdered during this period (this is in addition to the 1,500,000 who were murdered in Maidanek). Here, far away from their sunny home, unable to comprehend or obey the life-and-death commands spoken by their captors in German or Yiddish, the Salonican Jews were exterminated. The number of survivors who escaped by flight or by some other means[1] was infinitesimal.

It is to be reported with the most profound regret that the general population of Salonica did not show that degree of practical sympathy with their harried fellow townsfolk which was encountered in some other cities, and many did not shun a profit from the Jewish distress. On the other hand, there were some among them, if not many, who did what they could to help, even at the risk of their lives, and it was to them that most of the tiny handful of survivors owed their escape. This was the case especially, it may be remarked, in the surrounding countryside, where the Germans applied the same regime as in the city itself. Out of thirty-three Jews at a little place named Aicatherine, for example, all except three who had been shot were able to take refuge in the neighborhood villages, disguised as peasants.

On a far larger scale was the help given by the Italian authorities, both military and civil, who, true to their finest and happiest tradition, refused to collaborate with their German allies and did everything that they could to help Jews escape by giving them false papers of nationality, sending them away in military convoys, or declaring them members of their own families. On the other hand, the Bulgarians, who indeed refused to collaborate in any excesses of anti-Semitism in their own country, had no such scruples in the portions of Greece which they occupied. Here, the annihilation of the Jews was almost complete, rising to 96 per cent, 98 per cent, and even (as at Xanthiex, where there were only six survivors out of a community of 550) 99 per cent.

From March 15 onwards, there were only the briefest interruptions in the deportations. Further convoys, each of the regulation size, left the Salonica railway station at intervals of two or three days in the second half of March; nine in April; and two at the beginning of May, these including persons who had been rounded up in other cities of Macedonia where there were Jewish communities, such as Florina, Demotica, and Verria. The Jewish ghetto police force, of which the Germans had made considerable use for enforcing their orders, was now superfluous, and its members, who no doubt had hoped for preferential treatment, were sent to join their co-religionists. The most despicable figure of all, Vital Hasson, suffered from no illusion and fled in good time, to be rounded up and condemned to death, however, after the German defeat (though the execution of the sentence was inexplicably delayed). Certain persons whose services had been used by the Germans for purposes of communal organization and discipline, were dispatched, as they were informed, to the relatively favoured fortress-ghetto of Theresienstadt in Czechoslovakia, where a good number of Jews in fact survived, but they too ended in the crematoria.

At the end of June, those Jews who were of Italian nationality were sent to Athens, though after the fall of Mussolini they too were rounded up and deported. Those who, owing to the romantic Judeophilism of the Spanish government before Franco, could claim Spanish protection but were not wanted in Spain, went to Bergen-Belsen; a number ultimately managed, however, to get to Casablanca or even to a new life in Tel Aviv.

Of the Salonican community, there were left, now, only the survivors of those who had been sent to forced labour. They were now rounded up, malaria-stricken, emaciated, and half naked, and on August 7 they too were deported, to the number of 1,200. This was the nineteenth convoy. It was also the last, for there were no more Jews left.

All told, there had been deported from Salonica in these few months (the exact figures are available) 46,091 Jews, of whom approximately 44,000 were natives of the city and the remainder from the surrounding countryside and neighbouring towns. Of these, 45,650 were sent directly to Poland where they were exterminated; the remaining handful went to Bergen-Belsen, where some of them survived – including Rabbi Koretz, who, however, died, perhaps fortunately for himself, on the morrow of liberation. Of the 5,000 Salonican Jews not deported, many had already succumbed to their sufferings in forced labour; others had found refuge in the surrounding countryside or else in Athens, where (largely owing to the noble lead of the Patriarch Damascenos, who alas had no imitator in Salonica) a goodly proportion of the Jews were saved by the complicity of the Christian population.

In October 1944, Salonica was recaptured by the Greek and Allied forces. A handful of Jews drifted back, in due course, to the city whose history had been intertwined so closely with their own for two thousand years. They found their homes occupied, their property looted, all but two or three out of their nineteen synagogues destroyed, their five-century-old cemetery still used as a quarry.

Amid the ruins, this remnant set themselves to build up their lives anew. Perhaps they may succeed in reconstituting a community, but it will be one like any other small Jewish congregation anywhere in the world. The Jewish community, which once numbered nearly 50 per cent of the total city population of 173,000, is now insignificant, less than one per cent out of the present 250,000. Moreover, all that Salonican Jewry had stood for – that strange island of 15th century Spain in a setting of 20th-century Greece – is gone forever. With it has gone, unnoticed and unlamented, the cultural environment which made the city for so long a centre of interest for philologists, historians, folklorists, and lovers of the picturesque. It is not only a community that has been annihilated, but also a way of life.

In the summer of 1946 I went to Greece on behalf of the British War Office to lecture to the troops, and had the horrible experience of visiting this charnel house of historic memories. In the synagogue on Sabbath morning, there was barely a minyan. There was as yet no religious education for the children. There was hardly any provision for other fundamental religious requirements. Everywhere one could see traces of loot. I found a child in the street sitting on a synagogue chair carved with a Hebrew inscription; I was given a fragment of a Sefer Torah which had been cut up as soles for a pair of shoes; I saw carts in the cemetery removing Hebrew tombstones on the instructions of the Director of Antiquities for the province, for the repair of one of the local ancient churches.

But a Greek hawker in the street was selling eggs cooked in the traditional Sephardi sabbatical fashion, *huevos enjaminados*, which had now become a local delicacy. Jewish life had been all but exterminated, but this relic of the Jewish cuisine curiously survived.

First published in *Commentary*, New York, July 1950.

NOTE

1. In Italy in 1945, and in the Balkans in 1946, I met Salonican Jews, their wrists tattooed with their prison-camp numbers and still in their eyes looks of horror which would never pass away; they owed their lives to the fact that they had been employed to stoke the furnaces of the crematoria. (CR)

32 A Solution to the Mystery of the Scrolls

A spirited discussion that has been going on during the past ten years regarding the historical background and implications of the Dead Sea Scrolls – with the sensational conclusions which we all remember – has been conducted by theologians and philologists, with occasional help from archaeologists. Historians have been conspicuously absent from the argument. But the mystery of the scrolls is properly a historical question, which should be dealt with on the same footing and by the same means as other historical problems.

Here an attempt will be made to do this, with the assistance of the information provided by our solitary extended authority for the period of the Second Temple, to which time it is generally agreed that these newly found documents belong. That authority is, of course, the Jewish chronicler and apologist, Joseph ben Mattathias the Priest, generally known as Josephus; there is virtually no other source of information at our disposal. But a word of warning must be added. Josephus was a revolutionary general turned traitor, who had come to the conclusion that the Jewish revolt was a crass mistake and who tried to justify himself by denigrating its leaders, whom he depicts as bandits and cutthroats (much as the Germans did to the partisan leaders in occupied Europe between 1940 and 1945). His facts are probably correct – anyway, lacking contradiction we have to accept them. But his interpretations are obviously biased, and his portraits of the Jewish leaders who were more steadfast than himself are sheer caricatures. We have to look at the information he gives through an inverted telescope, as it were.

There are, in the Dead Sea literature – in particular in the now famous Habakkuk Commentary, which provides such a wealth of cryptic detail – two principal *dramatis personae*. One is the Teacher of Righteousness, who was at the head of the Qumran sect. The other is the Wicked Priest, who persecuted the Teacher and, in the end, brought about his death on the Day of Atonement. It will be remembered how this episode has been associated with the time of King Alexander Jannaeus (103–76 BCE), how it was suggested that the execution was carried out by crucifixion, and how the commentary's statement that the Teacher was to 'rise at the End of Days' was assumed to imply a belief in his resurrection. Thus the whole episode seemed to anticipate the pattern of the origins of Christianity a full century or more before the time of Jesus of Nazareth, and theological dovecotes throughout the world were set in an uproar. There were various other conjectures which also placed the scene at about this time.

But one most important consideration was overlooked. Alexander Jannaeus and the members of his house were indeed high priests (though it has been questioned whether they belonged, in origin, to a priestly family), but only by usurpation. Moreover, essentially they were kings; and the more devoted elements in the Jewish people strongly resented their concentration of the royal and priestly power in the same hands, which had never happened before in Jewish history. That this should not have been mentioned, however, obliquely, in the Dead Sea documents, and that their royal functions should have been wholly overlooked, is inconceivable. We must in fact look for a period when the priesthood, qua priesthood, was in authority and in a position to indict a sentence of death; and when moreover they were at loggerheads with some religious sect among the Jews, with its headquarters in the Dead Sea region. There is one other historical factor to be taken into consideration. That is the Kittim, who pervade the whole of the Qumran literature. They are a people coming from overseas, of overwhelming military might, furnished with irresistible equipment and siege-trains, utterly merciless in their methods.

There cannot be any doubt that this refers to the Romans – the picture applies to no other people; and besides, a document fragment recently discovered makes it plain that the Kittim came after the kings of the Greeks. There is no need to seek the philological or geographical origins of the name; the term is obviously based on the last verse of the Prophecy of Balaam in the Book of Numbers and implies the ultimate enemy of the Jewish people, whose overthrow would (in the eyes of the writer) usher in the final deliverance and the 'end of days'. Moreover, the menace is not remote and academic. It is something imminent and pressing. The allusion must therefore necessarily be to the period after Pompey's conquest of Palestine in

63 BCE, or more probably, to the period after direct Roman rule was established following the death of Herod. We must, therefore, locate the episode of the Master of Righteousness at a time when the menace of the Romans was pressing, but when they were not actually in control, local authority being exercised by the priesthood.

With this in mind, we turn back to Josephus and find the answer to our problem, though he presents the story in his usual biased fashion. He indicates precisely when a priestly junta, who could not be considered as anything other than priests, held authority in Jerusalem in the period we have to consider; and while they were in authority, such an episode as the Habakkuk commentary describes did in fact take place. In the summer and autumn of the year 66 CE, there began in Jerusalem the great revolt against the Romans, who were ejected triumphantly from the city. It was in fact properly considered not merely a revolt, but also at the same time a revolution, like the French Revolution of 1789 or the Russian Revolution of 1917 or (the closest parallel, for many reasons) the Puritan Revolution of the 17th century in England. The common factor in all these movements, as Crane Brinton showed in his brilliant work on the subject, *The Anatomy of Revolution*, is that they all started as reformist movements, afterward moving further and further to the left and becoming more and more extreme, with blood-baths and reigns of terror at much the same relative stage. Now the original 'aristocratic' leaders of the Jewish revolution of 66 belonged to the priestly class, as was only natural, for the high priests had governed Judea from the Return from Babylonian Exile down to the Hasmonean Revolt, and some of this element would naturally have been at the head of a movement such as this, which promised to restore their authority. The actual instigator of the political revolt was, in fact, one Eleazar ben Hananiah, the captain of the Temple Guard. It was he who had brought about the repudiation of Jewish allegiance to Rome, by refusing the sacrifices hitherto offered in the name of the Emperor. Subsequently he directed military operations against the Roman legionaries, and when a revolutionary government was formed – mainly made up of priests – he was appointed to one of the key positions. Here now we have the background.

But almost immediately after the outbreak of the revolution, the dominant position of the priestly aristocrats was threatened. Half a century before, one Judah the Galilean had founded the sect or party of the Zealots, about whose theoretical basis we know in fact very little, except that one of their cardinal principles of faith was that they considered the recognition of Gentile rule over the people of God to be a mortal sin. The sect was at present headed by Judah's son, Menahem. Now here is a point that must be noted very carefully: Josephus makes it quite plain that he hated both father and son – in particular the latter – but he calls them both, repeatedly, by the Greek term 'sophist'. This did not have, at that time, the contemptuous implication that it has since acquired. It then meant scholar, teacher, heretical leader if you will. One Greek writer uses it of Jesus; Josephus himself applies it elsewhere to rabbis. So Menahem was not a mere gunman or partisan chieftain, as the historian Josephus depicts him; he was at the same time an intellectual leader. At the outset of the revolution, he and his followers seized the former Herodian fortress of Masada on the Dead Sea coast, not far from Qumran, where the Dead Sea Scrolls were discovered. Thence, after equipping themselves from the great armoury there, they marched on Jerusalem, where Menahem, thrusting the captain of the Temple Guard and his associates into the background, assumed military command and soon forced the surrender of the Roman garrison, beleaguered in the royal palace. This took place in the early autumn. Josephus gives the date as the sixth day of the month Gorpiaeus, which has been calculated as being equivalent to the 3rd Tishri.

Precisely what happened afterwards is not easy to determine. Josephus implies that Menahem developed a megalomania and wished to impose his authority as king; perhaps, indeed, he had Messianic ambitions. There is reason to believe that his sect had a different religious calendar from other Jews, and that he tried to impose it in the Temple on the most solemn day of the Jewish year. But whatever happened, tragedy ensued. Attended by some of his devoted followers and sumptuously arrayed, Menahem went up to the Temple to perform his devotions, notwithstanding the fact that he thus placed himself in the power of his enemies. Eleazar, the captain of the Temple Guard, who resented his growing influence and feared for his own position, stirred up the people against him. A riot began, in the course of which many of the Zealots were killed. Menahem took refuge on the Hill of Ophel, where shortly afterward he was found and dragged out to his death. Surely this episode coincides precisely with that which is alluded to in the Habakkuk

Commentary. Here we have, in fact, a teacher (obviously, from his followers' point of view, a 'Teacher of Righteousness') who was killed by a priest (obviously, from his opponents' view, a 'Wicked Priest') – and, to boot, nearly enough on the Day of Atonement, though we are not informed by Josephus that it was actually on this day. Moreover, both Menahem and the Teacher of Righteousness had an unreliable associate of the same name. The Habakkuk Commentary tells us elsewhere that 'the House of Absalom' treacherously maintained silence, when they should have backed up the Teacher of Righteousness on some occasion. Josephus informs us that among the associates of Menahem (not, however, among his lieutenants, apparently) who were killed in these disorders was a man called by the same, then unusual name, Absalom! Presumably, his followers ('the House of Absalom') switched their allegiance after his death.

What evidence is there that Menahem let a sect behind him to revere his memory? The point, obviously, is vital, but the answer is not in question. For after the sanguinary episode in Jerusalem, the survivors of his Zealot following retreated back to Masada under the leadership of his nephew, Eleazar ben Jair. Here they sulkily remained, having nothing whatsoever to do with the central revolutionary government in Jerusalem, although some less intransigent members of the sect came to terms. They did not participate in the defence, they did not organize any diversionary activities during the siege, they carried out their own private campaign against the Romans, and even against Jewish groups who acknowledged the authority of the central government, and they continued to hold out even after the fall of Jerusalem, until the year 73 CE. Now at last they succumbed, Eleazar ben Jair being the last hero of the revolt. Obviously they must have cherished the memory and the teachings of their assassinated former leader, Menahem. Furthermore, there is abundant evidence that they extended their little republic over the adjacent areas, though we have no definite proof that this 'empire' of theirs included Qumran (whose name in antiquity, indeed, is as yet unknown).

Here then we have a group which, like that at Qumran a few miles to the north, revered the memories and doctrines of a teacher (of righteousness) who had been killed by a (wicked) priest who could only be thought of as a priest, on or about the Day of Atonement, and who similarly had an associate named Absalom.

Surely, there can be no question about the identification. Or let us put it in another way. Unless this identification is accepted, then we must conclude that in the years 66–68 CE, (the archaeologists insist that the Qumran remained in Jewish hands until this period) there were both at Masada and at Qumran – also on the Dead Sea, a little way to the north – two separate groups, each with its own doctrine, each of them (1) venerating the memory of a Teacher of Righteousness (2) who was killed by a 'Wicked' Priest, (3) and who perished on or about the Day of Atonement (4) and an associate named Absalom. The arm of coincidence cannot be as long as that!

Thus we are given, at last, albeit incidentally, an assured dating for one of the Dead Sea documents. The Habakkuk Commentary, in which the martyrdom of the Master or Teacher of Righteousness is described, cannot have been written before 66 CE, when the episode took place, nor after 73 CE, when Jewish life in this region was blotted out; and the archaeologists are convinced that the sect's library was concealed and abandoned about this time. There is, indeed, good reason to believe that the work was written by Eleazar ben Jair himself. On the basis of this dating, which is assured, it should be possible to fix the age of the other Dead Sea Scrolls objectively at last – the new dogmatism which assigns them to narrow limits of time being mere conjecture, so long as we have no comparable dated specimens to serve as a point of departure. As to the antiquity of the Biblical codices, which has been so bitterly discussed, there is no need to pass any opinion here; it will have no bearing on the present argument even if they can be proved still older than the wildest partisans now claim. It is enough for our purpose to have demonstrated, so far as anything of the sort ever can be demonstrated by the use of normal historical methods, the identity of the assassinated Teacher of Righteousness with Menahem ben Judah, the assassinated Zealot leader.

This leads inescapably to a logical conclusion which is of the utmost importance for Jewish historiography, far more important than the Teacher's actual identification: If the Teacher of Righteousness of the Qumran literature was, as here posited, Menahem the Zealot leader, then the mystery of the Qumran sect is solved. The sect's members must have been (as Joseph Klausner has already conjectured) the Zealots.

This may seem surprising, in view of the normal impression of the Zealots as a hyper-patriotic political party. But here, once again, we have been misled by Josephus, who colours his picture of them by his personal prejudices but nevertheless allows the facts to escape, partially, when he designates their principles as 'the fourth philosophy', and speaks of their leaders in successive generations as 'sophists', or scholars. Indeed, it is erroneous to imagine that Josephus gives us an actual descriptive account of the Jewish sects of his time; he rather gives a slightly amplified inventory of them, to serve as a foil to his lengthy, hyperbolic, and highly idealized picture of the Essenes. The Qumran sect has, indeed, been identified with this body and doubtless came under their influence, but scholars have already pointed out that there were basic differences between them, as for example in their attitude to war (the Qumran sectaries were highly bellicose) and to property (which at Qumran was certainly not held in common). Similarly, it is demonstrable that the Qumran sectaries were not Pharisees (for their *Halachah* was different in important respects), nor Sadducees (with their Temple-centered outlook). The conclusion that they were Zealots is now inescapable.

On the basis of this identification, we are in a position to apply the literature discovered at Qumran to the circumstances of Zealot history, with its culmination in the period of the great revolt against Rome in 66–73 CE. The results are amazing. The whole of the new data now slide into position with almost uncanny neatness, dovetailing precisely with the archaeological findings and with the information already available to us from the writings of Josephus. To such an extent, in fact, is this so, that even if my original identification of the Teacher of Righteousness with Menahem were overlooked, there could be no doubt that the Zealot revolt provides the proper historical setting. I cannot go into all this here in detail, nor can I be expected in a paper of this sort to provide references and detailed demonstrations, but will only outline the new picture that is now beginning to emerge.

It will be recalled that the discovery in the Qumran caves of many fragments of what was once called the Zadokite Document, as well as various common terms and features which it shares with the Qumran literature, has made it certain that this extraordinary compilation, brought to light by Solomon Schechter half a century ago or more, among the hoards of the Cairo Genizah, belongs to this same milieu and therefore emanates from Zelaot circles. Now Judah the Galilean, the founder of the Zealot sect, headed a revolt in his native Galilee after the death of Herod in 4 BCE, seizing Sepphoris. The city was soon recaptured by the Romans, and he disappeared from view for ten years. It would have been natural for him to have taken refuge in Damascus, nearer to Sepphoris than Jerusalem and presumably safer. Here he and his followers could have drawn up the Damascus Covenant that is so often referred to in the Zadokite Document.

There is no need to assume, as some savants now do, that the Damascus place name is fictitious or figurative; it is a foremost failing of modern scholarship to claim that documents mean the reverse of what they actually say.

In or about the year 4 CE Judah reappeared in Judea, and there launched his doctrines and his sect, according to Josephus. At precisely this time, according to the archaeologists, the Qumran monastery, which had been abandoned since the earthquake of 31 BCE, was reoccupied. This was done, I suggest, by the returned Covenanters, who used it thereafter as their base, not improbably figuring they would be considered pacific Essenes by the outside world. The Thanksgiving Psalms found at Qumran, with their references to hair-breadth escapes, to bitter exile, and even possibly to the Verdure of Damascus, seem to reflect Judah's personal experiences and may conceivably have been compiled by him before his death in the rising against the Romans a short while later.

He was succeeded in turn by his sons, Jacob and Simon, crucified under Tiberius Alexander, the apostate Procurator of Judea (and Philo's nephew) in 46–8 CE, and then by Menahem, their brother. The latter – a singularly forceful personality, as it seems – figured, in the recollection of his disciples, as the Teacher of Righteousness, and may have been responsible for some of the sect's other literature – in particular, for the attempt to see the picture of the 'End of Days', now so imminent, in all the Biblical prophecies. The Discipline Scroll, which laid down the basic regulations of this monastic community at Qumran, probably dates to this period and even seems, at one point, to reflect the institution of the activist group of *sicarii* whom Menahem organized in 56–60 CE.

One of the basic theories of the sect, not mentioned by Josephus because it was of no interest to his Gentile readers, was the adherence to a religious calendar of their own (solar, according to the latest reports), akin if not identical to that outlined in the Book of Jubilees. This assumed great importance, especially as regards the

Day of Atonement. In their view, until this was observed in the Temple at Jerusalem with all due ceremonial, on the proper calendar day enjoined by God, the Jewish people would necessarily lie under an accumulated burden of unexpiated guilt and could not expect the Divine favour.

Upon the outbreak of the revolt against Rome in 66, Menahem captured by a *coup de main* the Herodian fortress-palace at Masada, which would henceforth be the military centre of the sect, though the *scriptorium* at Qumran remained active. Thence he led his followers to Jerusalem, where he took an outstanding part in the military operations but aroused the jealousy of the ruling priestly junta, hitherto in control. His ill-fated visit to the Temple early in the month of Tishri – i.e. on the Day of Atonement according to his own reckoning – may have been connected with his desire to impose his sectarian calendar there. On his death, his surviving followers withdrew under his nephew, Eleazar ben Jair, back to Masada.

There are some scholars who question whether the language of the Habakkuk Commentary justifies the conclusion that the Teacher of Righteousness was actually slain. In that case, he is to be identified not with Menahem himself, but with Eleazar, in whom all the other requisite conditions (assault by a priest on the Day of Atonement, association with Absalom, leadership of a sect on the Dead Sea, etc., etc.) are identically fulfilled.

The area Masada-Qumran was henceforth a sort of independent republic, exhibiting determined opposition to the central authority in Jerusalem and pursuing its own way. Its inhabitants were convinced that the End of Days foretold by the prophets had begun – the 'End of Days', when their Teacher of Righteousness had risen (not 'risen from the dead'). Divine succour for them was certain – but only when the sinful administration in Jerusalem had been swept away and the remnant of the Jewish people had turned to the perfect service of God in accordance with the Zealot doctrine. The magnitude of the general disaster did not affect this reasoning, for God could give victory to the few as to the many. The advance of the Romans served to strengthen their conviction, rather than the reverse, and as the latter swept over the land the Zealots remained aloof at Masada and at Qumran (which held out as it seems for some while after 68; there is no actual evidence that it was captured by Vespasian in precisely that year). Thence they eagerly watched the progress of events, writing meanwhile their wild apocalyptic works

– the series of commentaries applying the Biblical prophecies to current events, and the 'Wars of the Sons of Light and the Sons of Darkness', with its preposterous combination of military awareness and apocalyptic dreaming, going so far as to prescribe the pious legends that were to be inscribed on the banners of the Hosts of the Lord when they went forth to battle.

The picture is not dissimilar to that of the Fifth Monarchy men in 17th-century England, who after fighting manfully in the ranks of the New Model armies against the king, retired into belligerent aloofness, as antagonistic now to Cromwell as they had once been to Charles Stuart, confident that God was on their side and writing wild mystical pamphlets as they awaited the Divine intervention which would introduce the Great Deliverance.

Looking at the Qumran literature again, with the suggestions that have been made above in our minds, we find passage after passage which seems to refer clearly to contemporary events. Mention is made in the documents of the Kittim of Syria and the Kittim of Egypt; in fact, Vespasian led his forces from the former country while despatching his son, Titus, to bring up the fifteenth legion from the latter. They came together on the Plain of Acco, which is specifically mentioned in a hitherto obscure fragment at a base of military operations before the advance on Jerusalem. The rulers of the Kittim follow one another in rapid succession, we are told: aptly said in 68 CE, the Year of the Five Emperors, when Vespasian began his reign. The Wars of the Sons of Light and Sons of Darkness mention tactics which the Romans had only just adopted, and weapons which were only now coming into use. The Kittim are said to offer sacrifice to their standards, which the Roman legionaries did for the first time on record in the Temple Court, after the capture of Jerusalem. (Remote parallels from other parts of the world may be discovered with difficulty, but obviously the Zealots were interested only in what was happening within their own orbit.)

We learn of the end of the Wicked Priest, who after despoiling the country fell into the hands of his enemies (apparently Jews, not Romans – these documents are very precise in their use of language) and who was then judicially tortured. Josephus in fact gives us no details regarding the end of Eleazar ben Hananiah, but many of his colleagues were condemned by the merciless tribunal set up when the revolution in Jerusalem entered on a more extreme phase, and it is probable that this was his fate as well. The person mainly responsible for this reign of terror was John of Gischala, the fiery patriotic extremist. The latter seems to be referred to in this literature, very aptly, as the Lion of Wrath, his followers being 'the House of Ephraim' – i.e. the belligerent refugees who had escaped south with him after the military debacle in Galilee. The revolutionary tribunal which the Lion of Wrath established, and the executions which it carried out, are spoken of in scathing terms, though the writer of the scrolls expressed little sympathy for 'the Makers of Smooth Interpretations' (i.e. apparently the Pharisee pacifists), who were among the victims. The Lion of Wrath received his punishment in the end, being 'delivered into the hands of the Terrible One of Gentiles for judgement'; in fact, John of Gischala was ultimately captured by the Romans and condemned to life-long imprisonment.

One of the Lion of Wrath's internal opponents was the last priest, or priests (obviously not the same as the Wicked Priest), who had at his (their) disposal 'the wealth and booty from the spoil of the Gentiles' but ultimately lost control of it; they fought with the Lion of Wrath but were saved from him. It is obvious to identify the last priest with the last high priest, Phineas ben Samuel, who was appointed by the Zealots by lot (the normal Zealot method) during the revolutionary period, and subsequently was associated with the non-monastic Zealot leader, Eleazar ben Simon, who had control of the Temple. These two and their followers in fact carried on a long armed struggle against John of Gischala, but though they were defeated their lives were spared, and the two forces ultimately coalesced; as the Habakkuk Commentary says, they were 'redeemed by God'.

Josephus informs us that at the time of the revolt, Eleazar had seized the Roman pay-chest and much of the public treasure, owing his subsequent importance to this fact. This definitely seems to be the 'wealth and booty of the Gentiles'. (The precision of the language of the documents is again to be noted.) While he and his associates controlled the Temple, some of the sacred vessels were doubtless added to this treasure, and there was access moreover to the priests' stores of incense. It does not seem preposterous to suggest that when danger became imminent this may have been buried, and a list of what had been concealed rudely inscribed, for better preservation, on a strip of metal that was sent ultimately for safe custody to the Zealot centre at Qumran. This could explain the preservation there of the remarkable and mysterious copper rolls containing details of the place of concealment of vast quantities of precious bullion, utensils, and incense – obviously not what one would normally associate with an ascetic monastic serf. One does not wish to seem too ludicrously romantic, but at least the hypothesis makes sense.

The same is true, in this context, of the rest of the Qumran records and literature. The hurried conspectus that has been given above is obviously not final and will need correction and supplementing at frequent points. But it gives the possibility, as the author ventures to believe, for adding a new and unexpected chapter to Jewish history in the 1st century.

There is a final point to be considered. What of the light thrown by the Dead Sea Scrolls on the origins of Christianity? Everything, of course, which illustrates the background of Jewish religious history in the 1st century obviously throws light on the circumstances in which Christianity developed. But that is all. Indeed, in the light of the evidence brought together here, it appears that whatever the personal heroism of the Zealots, a great deal of their literature is unbalanced in conception and petty in outlook, and Pharisaism no less than Christianity was fortunate to lose this incubus. On the other hand, the somewhat unfortunate publicity given to the original attempts to identify the Teacher of Righteousness led to the elaboration of a sensational theory, as already mentioned, that this episode provided the pattern for the central episode in the story of the origins of Christianity.

Personally, all my predilections, as well as my romanticism, led me to welcome the theory. But when I began to investigate the sources, it became clear to me that it is entirely lacking in basis. There is no shadow of a doubt that the central episode in the history of the Qumran sect is not pre-Christian, but post-Christian, as has been shown above; even without the identification of the Teacher of Righteousness with Menahem which has served as a point of departure, the historical setting and circumstances suggested are completely coherent and rule a pre-Christian dating out of the question.

Moreover, there is no evidence whatsoever that the Teacher was crucified – even if the phrase 'to hang up alive' denotes crucifixion, some other episode and some other victim is obviously envisaged. Nor is there the slightest evidence that the sect anticipated the doctrine of the resurrection, expecting their Teacher to 'rise again in the remote future at the End of Days'. What the documents state is that the Teacher has arisen at the End of Days, which is the apocalyptic period then just beginning. It does not seem to me that any unprejudiced reader can dispute this, in the light of the material that has been assembled in a preliminary survey in the foregoing pages. But I do not anticipate that my views will command universal agreement, for so many scholars have already nailed their colours to the mast.[1]

First published in *Commentary*, New York, Vol. 24, October 1957.

NOTE

1. Dr Roth, as evident from the final sentence of this chapter, acknowledged the controversial nature of his views on this subject.

33 The Backround Story of the Fall of Jerusalem in the Year 70 CE

The story of the last days of Jerusalem, before its capture by the Romans in the summer of the year 70, is one of the most familiar in ancient history. We have minute details of it in the writings of Josephus, who positively gloats over the rivalries, the bloodshed, and the fighting between ambitious partisan leaders which dissipated the strength of the defence and made disaster inevitable. Christian theologians, later on, were eager to emphasize the lesson, thereby crystallizing his presentation of the story. The Jews, so recently responsible in their eyes for the most grievous of crimes, were now to receive their punishment, and God first maddened those whom He wished to destroy. Hence the modern reader is given the impression of a tangle of fratricidal strife and murder, only occasionally relieved by episodes of savage heroism.

As I have said, this is largely due to the fact that the judgements of the quisling historian Josephus – one of the few persons of antiquity for whom I nourish a cordial personal hatred – have been accepted blindly by most writers. In Jewish history of the period, he played a role not dissimilar from that of Benedict Arnold, the renegade general in the War of American Independence. How Josephus's work should properly be regarded can be illustrated by a 'spoof' quotation from a non-existent *History of the American Rebellion*, as Arnold might have written it:

> In the winter of 1779 large numbers of these brigands gathered together in the hill country near Philadelphia, at a spot named Valley Forge. They were led by an ex-officer named Washington, who had been impelled by ambition to repudiate his oath of allegiance and placed himself at the head of the rebels. From this favourable position they carried out raids on the peaceful farmers in the vicinity who remained loyal to the government. The brigands received much encouragement from the scribblings of a dissolute mechanic

named Benjamin Franklin, now almost senile, who in
consequence of having printed a number of almanacs for the
lower classes considered himself a man of letters.

Imagine this spirit extended over an entire work, and you have a fair
impression of Josephus's account of the Jewish War of 66 to 73.

It is the historian's task to ascertain the true motives and attitudes
that lay behind the actions and personalities described by Josephus,
which we know only from his jaundiced pages. The events in
Jerusalem during these years are to be considered in the context
directed of a revolt not merely against the Roman Empire, but one
which began with a popular uprising against the Roman forces in the
summer of 66 – which was first directed against the occupying
Roman power, then against the social ruling classes, then against the
merchant bourgeoisie as a whole.

This sequence of events follows, exactly, the normal pattern of
revolution as described by Professor Crane Brinton of Harvard in his
classic work, *The Anatomy of Revolution.* Surveying in detail a
number of revolutionary movements in history – above all the
Puritan Revolution in England in the seventeenth century, the
American Revolution and the more notorious French Revolution in
the eighteenth, and the Russian Revolution in the twentieth – he
finds that all followed much the same course.

The classic revolution begins, almost always, as a reformist
movement, insisting on loyalty to the regime but agitating for the
removal of administrative abuses. In the second stage the movement
becomes truly revolutionary, and popular leaders assume control
(e.g. the Girondins in France, and Kerensky in Russia). Later on,
these moderate leaders are thrust aside and a social revolutionary
movement begins. The moderates who oppose this are accused by
the extremists of being counter-revolutionaries. This generally leads
to a reign of terror, for at such a time it is obviously dangerous to
show compassion or to allow justice to take a leisurely course.
Ultimately the threat to the state, whether from within or without,
makes necessary desperate measures, such as entrusting the
government, for the sake of efficiency, into the hands of a single
person. Thus we arrive at the fifth and final stage – the dictatorship,
exemplified in the towering figures of Oliver Cromwell in England,
of Napoleon Bonaparte in France, of Lenin or Stalin in Russia. Thus
the face of the revolution is entirely changed. The wheel has gone

full circle, and from certain points of view the position is not dissimilar from that at the outset.

The history of the Jews in the heroic years from 66 to 73 is to be interpreted in these same terms. It was a revolutionary movement, as well as a patriotic movement; it followed, exactly, the standard pattern of revolution; it had as its sequel the same political extremism, with exactly the same violent outcome; and in the end it showed symptoms of the classical anti-revolutionary climax of revolutionary movements.

The classic revolution generally has its birth in financial grievances, and so in the case we are now examining. The Roman administration culminated in the heartless exactions of the procurator, Gessius Florus, who in the end plundered the Temple treasury. In consequence of this, a series of riots broke out which ultimately spread to such an extent that, in the summer of 66, the Romans had to evacuate Jerusalem. A punitive force, sent to re-establish order, was annihilated. This brilliant victory gave the insurgents confidence, as well as an excuse to liquidate some avowedly pro-Roman ruling elements. The revolution was now irrevocably launched on its path.

After the first outbreak, as Professor Brinton points out, the revolution often throws up pressure-groups (such as the Jacobins in France) who, while claiming to keep the movement on its true course, drive it in fact further and further towards the left. In first-century Palestine, such a pressure-group was already active. The Zealots had emerged some while before as a separate faction among the Jews – the 'Fourth Philosophy', Josephus calls it – with the cardinal principle that the Jews had no King but God alone, so that any show of allegiance to a non-Jewish authority was a fundamental breach of the Jewish religion. The activist wing of the Zealot party Josephus terms the sicarii, or daggermen. One may compare the 'gunmen' of the time of the struggle for Irish independence, or the 'terrorists' in most contemporary revolutionary movements, who if the revolution succeeds become immortalized as revolutionary martyrs.

It appears from Josephus's story that the *sicarii* had a social and economic, as well as a political programme. This emerges from what happened at the beginning of the revolt against Rome, when the political malcontents who were holding the Temple were reinforced by a body of *sicarii*, with whose help they assaulted the Upper City, which we might term the fashionable and business quarter. Here they destroyed the palaces of the members of the upper class and set fire to the public archives – their object, according to Josephus, being 'to destroy the money-lenders' bonds and hinder the recovery of debts'. Hard pressed at the outset, the scales were ultimately turned in their favour by the arrival in Jerusalem of the followers of the Zealot leader, Menahem, who had stormed King Herod's fortress-palace at Masada, overhanging the Dead Sea, and equipped themselves from the great armoury there. Incidentally, recent evacuations here have minutely confirmed Josephus's account of these buildings.

In the 'pattern of revolution', it often happens that the initial victory owes a good deal to the extremists, who later on are suppressed. (Think, for example, of the storming of the Bastille by the mob at the outset of the French Revolution.) So it was, too, in the Jewish revolution of CE 66. Flushed with his success, Menahem endeavoured to seize power, but was worsted and killed by the alarmed 'moderate' and respectable elements, led by the Captain of the Temple. His surviving followers now withdrew from the city back to the Dead Sea area, under the leadership of his nephew Eleazar ben Jair – who was almost certainly (as it seems to me) the Teacher of Righteousness of the Dead Sea Scrolls.

After the suppression of this attempted *coup de main* on the part of the extremists, a provisional government, representing a coalition between priestly and bourgeois elements, took over the administration, the leading figure being the former High Priest, Anan son of Anan ('Ananus' in Josephus). He ruled with a heavy hand. Extremists, even those who had played outstanding parts in the recent victory against the Romans, were excluded from office; military forces were sent to suppress some of the partisan groups; there is evidence of violent action against the sicarii of Masadah and Qumran; and the Jerusalem Zealots were hemmed up in the Temple area. Meanwhile, in the Galilee Josephus, the priestly nominee sent to take command of the Jewish rebel forces in the North, collided with what he depicts as subversive elements in the population.

There is no need to go here into any details of the campaign which he directed anaemically against Vespasian's forces, or of the final *debacle*, when he shamelessly went over to the enemy. From the point of view of the revolution in Jerusalem, this had results precisely opposite to what might have been anticipated. The priestly junta was now apparently willing to come to terms, like Josephus. However, the influx of war-refugees from Galilee, under the patriot commander,

John of Gischala, reinforced the extremist elements and swung the scale decisively against the moderates. Though associating himself at first with the party in power (presumably with 'a unified front' or a 'win the war' program), John ultimately realized their anti-national objectives and joined the Zealots. On his advice, the latter faction sent for help to the Idumaeans or Edomites, who although but recently converted to Judaism, were now hyper-nationalist. They marched on Jerusalem, entered the gates, and weighed the balance decisively on the side of the 'democratic' elements.

The revolution now entered into its second and more extreme (one might say 'Jacobin') phase, accompanied by the wave of violence characteristic of this stage – partly directed, as usual, against the original revolutionary leaders. Already, in the disorders which preceded the Zealot triumph, a series of executions had been carried out by extremists, who broke into the prisons and put to death persons awaiting trial. This had the same justification as the September Massacres in Paris in 1792 – that with the menacing advance of the enemy, the revolution was in danger. Now what may be termed a Committee of Public Safety (to use the French term) was set up, to 'save the revolution.' Ananus, who had formerly headed the provisional government, was executed without trial, together with many other persons who had played an active part in the early stages of the revolt but were now suspected of disloyal intentions.

A further democratic step taken at this period was to remove the High Priesthood from the hands of the closed circle of aristocratic families who had so long monopolized it. This was done by the classical democratic method of the ancient world, selection being made by lot. Josephus tells us contemptuously how, in consequence of this, a simple descendant of Aaron, names Phineas, was dragged from the plough to serve at the altar. A man of the people now occupied the highest office in the State.

John of Gischala's assumption of the leadership of the patriotic extremists perhaps implied a slowing down of the revolutionary programme, in favour of a more active military policy. For the extreme elements – the 'pure' Zealots – such steps were a superfluous labour so long as the implications of the revolution itself, in the social and religious sphere, had not been realized. They now became reorganized under their old leader, Eleazar ben Simon, who had seized the Roman pay-chest at the outbreak of the revolution but had been excluded from the provisional government. He now 'seceded from the party,' together with others who shared his ideas, and seized the inner court of the Temple.

His doctrinaire attitude is in obvious contrast with the purely political motivation (as it appears) of the more secular John of Gischala. It is by no means surprising that the latter, with his strong personality, political adroitness, and fine resistance record, as well as his devoted following, was able to reassert his authority over his rivals. Josephus possibly exaggerates the degree of violence by which this was achieved, as the two factions now drew together again, the Zealots fighting henceforth to the end under John's command.

Meanwhile, another revolutionary party had appeared in the city, led by Simon bar Giora, who at the beginning of the revolt had also taken a distinguished part in the fighting. A democrat in the fullest measure, and in a sense that was true of none of the other leaders of the revolution, he believed in equality for all, for we are informed how he proclaimed liberty from the slaves, who therefore flocked to his standard. Taking advantage of the difficulties of the central government in Jerusalem, after the fall of the priestly junta, he began to establish his authority in outlying areas. The Zealots ensconced in Jerusalem continued to oppose him and his programs steadfastly. On the other hand, the remnant of the moderate party, headed by the recently deposed High Priest, saw in him a possible ally, who might save them, no doubt hoping that he would ultimately be sobered by responsibility.

The phenomenon of the moderates summoning aid from extremists, in time of emergency, is again well known: Kerensky released the Bolshevik leaders in order to gain their support, and thereby signed the death-warrant of his administration. Nothing loath, Simon and his levies marched on the Holy City, freeing the slaves, opening the prisons, and gathering force as he advanced. Obviously he wished to carry the revolution yet a stage further. In the spring of 69 he entered the gates of Jerusalem, and before long was able to make himself master of the entire walled area – with the exception of the Temple Mount, where John of Gischala was still in control.

Bar Giora is henceforth to be reckoned as head of the attenuated Jewish State. His administration seems to have been efficient, though stern. But it was inevitably a one-man rule. We have the normal paradoxical climax of the pattern of revolution, as it so frequently evolved in the final phase.

At this stage there was carried on the fratricidal warfare within the walls, which sealed the doom of the beleaguered city. This was in a way inevitable, for the various factions were struggling not merely to defend the city against the Romans, but as they imagined, to establish the reign of God on earth. Once they had done this, God would Himself descend on the city and deliver it. Until they had done so, none of their efforts could be successful. It did not matter how extreme their case was – the Divine power would be sufficient to save them.

But the Divine power would not manifest itself until all iniquity had been purged away, and justice and righteousness fully established in the Holy City among the remnant of the Holy People. They did not fight among themselves, despite the fact that conditions were so extreme. It was precisely because conditions were so extreme that it was necessary for the left wing of the social revolutionaries to fight against those who were obstructing their program. Only if the Law was observed fully, and social justice was implemented according to the prophetic vision, would the Lord descend on the ramparts to save His once-chosen people. Thus the slaves were set free; the Biblical laws protecting the poor were put into force; interest was no longer exacted on loans to those who needed help; and every man was required to deal justly with his neighbour.

Meanwhile, in and around the Dead Sea the Zealot extremists, whose views and opinions seem to me to be reflected in the Dead Sea Scrolls, still maintained themselves aloof, cherishing the personality of that leader who had been murderously assailed in Jerusalem by the priestly junta at the outbreak of the revolution, and convinced that it was themselves and their doctrines that God would firmly establish in the 'end of days,' when their rivals had been swept away in the maelstrom of war.

In the event, it was the Roman military machine that triumphed. Jerusalem was captured, to be followed three years later by Masadah. The Jewish revolutionary leaders either perished sword in hand, or were subjected to the ruthless judgement of the Roman conqueror. The Temple lay in ruins, the once-dominant priesthood thus losing its *raison d'etre*. Not only did the Jewish revolution against Rome collapse, but more than that – its memory disappeared, for its arch-enemy wrote its epitaph.

34 The Slave Community of Malta

For more than two hundred years, and as late as the eighteenth century, there existed on the island of Malta a community of Jewish slaves, protected by the Inquisition and presided over by a Gentile: this is the essence of a fascinating story which has been hitherto virtually unknown and which is now fully disclosed for the first time from documents in the hands of the present writer.

Malta had harboured a Jewish community for almost fifteen centuries after the visit of Paul of Tarsus to the island. Catacombs commemorate its existence in Roman times, and government records mark its medieval history. But the island fell, together with Sicily, under the rule of the royal house of Aragon, and the community of Malta shared, in 1492, the fate of the Jews of Spain. There was a brief interval during which there were no Jews on the island. Then followed the amazing interlude of the slaves.

In 1530, Charles V made over Malta to the Knights Hospitaler of the Order of St. John, who had been driven from Rhodes nine years earlier by the Moslems. The whole raison d'être of the body and of its tenure of Malta lay in the supposition of a continual state of hostility between the Moslem world and Christendom, of which its members of the Order were, in a sense, the knights-errant. Accordingly, they waged continual maritime warfare, hardly distinguishable from piracy, against the Moslem powers. Seaports were raided and their inhabitants carried off. Shipping was preyed on indiscriminately, captured vessels being brought to Malta, and crews and passengers sold into captivity. Throughout the rule of the Knights, which lasted until they capitulated to the French in 1798, the island was thus a last European refuge of slave traffic and slave labour.

The victims were any persons, of whatever standing, race, age or sex, who happened to be sailing in the captured ships. Jews made a large proportion of the Levantine merchant class and were hence peculiarly subject to capture. Because of their nomadic way of life, disproportionately large numbers were to be found in any vessel sailing between Eastern ports. Also, they formed a considerable element in the population of the Moslem ports subiect to raids. So, soon after the establishment of the Knights there, the name of Malta begins to be found with increasing frequency in Jewish literature, and always with an evil association.

The island became in Jewish eyes a symbol for all that was cruel and hateful in the Christian world. Whatever the truth of the contemporary rumour that the Jews financed the great Turkish siege of Malta in 1665, certainly they watched it with anxious eyes and their disappointment at its failure must have been extreme. 'The monks of Malta are still today a snare and trap for the Jews,' sadly records a Jewish chronicler at the end of his account of the siege. A Messianic prophecy current early in thc seventeenth century further expressed the bitterness of Jewish feeling, recounting how the Redemption wonld begin with the fall of the four kingdoms of ungodliness, first among which was Malta.

A typical capture, and one of the earliest mentioned in Jewish literature, is related in the *Vale of Tears* by Joseph haCohen:

> In the year 532 [1552], the vessels of the monks of Rhodes, of the order of Malta, cruising to find booty, encountered a ship coming from Salonica, whereon were seventy Jews. They captured it and returned to their island. These unhappy persons had to send to all quarters to collect money for the ransom exacted by these miserable monks. Only after payment were they able to continue their voyage.

In 1567, large numbers of Jews, escaping to the Levant from the persecutions of Pius V, fell victims to the Knights. 'Many of the victims sank like lead to the depths of the sea before the fury of the attack. Many others were imprisoned in the Maltese dungeons at this time of desolation,' writes the chronicler. It was not only those who went down to the sea in ships over whom the shadow hung. Of the Marranos of Ancona who fell victims to the fanaticism and treachery of Paul IV, thirty-eight who eluded the stake were sent in chains to the galleys of Malta, though they managed to escape on the way.

Arriving in Malta, the captives were only at the beginning of their troubles A very graphic account of conditions is given by an English traveller Philip Skippon, who visited the spot in about 1663:

The slaves' prison is a fair square building, cloister'd round, where most of the slaves in Malta are oblig'd to lodge every night, and to be there about Ave Mary time. They have here several sorts of trades, as barbers, taylors, etc. There are about 2,000 that belong to the order, most of which were now abroad in the galleys; and there are about 300 who are servants to private persons. This place being an island, and difficult to escape out of, they wear only an iron ring or footlock. Those that are servants, lodge in their masters' houses, when the galleys are at home; but now, lie a-nights in this prison. Jews, Moors and Turks are made slaves here, and are publickly sold in the market. A stout fellow may be bought (if he is an inferior person) for 120 or 160 scudi of Malta. The Jews are distinguish'd from the rest by a little piece of yellow cloth on their hats or caps, etc. We saw a rich Jew who was taken about a year before, who was sold in the market that morning we visited the prison for 400 scudi; and supposing himself free, by reason of a passport he had from Venice, he struck the merchant that bought him; whereupon he was presently sent hither, his beard and hair shaven off, a great chain clapp'd on his legs, and bastinado'd with 50 blows.

The Holy One, Blessed be He, says a well-known rabbinic proverb, always prepares a remedy before the affliction. So it was in the present case. Among Jews, the idea that a coreligionist should be enslaved by a Gentile and forced to disregard the practices of his religion, with life and honour in constant danger, was altogether abhorrent. Thus from earliest days the Redemption of Captives had ranked high among the acts of charity which a Jew was called on to execute, and it was considered proper that, should a dying man leave money 'for the performance of a good deed,' without further directions, it should be devoted to this purpose, known in Hebrew as *Pidion Shevuim* as best deserving the title.

Throughout the Middle Ages this activity continued, leaving ample traces in Halakhic and historical literature. Generally the organization of relief had been purely sporadic. Whenever need arose, an emergency collection would be made and assistance proferred to the needy. With the establishment of the Knights of Malta, the depredations on Mediterranean shipping were systematized and came to have one main centre. It therefore became useful and neccssary to set up a permanent organization to cope with the new permanent situation.

Now, the great entrepôt of Mediterranean commerce was still Venice, whose trade with the Levant was carried on largely by Jews. It happened, too, that there was at Venice an important settlement of Jews hailing direct from the Iberian Peninsula, whose genius for organization was famed. Thus it came about that there was set up in Venice in the course of the seventeenth century the first of Confraternities for the redemption of Captives – *Hebrath Pidion Shevuim* – which, in the course of the next hundred years were to spread throughout the great Sephardi communities of the West.

Apparently the terrible Chmielnicki persecutions in Poland and the Ukraine in 1648 served as the immediate occasion. Thousands of Jews were sold into slavery at this time, and at Venice the charitable brothers Aboab started a fund which became permanent. By 1683 it was so successful as to be described as the most wealthy and most highly regarded among Jewish associations in Venice. The organization was under the auspices of the Levantine and Portuguese congregations; the German and the Italian congregations, though they contributed liberally to the fund, took no official share in the labours of Confraternity. This was not due to any lack of solidarity: it was that the two Sephardi communities had commercial and social intercourse with the Levant, and were most immediately concerned.

For its funds the association depended only partially on benevolence. Voluntary donations came in, of course, from Venice and from foreign cities as the fame of the association spread. The charitable Zaccharias Porto of Florence, among his immense charitable bequests, left it 1500 piastres. Abraham Texeua, Swedish resident at Hamburg, made an annual subscription during his lifetime, which was continued by his son after his death. Moses Pinto, another wealthy Hamburg Jew, a yearly subvention of twenty patacas. The Hamburg community even established an auxiliary society under the name of the *Camara de Cautivos de Veneza*, with its special treasurer or *Gabbai*. On occasions of great urgency, the Confraternity would appeal for help to unities as far afield as London and Amsterdam, which were generally glad to assist. On one occasion, in 1705, every community in Italy, except that of Rome, which was racked with oppressive taxation, contributed to the fund. Sometimes, the native city of a captive would be asked to help raise his ransom.

But all this was regarded as extraordinary income. The ordinary came as a matter of business rather than of charity. In the first place members of the Confraternity paid into its funds a certain proportion of their annual profits. But, above all, a special tax of .25 per cent was levied on all goods dispatched from Venice (presumably by sea) to Jewish correspondents, and .125 per cent on all goods taken away in person. This high tax is not so surprising as might appear at first sight. For those who paid it were precisely the Levantine merchants who might have occasion for the services of the Confraternity. It was, as a matter of fact, a form of insurance. That this was the case is shown by the fact that, whenever the fund was curtailed, trade with the Levant was seriously hampered.

The funds were kept in two separate chests or *caixete*, for the 'Levantines' and the 'Ponentines' (Portuguese) respectively. The amounts varied from time to time. About 1742, the total was 3,500 ducats, of which nearly two-thirds was in the possession of the Portuguese. The combined funds were administered by five officials, the *Deputados dos Cautivos*, of whom three were 'Ponentine'. These were empowered to dispose of sums up to fifty ducats on their own authority. For the disbursement of larger amounts general approbation was required. The separation of the funds having led to constant dispute, in 1742 recourse was had to the Venetian magistracy to make a settlement. It was decided that the two *caixete* should be combined, that the joint organization should continue to be governed by three 'Ponentines' and two 'Levantines'; and that any sum could be disposed of by four voices out of five.

This parade of internal differences had revealed the wealth of the Confraternity and aroused Gentile cupidity. The consequences were not long in showing themselves. In the same year, the *Inquisitori sopra gli Ebrei*, seeking to bolster the failing loan-banks which the Jews were forced to maintain as a condition of their toleration in Venice, confiscated the whole of the fund. A touching appeal was lodged against the raid. The sums, it was urged, were too small to benefit the banks substantially, while the Levantine merchants, deprived of their insurance, would refuse to trade with Venice. Perhaps, also, reprisals would be made in Turkey. The representations were not without effect. Henceforth, however, the organization came under the control of the *Inquisitori*, whose permission became necessary before any disbursement could be made.

The range of the society's activities was immense. In addition to captives in the Mediterranean trade, prisoners in the constant wars on the mainland of Italy or as far afield as Hungary and Poland, slaves rowing in the galleys in the Adriatic and Tyrrhenian seas from Marseilles and Elba to Corfu and Zante, victims of the Cossacks to the north and of the Tartars to the east, unfortunate Jews groaning in servitude in distant Persia or on the Barbary Coast, all turned for succour to the *Parnassim dos Cautivos* in Venice, certain to receive sympathy, and, if humanly possible, deliverance. But though many galleys slaves were redeemed at other ports, three-quarters of the Confraternity's work was done at Malta. The story of this work, as disclosed by the original documents, is not only a monument of Jewish charity at its finest but also a pathetic record of the persistence of Jewish life under conditions which could not have been more adverse.

Communication was precarious; sometimes a letter took two or three months in transmission from Venice to Malta. It was therefore necessary to have on the spot someone to represent the Confraternity. Under the Knights the exclusion of Jewish residents from Malta was not absolute (the plot of Marlowe's *Jew of Malta* was not so entirely impossible as has generally been assumed). They were, however, admitted only temporarily and under great restrictions. But the Venetian merchants had at Malta correspondents willing enough to do them a service, and a succession of these acted on their behalf as 'consuls'. They rceived no salary but must necessarily have benefited as a result of their good offices, acquiring through them business correspondents of absolute reliability whose support was valuable in dealing with Jews in other parts of the world. They had, moreover, the right to charge a commission of five piastres for every slave liberated through their offices.

The first of these agents of whom there is any record is a certain Baccio Bandinelli, namesake of the puny rival of Michelangelo, who acted perhaps from the establishment of the Confraternity down to about 1670, when he was forced to give up by reason of his years. He was succeeded by a French merchant, François Garsin, a Judge of the Tribunal of the *Consolato del Mare*. That the agency was considered desirable is shown by the fact that Thomas Luis da Souza, who had assisted Bandinelli, proferred his services in addition. He was accordingly associated with Garsin for a while (1673–74), until the latter indicated that he would prefer to dispense with assistance. Garsin's zeal was not a selfish one. He refused the commission which he the right to charge for slaves released through his efforts. 'All the greater will be your merit before God,' wrote the grateful Deputados, 'and by Him will you be rewarded all the more, these being of a nation diverse from your own.' Nevertheless, Garsin profited from his connection. The Deputados acted as his agents for the dispatch of merchandise from Venice, and in 1671 did their utmost to procure the intervention of the rabbinate of Alexandria with some of Garsin's recalcitrant debtors in that city. Moreover, he received occasional gifts in token of their gratitude.

Garsin died in the autumn of 1706 after more than thirty-five years of devoted service. His son, Jean-Baptiste, writing to tell the Deputados of his loss, offered to carry on the work. This he did until his death thirteen years later. His successor was a certain Filippo Antonio Crespi, who served for a decade. For some years during this period, a Jewish merchant from Leghorn, Samuel Farfara, resided at Malta and aided the 'consul'.

When the Maltese galleys returned from a marauding expedition, the 'consul' would visit the prison to see whether Jews were among the captives. Frequently there were – usually merchants or travellers sailing peacefully between Levantine ports. Sometimes when Jewish booty was in prospect, not even the flags of Christian powers were respected. The case is on record, for example, of the seizure in 1672 by a Tuscan privateer of ten Jews – seven men and three women – from a Venetian vessel sailing from Alexandria, under the pretext that they were Ottoman subjects. They were brought to Malta and shamelessly offered for sale. A petition presented by the Deputados to the Doge brought about diplomatic representations at the Court of the Grand Duke of Tuscany which were sufficient to procure their release.

This, however, was an exceptional case. Generally there was no shortcut out of the difficulty. Thus, on July 23, 1725, there arrived at the island eighteen prisoners captured while sailing from Salonica to Smyrna. All were poor excepting one – Jacob Fonseca, brother of Daniel Fonseca, Voltaire's friend, who had first been a Malano priest and later, as a practising Jew, physician to the Grand Vizier at Constantinople. Fonseca refused to pay ransom, and was subsequently released at the instance of the French court with which his brother had great influence. The rest were left to the charity of their fellow-Jews. Some time previously, in the autumn of 1675, ten poor Jews on their way to Palestine were captured by the Treasurer of Malta and brought into the island. Five died of the plague in captivity, and the rest were ultimately liberated for 480 pieces-of-eight. Another great influx came in 1685, when the city of Coron on the Dalmatian coast was sacked; twenty-one Jewish prisoners were brought in. But these are only a few of the most striking instances. Throughout the period, and especially in time of war (as, for example, during the heroic struggle between Venice and Turkey at the close of the seventeenth century) there was an almost constant influx of prisoners, mostly poor, to keep alive the Jewish connection with Malta and to give the Venetian community an opportunity of exercising its benevolence.

Whenever Jewish captives were found among a batch of new arrivals, the agent would give them a small sum on account of the Confraternity to satisfy immediate needs. Besides, each received an allowance of one ducat weekly until the limitation of funds forced a reduction. Even then, every Jewish slave received the equivalent of four pieces-of-eight in cash annually, distributed on the great festivals, particularly the Passover. In case of illness, they were given an additional allowance. They were housed in a special room taken for them by the agent in the *bagnio* or prison in which they were confined.

Meanwhile, word would have been sent to Venice at the earliest opportunity to inform the Deputados of the number and quality of the new arrivals and of the sums demanded for their release. When a single individual was in question, there might be enough in hand to ransom him straight away. When a whole shipload came in, it was necessary to have recourse to all sides to collect the amount required. It occasionally happened, too, that one slave would be set free to collect money for the release of the others, or that a wealthy merchant might be able to give satisfactory security for his ransom. But more frequently the victims were poor, and it was left to the Venetian society to look after their welfare and deliverance.

The mechanism of release was not always simple. The Jew was rarely as rich as he was reputed to be, but his reputation for wealth was greatest precisely where he was least known. The usual price standard of a slave tended, therefore, to disappear whenever a Jew was concerned. He was worth, not his value, but whatever could be extorted from his brethren. Ransom degenerated into blackmail. Fifteen centuries earlier, the Rabbis of the Talmud had realized that this was a case in which it was necessary to turn for once a deaf ear to suffering, lest a premium be put on the enslavement of Jews. They ordained, accordingly, that no captive be ransomed for more than his economic value. This was a rule to obey which was hard for Jews, 'Compassionate sons of compassionate sires', and generally the price paid for a Jew was higher by far than that of a Moslem.

On occasion, the Jews were mercilessly exploited. The owner of one Judah Surnago, a man of seventy-five whose value in the open market would have been negligible, was unable to obtain the sum which he demanded in ransom. Thereupon, he shut him up naked in a cellar for two months, giving him nothing to eat but black bread and water. The old man came out blind and unable to stand. His master then threatened to load him with chains and to pluck out his beard and eyelashes if the sum asked were not forthcoming. Ultimately, the Deputados redeemed him for 200 ducats. For a certain Aaron Afia of Rhodes, bought in 1793 by a speculating owner, 600 ducats were demanded. To stimulate the zeal of his coreligionists, Afia's owner kept him in chains and threatened him with the galleys. The owners would not believe, wrote Garsin in despair, that they were poverty-stricken. The Deputados were horrified. 'We are not in a condition,' they wrote, 'to make such exorbitant expenditure. If they do not moderate their price there will be disaster for the poor wretches, who will die in slavery, and the owners will lose their capital.' For a certain Rabbi Isaac Moreno of Belgrade with his wife and three children, the Deputados were willing in 1673 to pass their usual limit and pay 300 piastres for which (so low were funds) they would have to dip into their own pockets. The owners demanded 575 piastres. 'If the said masters expect to obtain more for a useless old man and a sick woman and three children, one of whom is blind, who have had nothing out of him (saving your reverence!) but lice, they are much mistaken,' they wrote to the 'consul'. The owners retaliated by attempting to convert one of the children, but the Deputados, on principle, refused to raise their offer. In another case, when one Abraham Perez and five companions were taken, one, Joseph Levy, was killed under the lash to stimulate the others to greater liberality. The rest were ultimately released, partly through their own efforts.

In 1702, a speculator had purchased three men and a woman of sixty for 350, 304, 299 and 72 ducats respectively. 'It astounds us that they could be sold at such extravagant prices,' wrote the Deputados. 'They can be sure that they will remain on their hands as long as they live, for our resources do not allow us to order their redemption even for as little as sixty... It would be as well to publish abroad what we have told you in this matter, so that no one will desire in the future to pulchase at such rates.'

Encouraged by a governmental order that Jewish slaves should not be sent to the galleys, an attempt was even made (with the help of a few judicious gifts) to obtain an edict fixing a fair price for Jewish slaves and forbidding their being put up at public auction. Apparently nothing came of it, for complaints continued without inermission. 'Though it displeases us to see the miseries which those unhappy wretches suffer,' wrote the Deputados in 1703, 'we do not see how to contribute to their release with more than we have offered the past, by reason of the calamitous times which are on us and the restriction of business. Their masters should moderate the rigorous pretensions which they have for their ransom: for if they do not they will assuredly lose all, by reason of their inevitable death in consequence of their miseries.'

Such was liable to be the fate of any wretched Jew who fell into the hands of an extortionate master. Every effort was made, therefore, to purchase prisoners before they had been put up at public auctions. In the auctions, the 'consul' was empowered (when there was money in hand) to pay up to sixty or seventy ducats without preliminary authorisation, or, at moments of especial affluence, even more. Some of the original deeds of sale are extant, or were until recently, for example, that of Abraham de Mordecai Alvo, 'white', of Smyrna, aged twenty-two, disposed of by his captors for a sack of bones 'according to the use of the corsairs' and bought by the 'consul' for the sum of 110 ducats. In 1677, six slaves belonging to the Treasurer were released together for 480 pieces-of-eight. For every sale a notarial agreement and the license of the Grand Master was essential. Sometimes, the unhappy prisoners were sent to the galleys, in spite of the governmental order to the contrary, and so it occasionally happened that the Deputados had the opportunity of ransoming slaves from Malta in Venice itself. Thus, in 1704, they appealed to the community of Leghorn for assistance in raising 2,000 reals for the release of three victims on a vessel then in port from pains 'worse than those of death'.

Despite all efforts, a long period frequently elapsed before slaves could be liberated. Thus a certain Isaac Esicrit who was released for one hundred ducats in 1716 had been captive for five years and worse cases are recorded.

Consequently, there was frequently in Malta a veritable community of slaves, as distinct from an agglomeration of isolated individuals. In 1672, for example, there were no fewer than sixteen left unredeemed at one time, while the total number of persons bought in that year was twenty-nine. Perhaps the most remarkable feature in the whole pathetic story is the way in which these miserable captives found it possible to carry on their religious life under such atrocious circumstances.

The authorities on the island were tolerant, as the ecclesiastical arm generally was, regarding Jews. There was an old authorization permitting the Jewish slaves to have their cemetery and synagogue, with scrolls of the Law. Slave-owners, however, were often less sympathetic, compelling their chattels to work on Sabbaths and holidays. The Deputados professed themselves unable to comprehend how they could do this, since they had acquired only corporeal dominion over their slaves. On March 3, 1673, they wrote to the community of Rome suggesting that some action be taken there, at the center of the Catholic faith and of ultimate authority over the Knights, to remedy this state of affairs. It would seem that something was effected, though none too speedily. In 1675 the Inquisitor of Malta issued an order prohibiting that Jewish slaves be compelled to work on their religious holidays. Thus facilities for a minimum of observance were ensured.

In consequence of this tolerant attitude on the one side and of remarkable tenacity on the other, there came into existence what is surely the most remarkable Jewish community that has ever existed – one composed exclusively of slaves, with its numbers continually recruited by prisoners brought in by sheer force, or depleted by releases effected through death or ransom. The Deputados address them in Hebrew in full form: *'To all the congregation of the groaning and captive which are in the city of Malta – may the Lord bring them out from anguish to enlargement; Ame, this be His will!'*

The community, however small, required services which could be rendered only by one who was free. Who else was available but the agent of the Venetian society? It is strange to see how this Catholic man of affairs looked after the religious welfare of these unfortunate creatures of a different faith. He worked with a conscientiousness and a fervour which would have been praiseworthy even in a Jew.

On the occasion of the Holy Days, he distributed among the slaves some small gratifications, sometimes without the express consent of his principals, who, he knew, would honour whatever he did. It was the agent, too, who made provision for a modest place of worship. He took a room in the *bagnio* which was fitted up as a synagogue. At first it was used as such only on festivals; later, on the Sabbath as well. Originally, the Jewish slaves slept here, but subsequently a couple of additional rooms were taken for their accommodation. The goaler acted as caretaker, receiving regular payment. In the autumn of 1673, the Deputados authorized Garsin to have necessary repairs done to the doors of the synagogue, and, two years later, to the reading desk. In the *bagnio*, too, the slaves had their oven – which in 1685 Garsin had been ordered to provide – for baking unleavened bread for the Passover. In 1707, when the number of slaves was small and regular religious worship momentarily ceased, one of the two rooms was given up.

There was a copy of the Scroll of the Law for the use of the slaves, doubtless originally sent from Venice, though it was not unknown for one to find its way to the island with other booty. If the number of slaves fell below the quorum of ten necessary for the full formalities of public worship, the Scroll was looked after by the agent. Thus, in 1696, when the last Jewish slave then in Malta died, the agent was instructed as to the preservation of the Scroll of the Law and other appurtenances of public ritual. When the younger Garsin entered upon his voluntary duties in 1707, he was recommended to take care of the Scroll and other Hebrew books until they were needed.

But, whatever might have been hoped, the days of the Congregation of Slaves were not yet over, for there was a recrudescence of piracy. 'Yesterday,' wrote the Consul, on May 6, 1713, 'they came to take the Law, wishing from now onwards, being eleven in number, to say their Mass. I gave them also stuff to make the mantle: and they stand in need of a table, with the pulpit.' Besides these bare necessities, they went to the extravagance of having a Perpetual lamp to burn in their synagogue and bells wherewith to adorn the Scroll. They had a curtain, too, to hang for the Ark.

Another necessary adjunct of settled religious life was the cemetery, for the conditions of life under which the slaves lived in so insalubrious a climate (Malta is notorious for its fever) made this requisite out of all proportion to their numbers. In 1674, without applying to headquarters for authorization, Garsin paid for the burial of two poor Jews who had died in an English ship going to Constantinople. This was done, however, in unconsecrated ground. For a short time afterwards the slaves complained to the Deputados that they had no place in which to bury any of their number who might die. On October 26, 1675, Garsin was authorized to purchase a plot of ground for this purpose at a price not exceeding fifty ducats. A couple of years later plague broke out in the island, and, since it was impossible to bury the dead in the ordinary cemetery, a special piece of ground had to be acquired as a plague pit. It was on March 17, 1677, that Garsin, for seventy-five ducats, purchased a plot outside Vittoriosa in the name of the Spanish community at Venice. Five slaves had been buried there previously. Arrangements were made for surrounding the cemetery with a wall. Despite this, in 1727 it was found that it was being treated as a private garden, and Filipo Antonio Crespi, the new Consul, urged the Deputados to find the title-deeds. A permanent cemetery was established in 1784 at the expense of the community of Leghorn for the benefit of the freedmen as an inscription over the bricked-up gateway still testifies.

Even in the depths of their misery, the slaves found an opportunity to indulge in the Jewish luxury of charity. A touching appeal was made by two of the slaves, both fathers of families, on behalf of one of their companions Solomon ben Isaac Azich (Aziz?), of Leghorn, a youth of seventeen who had been captured while on the way home from Smyrna. He was in the service of the Grand Master, being forced to carry intolerably heavy burdens and to work beyond the limits of his strength. The two elder men urged that intervention should be made on his behalf, not mentioning their own plight. Despite their miserable material condition, the slaves somehow found the opportunity to translate their charitable sentiments into works, though they were not always well-directed. The case is on record of one unmitigated scoundrel, Isaiah Orefice, pobably a galley-slave, who was in the island in 1716 pretending to be a captive like the rest, and without doubt obtaining relief from the agent on that score. The tale he told was so piteous that the compassion of the other slaves was aroused. They assisted him to get away, not only by entreaties to the agent, but also with gifts from their own slender store of money. He rewarded their benevolence by taking with him the quilt and cloak of another slave, Abraham Ajet, and the prayer books of the Synagogue.

Even more touching was the pawning by the slaves in 1672 of the lamps and petty articles of silver which their synagogue boasted in order to assist in the ransoming of Moses Messini and Mordecai Maio, two of their brethren in distress. The Deputados rated them roundly for this action, which might have deplorable consequences in the future and ordered the Christian agent to redeem the articles from pawn. Nevertheless, there seemed to be an undercurrent of admiration in their rebuke.

The religious life of the captured was enriched frequently by the presence on the island of scholarly prisoners. The most eminent scholar of whom we have any record, as well as one of the earliest, was Jacob leBeth Levi (Jacob ben Israel the Levite), a native of the Morea and translator of the Koran into Hebrew. He was later Rabbi of Zante, where he died in 1634, leaving a considerable body of Responsa. Earlier in his career he was carried off with his household and all his property to the 'den of lions and house of imprisonment' at Malta. His deliverance he regarded as a special manifestation of Providence. More than one victim redeemed by the Confraternity is referred to as Rabbi or Haham; for example, Joseph Cohen Ashkenazi of Constantinople, who was redeemed at the close of the seventeenth century for 150 ducats. Another was one Samuel aben Mayor, purchased in Malta by a speculating Armenian and ransomed later through the congregation of Ferrara. 'Emissaries of Mercy,' on their way to collect alms in the Diaspora for the four Holy Cities of Palestine, were especially liable to interception at sea. Thus, an Emissary of Safed was captured irregularly with nine other persons in a Venetian vessel in 1672. In 1666, a party of rabbis from Jerusalem was captured while on their way to convey the glad tidings of the Messianic pretensions of Sabbatai Zevi.

An interesting and tragic figure appears among the slaves in the last decades of the seventeenth century. Moses Azulai was doubtless of the famous Moroccan family of scholars and mystics, some of whom had emigrated to Palestine. How he was brought to Malta it has been impossible to trace, but his presence there is attested at least as early 1671. He must have fallen into the hands of a mild master, for there is some indication that he engaged in trade on his behalf, nor did he make appeal for ransom. His preoccupations were not for himself but for others, and for a long time he was coadjutor to the worthy Garsin. He would report what captives had been brought in, what steps were being taken to release them and who had been ransomed. The Deputados had perfect trust in him, advising their agent to rely on him implicitly for the regulation of the internal affairs of the slaves. He seems to have been a man of some learning, who corresponded occasionally in Hebrew and could not support captivity without the solace of Jewish literature. He is, indeed, first mentioned in connection with the dispatch to Malta of a copy of the *Midrash Tanhuma*. He was probably ringleader of the slaves who requested a perpetual calendar (*Sefer Iburim*), and some time after we find him obtaining another calendrical work, the *Tikkun Issachar*. A work of practical utility in another direction which was sent him was the *Pitron Halomot*, or Interpretation of Dreams, as well as the liturgical subsidiary, *Maamadot*, with a commentary. His rabbinical knowledge was at times of practical use. In 1673 and again in 1685 he was called on by fellow-slaves to draw up bills of divorcement. It was owing to his insistence that the oven for unleavened bread was provided. When any of the slaves were refractory (as, considering their misery, quite apart from their race, was no matter for surprise), it was he who was enjoined to restore discipline. From all this it would appear that he acted as religious leader of the community during the period he was on the island.

Azulai seems for all these years to have made no effort to obtain his freedom. Apparently he was content to remain in his position as guide to the captive Jews who came and departed, to maintain his post – the one constant in the shifting population.

At the beginning of the last decade of the seventeenth century, however, there came about a change in the condition of the Jewish slaves in Malta that altered also his apparent determination to make the island his home. The maritime war in the Levant was not being carried on with much vigour. Victims were fewer. The slaves remaining on the island were released one by one. The calls on the Deputados at Venice became more and more rare, the total of their outgoing letters being reduced from a maximum of forty in 1673 to as few as two twenty years later. By the end of 1691, Azulai had only one companion left – a certain Moses Joseph of Safed. He began to feel lonely. And after twenty years of captivity, during which he had been in constant communication with Venice, he asked for the first time for his own release. He was advanced in years and had for a long time served unstintingly without recompense He had seen scores of fellow-slaves liberated while he remained in uncomplaining captivity. His demand now could not be refused. The Deputados of

Leghorn added forty reals to the fifty contributed by those of Venice, and Garsin was instructed to go as high as 120 if necessary. So that Azulai's companion should not be left in utter solitude, Garsin was to negotiate his release as well. In the latter case there was rapid success and the Palestinian prisoner sailed for freedom on a French ship for Tripoli after 180 ducats had ransomed him. But over the unhappy Azulai, thus left in complete loneliness, there was some difficulty, for the anxiety of the Deputados increased the expectations of his owner. An additional contribution was elicited without much difficulty from Leghorn, and Garsin was authorized to go up to 150 reals. Success seemed at last assured. Instructions were given for the care of the communal property. Garsin was to retain the keys of the Synagogue and the custodianship of the oven and burial grounds. The Scroll of the Law and books and other ritual objects were to be placed by Azulai in a sealed chest and entrusted to the agent's keeping until opportunity should offer itself for dispatching it to Venice. For the expenses of his voyage, Azulai was to be given five reals. At last, in July, 194, it seemed that his long sufferings were at an end. But when the Deputados at Venice were expecting to hear of his final release, they received instead the information of his death (April, 1696).

Out of the horrors of slavery there was always one easy escape – baptism. But this simple expedient was an alternative rarely chosen by the slaves. An exception was one Jacob Cardiel of Tunis. When the ship on which he was sailing was captured he fouht to defend it. Fearing ill-treatment in consequence, if his religion should be discovered, he passed as a Moslem for the first year or more of his captivity. Realizing, perhaps, that he had better chance of release as a Jew, he declared himself as one, after fourteen months. The Deputados, informed of this, instructed their agent to make inquiries. Ultimately his claims were accepted; but when matters moved more slowly than he had hoped, Cardiel decided to take the shortest road out of his trouble. After three years' captivity, he was baptized – more, wrote the 'consul', from desperation than from zeal. Another convert, Guiseppe Antonio Cohen (though there is no definite proof he was a slave), attained some fame, as well as a commemorative tablet and a small annuity, by betraying the Turkish Plot of 1749 – a curiously contradictory historical parallel to *The Jew of Malta*.

Once a person had apostasized, the Deputados naturally lost

interest in his fate. 'As for the young woman from Coron, whom you were to ransom,' they wrote the 'consul' in 1688, 'since she has passed to another religion, you are to remove her utterly from your mind.'

It was not only human captives that the association felt moved to redeem. At the raid in Coron in 1865, during the Turko-Venetian War, besides the twenty-one individuals captured (mostly women and children), large numbers of books, with Scrolls of the Law and their trappings, were carried away among the spoil. The Deputados were careful to instruct their representative on the island to attempt to redeem these. In 1699, Garsin gave a woman ten ducats for five Hebrew books of the nature of which he had no idea, sure of the approval of his principals. Rabbi Jacob leBeth Levi, a century before, was able to bring away from the island an ancient Scroll of the Law, no doubt a redeemed captive like himself.

Precisely how long the Community of Slaves continued its intermittent existence it is impossible to say. In 1749 the slaves in the island were still so numerous as to make possible the Turkish plot which nearly brought Malta under the Crescent at last. With the growth of international peace and humanitarian ideas, the traffic necessarily diminished, but conditions were not fundamentally changed. Slavery ceased in Malta only at the dawn of the nineteenth century, the slaves being freed on the overthrow of the Knights, and their release being confirmed officially on May 15, 1800. The Jew, as merchant and nomad, must have remained peculiarly subject to capture until the last. The case is recorded of the release by the Deputados of Venice of Daniel de Benjamin Silva and his wife Judith as late as 1752 for the sum of 200 ducats, probably from Malta. For Jewish victims at this place were still common. As late indeed as 1752, the community of London forwarded to Leghorn the sum of 200 ducats to assist in ransoming a batch of no fewer than fourteen prisoners, then in captivity at Malta. Similar conditions must have prevailed in some degree as late as the period of the French Revolutionary wars. By this time, however, travel at sea was becoming more secure, and the need for ransom less frequent. The duration of the Venetian hegemony covers, therefore, the most interesting portion of this community's history.

In their last days, the Knights began to show greater tolerance, ad a few Jewish merchants settled in this commercially attractive centre. Even some redeemed slaves remained and settled as freemen. So,

when the British came into possession in 1802, there was the nucleus
of a Jewish community already on hand. Under British rule it
prospered and increased. Though today on the downward grade, it
appears still firmly established, with a rabbi and a synagogue.
Among its members, perhaps, are still to be found descendants of the
slaves, who introduced a new and heartrending element into the
tragic story of Israel, and founded a community the like of which no
other place or age has known.[1]

First published by the Jewish Publications Society of America in
1929 and republished in L. W. Schwartz (ed.), *The Menorah
Treasury* (1964). Dr Roth's extended paper on the subject appeared
in the *Transactions of the Jewish Historical Society of England*, Vol.
12 (1931), pp. 187–251, following his lecture to the Society in
March 1928.

NOTE

1. The Maltese Jewish Community, which includes families who
    originally arrived there in the mid-twentieth century mainly from
    Central Europe and northern Africa, is a member of the (British)
    Commonwealth Jewish Council.

35 The Musical Academy of the Venetian Ghetto

'What does Music say to the Gentiles? "Assuredly, I have been stolen from the land of the Hebrews"' (Genesis xl, 15). Thus wrote the sarcastic Immanuel of Rome, imitator if not friend of Dante, at the beginning of the fourteenth century. It is today clear that the theft was incomplete, or else that the recovery has been extraordinarily rapid. If this is so, it is in no small measure due to Italian Jewry.

The Jewish community of old time did not signify merely an association for the performance of certain religious rites. Social activities, from the dowering of the bride to the visiting of the sick, were comprised no less among its activities; and the other amenities of life were not by any means forgotten.

As far as the Arts went, painting and sculpture were almost excluded by the over-rigid interpretation of the second commandment – though, indeed, by no means so absolutely as is generally imagined. Humanistic interests were therefore concentrated all the more in music, against which no similar objection could be raised. Hence, in any general consideration of the history of Italy at the period of the Renaissance, it is impossible to overlook the part which the Jews played in this important sphere of activity.

The centre of this activity was the Court of Mantua, under the patronage of the House of Gonzaga. Here, Jewish artists were able to figure definitely in their Jewish capacity. As far as music is concerned, it would have been possible to organise in Mantua at that period a concert-party of remarkable ability, composed exclusively of Jews. Abramo dell' Arpa and his nephew, Abramino, indicate clearly, by their name, the instrument at which they excelled. Isacchino Massarano (another delightful diminutive!) played the lute, sang soprano, and taught music and dancing. David Civita was a composer of some merit, who dedicated his 'Premitie Armoniche' (Venice, 1616) to Ferdinando Gonzaga. A contemporary, and probably fellow-townsman, of his was Allegro Porto, who published at least three volumes of original compositions, one of which was dedicated to the Emperor Ferdinand II.

But there was one Mantuan family which particularly distinguished itself at this period. Salamone de' Rossi was a prolific composer. He published, besides a number of non-Jewish works, the first volumes of Synagogal music extant. His merits were so generally recognised that, like Leone de' Sommi before him, he was exempted from the obligation of wearing the red hat of shame imposed upon the Jews by law. His sister, known by the somewhat operatic professional name of Madame Europa, was a celebrated singer; her son, Anselmo, was known both as an instrumentalist and as a composer.

The array of Jewish artists at the court of Mantua at this period was not limited to those above mentioned. Any deficiencies could be remedied by Simone Basilea, a ventriloquist, who enjoyed the same exemption as de' Rossi and is said to have been able to act an entire comedy by himself, without any assistance.

The prototype of the Italian Ghetto was that of Venice, which thanks to its position, its population, and its culture, was among the most important in the Peninsula. Naturally it was not inferior to the others in the field of music. Nevertheless, two tendencies were to be discerned here – the hyper-orthodox and a trifle Philistine, especially represented by recent immigrants from beyond the Alps; and the less uncompromising and mere aesthetic, which was more specifically Italian.

The outstanding representative of the latter was, naturally, Leone da Modena, that strange prodigy, the despair and delight of his age, who perhaps more than any other represented Judaism to the outside world. He is said to have had a good tenor voice. In his youth he studied music and dancing, and he taught the former art among the twenty-six professions which he unsuccessfully practised in manhood. In the city in which he exercised his influence, it is not to be wondered that the Jews played a notable part in artistic life.

This was, indeed, no innovation. As early as 1443 the Senate, alarmed at the success and the close social relations with the general population that were engendered by the schools of singing and music maintained by the Jews, ordered that they should be closed down; and it forbade any Jew henceforth to teach these subjects, under pain of six months' imprisonment and a heavy fine. The prejudice continued apparently, in governing circles, without any alteration. 'This night,' wrote Marin Sanuto, on March 4th, 1531 (it was the day, though he did not know it, of the feast of Purim), 'there was acted in the Ghetto amongst the Jews a splendid comedy, though no Christian was able to be present by order of the Dieci. They finished it at 10 o'clock at night.' Nevertheless, in 1559 and again in 1592, a play on Esther by the illustrious Marrano writer, Solomon Usque (alias Duarte Gomez), was presented publicly before a select company of nobility and gentry.

There was, thus, ample precedent for the eventual outburst of activity in this musical sphere which took place at Venice at the opening of the seventeenth century. In 1609 a singer named Rachel was a familiar figure in the salons of the Venetian patricians. Leone da Modena (whom we find, on another occasion, writing to a friend requesting him to secure him a good place for the regatta!), not content with adapting from the Spanish Usque's drama, 'Esther', composed an original pastoral comedy, 'Rachel and Jacob', of which we know, since on one occasion he was compelled to pledge his only copy to a friend. It was one of his pupils, Benedetto Luzzatto, who published at Venice, in 1631, a pastoral fable in five acts entitled 'L'Amor Possente', which he dedicated to Don Forosto d'Este, while in 1611 Modena edited a similar work, 'I Trionfi', by his friend Angelo Alatino.

In the midst of all this activity, it is not remarkable that (to the disgust of pietists like Azariah Picho and Samuel Aboab) a regular theatre was instituted in the Ghetto – apparently with Leone da Modena's approval, if not at his incitement – to which men and women of every class thronged promiscuously.[1]

Thus far, the puritans of the Ghetto had to stifle their annoyance, for only social life was in question. Once, however, the Synagogue was entered, and an attempt was made to introduce a more decorous employment of melody in religious functions, they immediately arose in arms, for was not this a patent imitation of the Gentiles – *hukkat haGoy*? The apostate, Giulio Morosini (who in his youth, when he had been known as Samuel Nahmias, had been a disciple of Leone da Modena) gives in his scurrilous polemical, the 'Via della Fede', the following graphic description of the scenes in the Synagogue at that period during the Rejoicing of the Law, which shows plainly how informally – not to say ludicrously – his one-time co-religionists endeavoured to give expression to their passion for music:

> In the cities in which the Jews have a Ghetto, the Synagogues are kept open all day and all night . . . Similarly in many places, and in particular at Venice, a sort of half-carnival is held on

this evening, for many maidens and brides mask themselves so as not to be recognised, and go to visit all of the synagogues. The synagogues are similarly thronged at this period by Christian ladies and gentlemen, out of curiosity, more than at any other feast, to see the preparations... There are present all nations: Spaniards, Levantines, Portuguese, Germans, Greeks, Italians and others, and each sings according to his own usage. Since they do not use instruments, some clap their hands above the head, some smite their thighs, some imitate the castanets with their fingers, some pretend to play the guitar by scraping their doublets. In short, they so act with these noises, jumpings, and dancings, with strange contortions of their faces, their mouths, their arms and all their other members, that it appears to be Carnival mimicry...

From this description may be deduced how urgent was the necessity of introducing greater discipline in the synagogal service. On the eve of Pentecost 1605, therefore, the congregation in the greatest of the synagogues – that frequented by the Portuguese – had the agreeable surprise of hearing a choir of half a dozen youths repeat certain hymns with all the artificial graces which can be acquired only by prolonged practice. The pietists immediately arose in protest against so un-Jewish an innovation. Modena, with some of his colleagues, retorted in a formal Rabbinic Responsum in which he convincingly demonstrated that no conceivable legal objection could exist to prevent any person who possessed a beautiful voice from exercising it as best he could, to the glory of God. Seventeen years later, this was printed by way of preface to the 'Shir haShirim' of Salamone de' Rossi mentioned above, together with an approbation in which he insisted, perhaps a trifle optimistically, that the words would not suffer by reason of the musical rendering. In another Responsum, he discussed the question whether it was permissible to repeat the name of God in the musical setting to a hymn. And when a new Scroll of the Law was consecrated by Modena, he composed, at the request of a friend, a special poem 'to be recited to music' in celebration of the event.

Hitherto, musical interest in the Ghetto at Venice had been merely sporadic. Some years later, however, political conditions afforded the opportunity for a more organised activity. In 1628, the house of Gonzaga, which ruled Mantua, became extinct, leaving no heir more direct than Charles de Rethel, Duke of Nevers. The

Spaniards, however, were unwilling to see a French prince established so near to the Milanese, and at their instigation the Emperor Ferdinand sent an army across the Alps to dispossess the new Duke. The Jews of Mantua, assured of the latter's favour, worked manfully on his behalf, taking part in the work for the fortification of the city, even at the expense of the sanctity of the Sabbath. After its capture, therefore, they were subjected to a persecution of the most severe nature, their sufferings being described by Abraham Massarano, son of the musician Isachino, in his work, 'haGalut vehaPedut' (Venice, 1634).

A good number of the members of the community had fled to Venice before the siege began. Among these, there must have been several of the musicians who flourished about the Ducal Court, of whom mention has been made above. It was to their ability and experience that there must be attributed the foundation for the first time, in the Venetian Ghetto, of a regularly organised musical society. Again, we must allow the renegade, Giulio Morosini, to use his own words:

> I well remember what happened at Venice in my times, about 1628 if I am not mistaken, when many of the Jews fled from Mantua through the war and came to Venice. Since every sort of study then flourished at Mantua, the Jews had similarly applied themselves to music and to playing. When these arrived at Venice, there was formed in the Ghetto of that city a Musical Academy, which met generally twice a week, in the evenings. It was frequented only by some of the principal and richest members of the community, who supported it, of whom I was one: and my master, Leo da Modena, was *maestro di cappella*. That year there served as Bridegrooms in this feast (the Rejoicing in the Law), as described above, two wealthy and splendid persons, one of whom was a member of this same Academy. They accordingly introduced into the Spanish *Seuola* (very richly prepared, and adorned with a great quantity of silver and precious stones) two choirs with music, after our custom. The two evenings, that is one the Eighth Day of the Feast and on the Rejoicing in the Law, part of the evening service was chanted according to a musical setting in Hebrew, as well as different Psalms; and the *Minhah*, that is Vespers, on the last day similarly, with solemn music which

lasted for some hours into the night. There were present many members of the nobility, both gentlemen and ladies, who greatly applauded. Among the instruments, an organ was also taken into the synagogue, but the Rabbis would not allow it to be played, it being an instrument which is ordinarily played in our Churches. But what! All this was a blaze of straw. The Academy lasted little, and the music soon returned to its former state...

Morosini goes on to insinuate that the reason for the failure of the attempt lay in the fact that the Jews were no longer a fit receptacle for the divine gift of song. In this he displays all of the spitefulness of the renegade, which renders him suspect also in the other more discreditable particulars which he gives.

In part, the decline of musical interest is to be attributed to the gradual restriction brought about by the slavery of the Ghetto upon the free Jewish spirit. However, the immediate cause of the failure of the attempt, as of its origin, is to be sought in external events. In 1630, there raged throughout Italy that terrible pestilence which Mazzoni has immortalised in his famous romance, 'I Promessi Spos', In Venice alone, in a period of sixteen months, there perished nearly 50,000 persons out of a total population of less than 150,000. The Jews suffered similarly, though not in the same proportions as their fellow-townsmen. The first victims were struck down in the Ghetto Vecchio in the autumn of 1630, during the Days of Penitence. From that date, the infection spread rapidly, so that within two months no less than 170 persons perished. Many of the wealthy Spanish merchants fled, especially to the Levant and to Verona. (No doubt it was because of this, and not as local legend asserts, through the deliberate spite of the general population, that the community of this city lost two-thirds of its members and was compelled to add another layer of earth in its cemetery to accommodate the victims.) Leone da Modena, with characteristic fatalism, remained at Venice without being attacked; his was the only family in the house in which he lived that had no victim to lament. Only in the winter of 1631 could the infection be considered at an end, and in all the Synagogues of Venice, services of thanksgiving were held, preceded by a penitential fast on the New Moon of Kislev.

Among the victims, there were, it seems, many of the members of the musical circle. This led to the suspension of the regular activity of the Academy, which henceforth continued a truncated existence, meeting only on rare occasions. Nevertheless, it survived for at least nine years, contrary to Morosini's spiteful assertions. This is proved by a letter of Leone da Modena himself, of which a rough draft is preserved, with that of other of his correspondence. It is written in an execrable hand, and replete with alterations and scratching out, so that the text and the sense cannot be restored with any degree of certainty. The general significance can, however, be recovered without too much difficulty. It appears that a non-Jewish amateur, recently arrived in the city, had founded a new musical society. Having heard of the similar institution which had once existed in the Ghetto, he wrote suggesting some sort of collaboration between the two societies – especially, it would seem, the interchange of original compositions. It fell to Leone da Modena, as *maestro di cappella* and a noted stylist, to compose the reply. The following is a translation, as far as it can be reconstructed, of the letter which he wrote:

Most Magnificent and Excellent Signore,
    Once our musical gathering rightly had the name of Academy, because it numbered some musicians, both vocal and instrumental, not unworthy of that title. The enterprise...received the motto *Dum recordaremur Sion*, out of Psalm cxxxvii, *Super fiumina Babilonii*, and its name was Degli Imperiti – all in allusion to the unhappy state of our captivity, which prevents the perfection of any virtuous action. But by reason of the disaster in the year of the Plague, when we lost the best members that we had, our company remained so solitary that it indeed deserved the name, for being no longer an academy, we meet together seldom and practised only imperfectly. Whatever it may be, it truly appreciates the goodwill that your honour shows it by yours of the 28th of the past month, and promises hearty reciprocation. It grieves us more than you, not to be able to profit ourselves of your settled abode in this city, which we are sure would give fullness of harmony to our poor attempts. We would willingly avail ourselves of your courtesy if you will communicate to us the mature fruits which will be produced in the new Academy which you announce; henceforth, we can offer nothing, having no fertile store of Composers. Nevertheless, you will always be loved, esteemed, and remembered worthily by us, as we hope to

be remembered by you, and we augur you all felicity from the Lord.

Your Magnificent and Excellent Honour's always most affectionate,

THE MUSICAL COMPANY OF THE GHETTO OF VENICE

The importance of this document is considerable. It is the only Jewish source thus far known which confirms the existence of this semi-mythical Academy, and of the part which Leone da Modena played in it. It demonstrates clearly the excellent relations which the institution (and, hence, the Ghetto as a whole) still maintained with the outside world, before the policy of repression became effective. We are informed for the first time of the real reason for the failure of the Academy's musical experiment – the result of a great general disaster, not merely of internal apathy; and we see that, nevertheless, it was able to protract its existence for at least another nine years.

Interesting, above all, is the fact that we are told the real title of the institution. It was known to the outside world by the name 'The Company of Musicians of the Ghetto at Venice', though it called itself, with mock modesty, 'The Academy of the Unskilled'. But every association in the Ghetto had an additional name, taken from some Biblical verse, ranging from the *Hebrath Hesed veEmet*, which emulated towards the dead the last 'kindness and truth' that Joseph swore to his father, down to the *Shomerim laBoker* – 'Watchers for the Morning', in the Psalmist's phrase – who saluted the dawn with prayers and hymns. The musical society of Venice drew its inspiration from that most beautiful and most moving of all the Hebrew poems (Psalm cxxxvii): 'By the rivers of Babylon, there we sat down, yea, we wept when we remembered Zion. We hanged our harps upon the willows in the midst thereof. For there they that carried us away captive required of us a song, and they that wasted us required of us mirth, saying, Sing us one of the songs of Zion. How shall we sing the Lord's song in a strange land?...'

From the last words of the first verse, the short-lived Musical Academy of the Venetian Ghetto took its name: 'When we remembered Zion' – *Dum recordaremur Sion*.

First published in the *Jewish Chronicle* September supplement, London, 1931.

NOTE

1. It may be mentioned that the histrionic interests of Italian Jewry were by no means confined to the seventeenth century. In Siena, on March 31st, Leone Forti was accorded permission to present a *tragedi asacra* during the forthcoming Passover, though men and women were seated separately, and it was planned to have one special presentation for the tender sex. In Venice, at the time of the Siege of 1848, the Jewish dramatic society gave a special performance to raise money for patriotic causes. (CR)

36 Paradoxes of Jewish History

Upon first receiving the invitation to come over to America to address the Menorah Summer School on this occasion, I began to compose an exordium in what was I felt to be the style properly indicated for the occasion. I drew attention, with the platitudinous pomposity always pardonable, or at least pardoned, in a transatlantic visitor, to the vastness of the Jewish population of New York – greater by far than that of any other city of the modern world, and exceeding by many times any agglomeration of Jews that has ever been found in one single spot of the earth's surface since Jewish history began. I dilated upon the new conditions which had been brought about by this vast concentration of Jews, and by the unparalleled migration which had brought it about. I called attention to the decay of the old prejudices, to the establishment of more intimate relations between the Gentile and the Jew, and to the new tolerance in which the rising generation can participate. I expatiated upon the problems of the new age, faced with new conditions and new questionings, and no longer trammelled by the tradition of the past. I spoke of the new developments – religious, social and cultural – which recent years had witnessed, and of the inevitable call for adjustment. I touched upon the novel type of spiritual leader which the new world had produced. I enlarged, in a word, with a careful marshalling of all of the providential commonplaces which seemed adapted to the occasion, upon the utter uniqueness of the present situation in this country, preparatory to launching out on my main theme.

As I arrived at this point, I felt a still, small voice disturbing my complacency. Whenever I embark, in the course of my writing, upon a specious generalization, or conclude a passage with some trite rhetorical peroration, I find this uncomfortable companion disturbing me, urging me to tear it up and write something sensible for a change. It is my Historical Conscience.

'Oh, do go away,' said I, with some annoyance. 'I am engaged upon a very important piece of work.'

My uncomfortable companion persisted.

'What is the matter now?' I inquired.

'Everything,' replied my Historical Conscience, concisely.

'What do you mean?' said I. 'Can you deny the facts that I have stated. I have compiled this survey of conditions in New York with the utmost care. I have consulted, for my data, the 'American Hebraite', the *Jewish Year Book*, and the published sermons of a popular Rabbi – a cumulative value, as you know very well, considerably superior in these enlightened days to that of the Bible. What authority have you got to challenge their statements?'

'Oh, nothing much,' said my Historical Conscience. 'Only that of a good-for-nothing pseudo historian named Cecil Roth.' And I felt myself impelled to go to my file and take out of it the manuscript of a newly completed work upon the history of the Jews in Venice. There, in the chapter entitled 'Life in the Ghetto', I found the following passage:

[In the Venetian Ghetto] relations with the outside world, whether amatory, social or literary, were close and constant. Rabbis had begun to speak of Jesus as one of the Jewish prophets, while Gentiles on their side flocked to hear the sermons in the synagogues. Pietists complained how Hebrew culture was neglected in favour of Italian. Ignorance of the sacred tongue was so far spread that there was a movement for prayers in the vernacular. The spirit of reform was rife. There was a strong current of opposition to the Talmud and Talmudic literature. Works were written attacking Jewish tradition, evoking a whole literature in Hebrew, Italian and Spanish in its defence. The ceremonial laws were not infrequently neglected. Ingenious arguments were put forward in favour of going in a gondola, or even riding, upon the Sabbath day. Mystical tendencies and the miraculous stories attached to them, were openly scoffed at. The spirit of the nineteenth century was anticipated in the disputes concerning the introduction of instrumental music in the synagogues. We even find the phenomenon of the card-playing Rabbi who was more concerned with justifying Judaism to the Christian, than with teaching it to the Jew. Literary and intellectual life, though centred in Hebrew studies, was by no means confined to them. We find vernacular playwrights, apologists, astronomers, mathematicians and economists vying in activity. From that day to this, it is doubtful whether so surprisingly modern an atmosphere has ever at any other time prevailed.

My perusal of this passage set me meditating. From seventeenth century Italy, I was carried back in imagination five or six centuries further, to Cordova in the age of the Caliphs. There I found an essential similarity to the conditions of today, which was in many ways more striking still than that which the Venetian Ghetto had provided. The Moslem Empire was, at that time, the centre of the world's civilization. A traveller who went from Paris to Cordova made the acquaintance of a higher civilization, just as one does who goes from Cairo to Paris today. There was a world-language and a world-culture quite as specious and as compelling as the Anglo-Saxon culture of the twentieth century. Every man who had the slightest pretension to education knew Arabic, which was more necessary by far than say, French is under similar circumstances at the present time. Accordingly, Jewish authors who wished to reach the enlightened world wrote their works in that language, utterly neglecting Hebrew. Even the minority which remained faithful to their ancestral tongue were influenced by the models and inspiration of their environment, to an extent far greater than is the case with Hebraists in any part of the world today. Arabic had indeed become a semi-sacred tongue. Its position was fully comparable to Yiddish of half a century ago, with the significant difference that it was used to some extent even in religious worship, and trespassed upon Hebrew as the medium for so characteristic a function as the composition of rabbinic *responsa*.

As for the Jewish observances, they were on the downward grade. Eminent rabbinical authorities in France of the period of the Second Crusade give evidence that, fifty years before, the practice of affixing the mezuzah on the doorposts had been virtually unknown; while in Spain, a visiting scholar found to his horror that the most complete ignorance prevailed with regard to the custom of wearing the phylacteries. It is true that Darwin and Darwinism were not yet thought of. However, their place was anticipated by Averroes and the Aristotleian philosophy which he taught. Just as our spiritual leaders of today and yesterday apologetically attempted to find Evolution indicated, or at least indicable, in the Bible, so Maimonides and his generation succeeded in proving, to their perfect satisfaction, that the Bible harmonized admirably with Philosophy, as it was then conceived. The perfect balance between Judaism and secular culture seemed, at last, to have been established.

This ideal state of affairs lasted for no more than a short period – short, at least, in comparison with the enormous antiquity of the Jewish people. Before long it became manifest that the glittering culture of the Moslems was not destined to prevail. Aristotle, as Averroes had interpreted him, had after all not said the last word in human knowledge. Arabic was not always to remain the medium of polished intercourse throughout the world. This epoch passed entirely away, and those who had pinned themselves to it found themselves in a backwater, neglected by the tide of progress in Jewish life. The theories and reconciliations which seemed so apt and so durable, in their day, have joined so many of their precursors in the limbo where such things finally come to rest. Those works written in the polished vernacular of the age, in order to reach the widest circle of readers and to ensure their durability, have been lost, excepting in those cases where their immortality was ensured by a providential translation into a barbarous Hebrew. It was fortunate that there had been residuum of the Jewish people, long despised as obscurantist, which had been left untouched by the specious tide of progress and which continued to its life absolutely unaffected by the rise and fall of Arab culture. Thus Judaism overrode the disaster, and the Jew pursued his way.

This, however, is by no means the closest parallel, in our past history, to problems and conditions of today. For that, we must go back ten centuries further still, to the age of Hellenism. If a New York Jew of today could be miraculously transported back into the Alexandria of nineteen or twenty centuries ago, he would find the general atmosphere, down almost to the last detail, familiar. The city, contained, perhaps, at this period some one hundred thousand Jews – not so many, indeed as New York does today, but equal approximately in the same proportion to the general population, of which they formed about one-third. Indeed, the actual numbers are definitely superior to the Jewish population of any city of Europe or America until perhaps half a century ago, and still exceed that of all but perhaps ten places (half of which are in the United States of America) today.

Alexandria was, like New York, a comparatively new city. It was an artificial creation, a colony erected in foreign, 'barbaric' territory which had rapidly developed into the greatest seaport and one of the greatest cultural centres of its day. If straight streets and town planning on the rectangular style lead to any intellectual reaction, that must have been common to the lot of the ancient Alexandrian and the modern New Yorker.

In this Alexandrian setting, a life indistinguishable in essentials form that of one in this most modern city of the modern world, was evolved. It was an age when Hebraic culture was in utter decadence. The last word in human knowledge seemed, at this time, to have been expressed in the current Greek philosophy, with which Hebraism had to be reconciled if it were to retain any permanent value. The use of Greek alone was fashionable. In order to have a chance in the world, Jewish literature had to be produced in the vernacular.

Modern phenomena such as social reform, social climbing, assimilation, Yom Kippur Judaism, and scientific anti-semitism, were rampant. When spirituality sought its material expression, it was in much the same way as today. The synagogues were huge; in fact, I cannot help thinking that the trustees of certain recent erections in New York must feel a little envious when they read of that extraordinary Alexandrian place of worship which was so huge that the beadles had to signal with flags in order to indicate to the worshippers that the time had come to say Amen.

The congregants were Jews of a sort with whom we of today would have much in common. We are informed that there were many who had forgotten their Judaism from one year's end to the other, recollecting it only on the occasion of the Day of Atonement, when they crowded the synagogues and sought pardon for their sins. The time honoured Palestinian names were replaced by the flashy Greek equivalents. Ignorance of Hebrew was general. The Bible was familiar only in a faulty Greek translation, the errors in which occasionally caused some perplexity to earnest inquiries. The New Translation of the Holy Scriptures, recently produced in this country (the United States – eds) in order to oust the venerable Authorized Version from Jewish homes, was anticipated long before by Aquila, whose deliberately harsh Greek rendering was intended to perform the same unkind office for the Septuagint. So far had Hebrew become forgotten that it did not figure even on the tombstones, with the exception, sometimes, of the ancient greeting Sholom, 'peace'. And if you visit some of our modern cemeteries you will find that it is precisely this familiar word that is seized upon, for identical purpose, by Jews ignorant of Hebrew today.

The literature which was produced – without exception, in Greek, was incredibly modern in tone. A whole plethora of works – expository, apologetic, and belletristic, without counting translations – were offered to the attention of the cultured world. There were anticipations of Graetz, of Mendelssohn, of Zangwill, of Houston Stewart Chamberlain; and all imagined that by writing in Greek and not in Hebrew, they were assured of immortality. There were historians, nationalist and assimilationist. There were philosophers who endeavoured to prove that Judaism was rational, and antiquarians who discovered that it anticipated all that was best in Hellenic lore. There were dramatists who elaborated biblical themes for their plots – the precursors of the historical novelists of today. There were antisemites who attacked Judaism, and apologists who defended it. It would never surprise me to find that there was an Alexandrian Jewish Publication Society to foster Jewish literature, or a Menorah Journal to present it in periodical form, maintaining, perhaps a Summer School which invited Caecilius Rossus from across the sea to deliver its inaugural address.

Communal organizations were no less familiar. There were Ethnarchs and Councillors and Elders and Fathers of the Synagogue. There was a feminist movement, which resulted in the appointment of the female counterparts of this last office, at least, who were perhaps the heads of the ladies' organizations attached to the synagogues. There were separate congregations established for those who hailed from different places in the 'old country', with intense rivalries between them. There was, provably, an Alexandrian Jewish Committee which was prepared, on occasion, to send delegations abroad for the defence of Jewish rights. Since there were Jews, there were, inevitably, anti-Semites. Need I add, to complete the picture, that the latter were recruited from the Jewish ranks? A notorious case was Tiberius Alexander, nephew to the great Philo, whose father was Ethnarch of Alexandrian Jewry, yet who acted as Chief of the Staff to Titus during the siege of Jerusalem?

The brand of Judaism which was practice in Alexandria was one which would be more familiar to us than to any generation that has intervened. Reform was rampant. Even the spiritual leaders, if we may take Philo for an example, were entirely ignorant of Hebrew. They had only a slight acquaintance with the living Jewish tradition as developed in Palestine, close at hand though it was. They made up for it, however, by a minute acquaintance with Greek literature, especially with contemporary drama, and they were familiar figures at the theatre. If they were familiar with the Bible, it was in the Greek version, and this constituted the whole of their knowledge of Jewish literature. This did not, however, narrow their outlook. It served them mainly as the text about which to group their ethical discourses. The fashionable doctrines of the time were that of Plato. Just as, ten centuries later, the sages of Cordova could harmonize the Bible with Aristotle, and as the spiritual lights of our modern world can prove that it maintains its value in spite of the march of modern science, so the Jewish philosophers of ancient Alexandria were able to show that it anticipated or supported, in any case did not necessarily oppose, the Platonic craze of the moment. The Law was read mystically, spiritually, symbolically, allegorically – anything but literally. 'In that case,' said the younger generation of that day, 'why continue to observe the precepts of the Law?' And the sages answered, just as many traditionalists do today, that observance at any rate does no harm, whereas neglect causes needless offence to those who view the matter in a different light; and above all, that a man should avoid weakening the solidarity of Judaism by isolating himself from the community in these matters. Two thousand years have passed since then, and as far as essentials go, we are just where Philo and his contemporaries have left us.

This too, however, passed away, so completely that, but for recent archaeological discoveries and the good fortune of a couple of the foremost writers of that age to qualify for inclusion amongst the Fathers of the Church, we would today know nothing whatsoever of its existence. The only permanent trace of Alexandrian Jewish life of subsequent ages is perhaps, in the philosophical interests of Saadiah of Fayyum, and in some esoteric doctrines of the Zohar, which may conceivably be traced back to an Alexandrian origin. Otherwise, Hellenistic Jewry has completely disappeared – vanished notwithstanding its vast numbers, its elaborate organization, its stately synagogues, its wealth, its culture, its intellectual champions. Hillel, the Palestinian contemporary of this age, remains a living force in Jewish life even today. Philo, though his intellect was perhaps more keen, and though the volume of his extant works is immeasurably greater, has become an antiquarian diversion, familiar only to assimilated Jews like ourselves.

How the phenomenon of Jewish Alexandria's downfall took place is another question. Its collapse into inconsequence is one of the mysteries of Jewish history. One thing may, however, be said with a considerable degree of certainty. It was *not* the result of any great cataclysm. There was no deadly persecution or vast political upheaval. The whole culture, long before the Arabs came, simply melted into nothingness. Perhaps this resulted in part, from altered economic circumstances, in part from the growing enmity of the environment. But above all, as it seems, it was due to the absence of Jewish backbone, which rendered it impossible to stand up against a hostile, or even less friendly world. And this happened – it is a point which Zionists will do well to note – in spite of the inspiration of a living Jewish tradition close at hand in Palestine, nearer and easier of access by far than it can be for the vast majority of the Jewish world today, despite the improved communications.

With an example such as this before our eyes, it is difficult to continue to speak so glibly, so confidently, about the future of any of the great Jewish agglomerations of the modern world, facing conditions precisely analogous to those which I have endeavoured to delineate and reacting to them in a manner so similar that the account sounds more like the fantasy of a political satirist than a sober historical description.

Already, indeed, there are signs that our modern synthesis is being dethroned in just the same way as that of Arabized Jewry in the twelfth century, and Hellenistic Jewry in the first. There are signs that Darwin, the fashionable idol of the moment, who formerly occupied the placed which Plato and Aristotle held in earlier ages, is being ousted from the unquestioned supremacy which he once held. The shallow rationalism of the Victorian era is receding. The charitable epoch in Jewish history has fortunately seen its best days. The attack on tradition, on the basis of Higher Criticism of the Bible, has been triumphantly repulsed, and the war has been carried back into the opposite camp. Higher Criticism itself does not stand where it did twenty years ago and there is an increasing recognition that the date and composition of the Scriptures need not necessarily affect their importance in modern life. The unquestioned supremacy of the German language and German method in Jewish scholarship appears to be waning. Mysticism, so decried by Graetz and his school, is coming back into its own. The fathers of Reform Judaism – Holdheim, Geiger or Wise – would feel, perhaps, more uncomfortable spiritually among us today than would the Vilna Gaon. The nineteenth century synthesis at which our fathers arrived is passing away before our eyes. Is all this the presage of a profounder decay which will carry us, too, away with it? And is our Anglo-Saxon culture, as a whole, necessarily more durable than the Arabic or the Greek of their day? It is not easy to answer the question with any degree of confidence.

Personally, I have a deep rooted belief (and here I am at one, I believe, with the vast majority of Jews, even in this unregenerate age) in the eternity and indestructibility of Israel. 'The Jews', asserted Disraeli in the House of Commons, in a famous speech, 'have outlived Assyrian Kings, Egyptian Pharaohs, Roman Caesars and Arabian Caliphs.' He went on to insinuate that they would in all probability outlive the gibes of the Right Honourable gentleman who had just sat down. We all, with very few exceptions, feel in very much the same way.

There is, however, no logical ground nor historical support for such belief. Around us, we witness assimilation going on, to a depressing degree. The losses to Judaism by intermarriage, by ignorance, by indifference, by actual conversion, are reaching proportions which are thoroughly intimidating. If we were to go by the actual conditions and indications of the present time, there would seem to be very good ground for believing that in America and Western Europe, Judaism and the Jews will have disappeared entirely within a century or two at the outside.

In the average Jewish family of today, the probable line of the graph is unmistakable. The old generation, in Poland, observed in gladness all of the six hundred and thirteen precepts of the Law and many others, and lived a life which was essentially Jewish. Their children, in America, begin to find it a little irksome. To discover members of the third generation vitally interested in their own racial tradition is, nowadays, almost exceptional. The fourth can remain Jews in anything more than name, only by accident. The same phenomenon is being repeated throughout the world. Logically, it seems impossible to escape the conclusion that, within a few generations, the whole body of the Jews of our Western countries will have gone the same way, and will be wallowing in the slough of assimilation. Ultimately, it seems, the time must come when nothing will be left excepting, in some cases, the merest recollection of the ultimate origin of a few scattered groups of families. This seems to be the natural consequence of the unmistakable tendencies of today.

There is only one reply which it is possible to make. The Jewish people has withstood the action of thirty centuries, and it is not to be imagined that it will suddenly collapse at the thirty first.

However, as a historian, I cannot but recognize that historical precedent does not permit the application of this belief to any one particular branch of the Jewish people, however numerous, deep-rooted, or long settled it may be. The human body, we are informed, reconstitutes itself entirely within a short space of years, at the end of which there is not a particle of its original components. The Jewish people, throughout its past, has been in much the same case. The whole of our history presents one constant procession of communities which have sprung up, then withered away entirely after a brief period of florescence. There is no guarantee that we in England, or you in America, will not follow the same path.

Permit me to draw your attention to a couple of characteristic precedents for decay. I will not speak of the Samaritans, once a powerful rival of Israel, but now reduced to a pious handful, whose main function seems to be the provision of an annual spectacle for Palestinian tourists. Let us approach closer to ourselves in place and time. When the Jews were chased out of France, a few survivors were permitted, by the tolerant policy of the Popes, to remain in Avignon and the surrounding territories which were then under their rule in the south of the country known as Comtat Venaissin. To this exiguous area, the ancient glories of French Jewry were henceforth restricted. Here, for many centuries, the tradition of Rashi and of the Kimhis were perpetuated. It is not simply a group of communities which is in question, but a whole distinctive Jewish civilization. The culture of the Jews of Provence was a unique one. They had their own customs, their own patois, their own folklore, their own tradition of synagogue construction, their own *hazanut*, their own site of prayers, their own style of calligraphy, their own method even of pronouncing Hebrew. With an incredible fortitude, this exiguous Jewish group – numbering perhaps between 3,000 and 5,000 at the most – was able to withstand the persecutions of centuries, preserving its traditions and its identity unimpaired. If perpetuity seemed certain for any branch of the Jewish people, it was assuredly the case with this, which had given over fifteen hundred years concrete proof of its fitness for survival. Yet this intense Jewish life, after withstanding persecution with incredible fortitude, was swept away almost in a moment after the French Revolution, by the first breath of freedom. Now, almost nothing is left to commemorate the existence of this pathetic remnant excepting a romantic tradition, a couple of ancient synagogues of exquisite beauty, and a vast number of liturgical manuscripts. As one views the ruin, it seems impossible to feel assured of the perpetuity of any branch of the House of Israel.

Let us take another instance. In China the Jews were already established at the period of the Han dynasty, perhaps from the date of the destruction of Jerusalem by Titus. From that time onward, the record of their settlement is more or less continuous. Communities existed in several of the principal cities. The Chinese treated their Jewish fellow citizens with every consideration. The latter showed their gratitude by sloughing off their foreign characteristics and entering into the life of the country. They were admitted into the Mandarin class. They wore pigtails in the approved fashion of the time Their synagogues were built in the Chinese style, and went by a Chinese name. They venerated their ancestors with the rest of their countrymen. On the other hand, they adhered punctiliously to Judaism, observing the Sabbath and feasts with all due rigour, cutting out meat from the sinew of the thigh (which they burned with great solemnity), and industriously copying the sacred books. The history of this extraordinary community is traceable for nearly twenty centuries. Now, according to latest reports, it is represented by a few individuals grouped about the ruins of a synagogue, who know that their fathers were once Jews, and a couple of clerks preserved in a Shanghai bank as an historical curiosity. Here is another Jewish civilization which has altogether disappeared.

The last three communities which I have instanced, I will be informed, were minute and isolated, and cannot therefore be taken as proper precedents for our present conditions and problems. This is not perhaps so sure. Nevertheless, in any case, they are not the most striking phenomenon of the sort. We have already seen the example of Hellenic Jewry, numbered by hundreds of thousands, living under conditions incredibly similar to our own, whose disappearance was even more complete than that of the other bodies which I have mentioned and that in spite of the inspiration of a living Jewish tradition in Palestine, within easy reach. If a Jewish civilization such as that can vanish, none of our upstart Jewries of today can consider itself safe.

The Jewish people will assuredly live – but not necessarily that particular section with which we are in touch, however vast and however wealthy it may be. One is reminded forcibly of that striking passage from the Book of Esther – from the literary point of view the most remarkable of all biblical works, though so much decried nowadays by those who, all oblivious of the existence sometimes of a higher truth, allege that it lacks historical accuracy. Mordecai, you will remember, is urging Esther to take action on behalf of her people. 'Think not within thyself', said he, 'that thou shalt alone escape, being in the King's house, out of all the Jews. For if thou holdest thy peace at this time, then will relief and deliverance arise for the Jews from another place, but thou and thy father's house will perish; and who knoweth whether thou are not come to royal estate for such a time as this?' We are in the same position today. Relief and deliverance and perpetuation will assuredly come about for the Jewish people from some place or other. Of that I am convinced. But, because we live in the lap of luxury and enjoy all possible material advantages, and have had the benefit of university education, that is no proof that it is we who will escape in any general catastrophe.

In a thousand years' time, the Temples of New York and the Yeshivoth of Poland may have followed the Jewish Mandarins of China and the Academies of Alexandria into oblivion and decay. Jewish Palestine may have withered and flowered and withered and flowered half a dozen times by then. Possibly, in that epoch, the Jewish tradition will be preserved by the descendants of the Falashas of Abyssinia, or the Arabized Jews of the Yemen, or the Sephardim of the Levant and northern Africa, whom we now tend to condemn as the degenerate heirs to a noble inheritance. Possibly the glories of Spanish-speaking Jewry will be revived in the Republics of South America, to which so vast a tide of emigration is now being directed.

But whoever preserves the tradition, the Jewish people will assuredly live. However, if we want to secure our own personal perpetuity as Jews, to guarantee our own identity, it is up to us to take steps – not on our people's behalf, for they can exist without us, but on our own.

The question is, wherein the salvation lies. It is not, necessarily, in Zionism, for Zion has not been able to save itself from overthrown on repeated occasions, nor (as we have seen in one especially notable instance) has it been able to preserve from decay the communities of the countries in closest touch with it. It is not, necessarily, religion, for there are numerous bodies of Jews, meticulous in their orthodoxy, which have entirely disappeared or almost entirely disappeared. But, if it is possible to generalize in such matters, one may perhaps make one categorical statement: it has never happened that any body of Jews, imbued with their ancestral culture, has withered away.

The Jews of China have left no literary monuments behind them, other than a few ancient scrolls of the law and other synagogal paraphernalia. The Jews of Avignon expended the whole of their energies in multiplying manuscript copies of their prayer book. The Jews of Alexandria were more concerned in justifying their religion to the Gentile, than in familiarizing it to the Jew. The ancient tradition of the genuine Jewish scholarship, has, alone, succeeded invariably in perpetuating itself and perpetuating those who immersed themselves in it.

The living record may be traced from the Palestinian authorities of the time of the Mishnah and the Rabbis of the Gemara, through the age of the Gaonim and of the Spanish codifiers, and of Rashi and his school in France, and the German expositors of the Middle Ages and the Polish Yeshivoth of more recent times, right down to our own day. Jewish learning, while it continues to be cultivated seriously, is the one tried preservative. It is, indeed, the solitary means through which these alternative panaceas, religion and nationalism, have themselves been preserved in our own day. It remains the only thing upon which it is possible for us to rely for our own continuity.

It is with some of these more permanent manifestations of Jewish life, in the main line of the tradition of our past, that we shall be concerned in the course of the lectures which I am to deliver at this Summer School. I shall endeavour to delineate the conditions under which Jews lived and Judaism was preserved during the past centuries in Europe, after the great centres of population in the East were broken up.

One fact will, I think, emerge. Historical Judaism has been in the past more than a religion only, more than a nationality, more than a philanthropic brotherhood. It has been a civilization and a culture, and without that civilization and that culture, it must inevitably have decayed as so many of its local manifestations have done. Personally, I am tired of the continual squabbling which is going on between

Reform Judaism and its opponents. The whole dispute obscures the real problem of today. Any Judaism, of whatever extremity of orthodoxy or liberalism, is to me a deformed Judaism so long as it lacks that cultural background which was, to our fathers, the inseparable adjunct of our national and religious life. The catchwords of nineteenth century polemics should be swept away into the limbo where such things belong. The only conceivable guarantee of our future is an informed Judaism.

It is because the Menorah stands (as I feel) for this informed Judaism that I am proud to be able to participate, in a practical manner, in the present Menorah School.

First published in the *Menorah Journal*, New York, Vol. 19, 1930. Substantially the author's address to the Menorah Journal Summer School, c. 1930.

37 Caveat Emptor Judaeus

The antique market is booming, and as one who purchased his collection long since, and in any case is in no position to purchase anything more now, I cannot but rejoice at the fact. The market in Jewish antiques, on the other hand, is not merely booming; it came into existence only a very short while ago, and it has already become affected by a runaway inflation.

It is little more than a half century since a few eccentrics in France, Germany, England, one even in the United States, began to be interested in the artistic relics of the Jewish past – objects of Bigotry and Virtue, as a friend of mine once paraphrased the French *bijouterie et vertu*: Chanukkah lamps for use in the home, pewter or majolica dishes for the Passover, the hanging lamps formerly kindled for the Sabbath, the brocades which hung before the Ark in the Synagogue, the silver adornments which decorated the Torah scrolls, the illuminated *megillot* or Books of Esther, the beautiful marriage contracts formerly common in Italy and elsewhere. But everybody knew that these collectors were eccentrics, and pitied them somewhat for not investing their capital in objects of more general interest or more profitable prospects. However, in a way such eccentricity was condonable, for the competition was so slight that the prices were negligible.

Now, however, the scene has changed. The universal collecting fever has spread to the field of Judaica. The economic well-being of Jews in some Western countries has made it possible for the circle of collectors to be immensely widened; and to some extent, doubtless, the abandonment of Jewish rituals has created a sort of guilt complex, which results in an attempt to assemble the vehicles wherein these rituals were expressed in the past. As a result, apart from the newly-developed major Jewish Museums in New York, Cincinnati, London, and so on, there are smaller museums of Jewish ritual objects attached to synagogues and temples all over the United States, as well as overseas; and travellers to Europe or the East are anxious to bring back some object of interest to add to these collections and thus perpetuate their own names. Moreover, a very, very large number of private persons, including many enthusiastic young married couples, are now engaged in beginning to build up private collections of the same type, based in the first instance on the objects they may be able to use in their domestic rituals, but later extending more and more.

As a result of the growing demand, there is a growing supply, but unfortunately it is of frequently dubious origin. (Some sales by auction, for example, at renowned auction galleries, which purport to be of important collections and to gain status thereby, turn out on investigation to be based on the recently and deliberately acquired stock-in-trade of professional dealers.) Since the supply of authentic antiques is limited (especially after the wholesale destruction of 1933–45, and the concentration of worthwhile specimens in the major museums), a lively manufacturing trade in Jewish antiques has sprung up in recent years, with its centres in Spain and (I regret to say) in Israel. Both are particularly suggestive centres for distribution, for what comes from Israel is even now imbued with some odour of sanctity, and what was purchased in Spain is ostensibly of very great antiquity – a relic of the ancient communities expelled from that country in 1492.

So far as this latter area is concerned, one may be quite categorical. To my knowledge, there is only one single authentic piece (or rather pair of pieces) of synagogue silver now extant, which goes back before the 16th century – a pair of *rimonim* (Torah bells) preserved in the Cathedral of Palma (Majorca), though in fact not Spanish but Sicilian in origin. Other pieces may be extant, but I do not know of them, and would want to have their date authenticated by expert opinion were I to spend any substantial sum on them. And objects of the sort dating from before the year 1600 are also very, very uncommon (and should be correspondingly costly.)

To the collector, I can give only one piece of advice: *never buy a Jewish antique in Spain!* (That is, *qua* Spanish antique, for indeed, a few authentic fairly old German-Jewish pieces have found their way into the Peninsula also.) Some little time ago, a pair of *rimonim*, described as being 15th-century Spanish, turned up for sale in New York; to the best of my judgment they are 19th-century Moroccan, and poor quality at that, and I do not think that if they were presented to me, I would put them on display.

The most ostensibly appealing and remarkable of the Jewish *objets d'art* now being put into the market has a romantic story attached to it. It is said to emanate from the Marranos (or crypto-Jews) of Spain and Portugal, who manufactured it in this way in order to conceal their observance of the rites of their former faith from the prying eyes of the Inquisition. (Sometimes, as a further embellishment, the purchaser is informed that it was formerly owned by a Grand Rabbi of Istanbul; the relevance is not obvious.) This precious object consists of a silver chalice (sometimes authentically old, and even of some value), which purports to be a *kiddush* cup. Into this are fitted ingeniously (1) a pair of candlesticks for the Sabbath, (2) a Chanukkah lamp, (3) a Scroll of Esther, (4) a *mezuzah* or some similar object, or whatever else appeals to the curious mind of the craftsman. Occasionally, this absurdity is even sold, without extra charge (the price used to be around $1,500!), with a written guarantee of authenticity! But it is obviously an absurdity, apart from the fact that most of the contents are patently of recent manufacture. For none of these things was absolutely necessary for Jewish life (any lamp, for example, could serve for the Sabbath, and Sabbath *candlesticks* are a recent innovation); and to be found with an agglomeration of this type in his possession would inevitably have condemned the owner to the stake. Nevertheless the manufacture goes on blithely, and I am afraid collections all over the U.S. count such horrors among their most treasured possessions.

Another trick of the industry is to adapt authentic objects by giving them a spurious inscription or embellishment, for it is easy enough to add a few Hebrew characters to an old piece of silver so as to qualify it for a Jewish collection. Thus, for example, a couple of words or a biblical verse in Hebrew can convert an 18th-century tea-caddy into a box for holding the *etrog* on the Feast of Tabernacles, or a silver beaker into a wine-cup for the *kiddush* on Friday night. Fairly old Scrolls of Esther are easily obtainable at moderate price; these are then handed over to an illuminator who embellishes them with a conventional design, and it is difficult to deny positively that the object is in fact 17th- or 18th-century, as the vendor claims. However, the number of craftsmen in the field is limited and it is not difficult to recognize their handiwork; it is generally in pastel colours, with a touch of gold, embodying a Gothic architectural design and the signs of the zodiac. Even if I saw this trademark attached to a silver or silver-gilt roller which appears to me to be authentic and desirable, I would hesitate to touch it; the entire object would now appear to me suspect.

Another very ingenious (and very common) method is to attach a newly made silver hand with outstretched forefinger to the tapering end of a Victorian (in one case that I know, even Fabergé) buttonhook or umbrella handle. This converts it into a very presentable antique yad, or pointer, used to follow the place in the Torah-scroll during the reading – and converts a price of a few dollars into a few hundred. These newly made silver objects are fairly easily recognizable: they are generally of rather base metal with a somewhat heavy *repoussé* pattern, and decorated with bosses of semi-precious or coloured stones. There is also a tendency for ivory, or imitation bone-ivory, to be used in the manufacture of some sections – a feature which immediately puts the collector on his guard. They are sometimes quite well-made and not bad value, and could well be used for ordinary synagogal purposes – but have no place in a Jewish museum.

Similarly, the Chanukkah lamps (and also hanging Sabbath lamps) of copper or brass are generally of quite good design – as they should be, since they are cast reproductions made last month of authentic old pieces, and worth no more than the price of any cast reproductions. However, when the reproduction is in silver the whole of the basis of the work, and its object, is falsified (though the price is correspondingly enhanced). Cast reproductions of the characteristic North African Chanukkah lamps have now become very common indeed. They are attractive and worth having – providing that they are not regarded as antiques. Stone is, of course, ageless, and Chanukkah lamps of stone were made in Yemen etc. for centuries past, though I would be inclined to ascribe some of them, which are now being offered for sale as belonging to the early centuries of the Christian era, to a date around 1870 or later.

Another category, now being widely imitated in the Orient, consists of *kemiot* or amulets, usually of base silver with long Hebrew inscriptions unintelligible in any case to the ordinary person. They are still being made, of course, but it is a wholly different thing, somehow, whether they are made for use or for sale.

When I first began to collect Oriental marriage contracts, the price was trivial (so, alas, I did not purchase as many as I should have). Now the value has gone up so enormously that a lively industry in falsification has sprung up. However, the Oriental craftsman being so economical of his time, and his opinion of foreign intelligence being so low, the text of the imitations that he now turns out is absurdly curtailed in length, so that it loses all significance, and as a marriage document would be legally invalid. The Italian *ketubot*, on the other hand, are far more beautiful, and therefore more valuable. Recently I saw one that obviously was copied from a photograph of a well-known original (replete with spurious signatures in, unfortunately, the wrong script).

Incidentally, there is one Jewish symbol from which the falsifiers are seldom able to abstain, but which should immediately put the purchaser on his guard. The *Magen David*, or Star of David, became recognized as a specific token of Judaism only relatively late, and if I see it on some *objet d'art*, I suspect that it cannot be earlier than the middle of the 19th century – and may be a good deal later.

It must be admitted that some of the contemporary fabricators show considerable ingenuity, or even learning. There is one highly complex and elaborately-inscribed article sold, at present, in Spain of which I can say no more than that it is of very recent manufacture and can have served no conceivable object. Except for this, it is quite desirable. In Morocco, there are now being turned out miniature imitations of medieval astrolabes (that is, instruments for use in astronomical observation), with Hebrew inscriptions which, if genuine, would be worth tens of thousands – but my search for the original has been unavailing.

Some of the elaborate gold and enamel betrothal rings now on the market (it is uncertain whether the originals, now very scarce and correspondingly valuable, were South German or North Italian) are so well executed that only an expert can advise definitely on their age. On the other hand, those ungainly and elaborate specimens in silver, which have become so common, are almost all fabrications, however romantic the elements they embody or the stories attached to them.

The auction price of Jewish *objets d'art* is soaring. There is no reason to complain about this. An antique is worth what it will fetch, or what it has fetched. Even if the enthusiastic purchaser pays what appears an astronomical price in competition with another enthusiastic amateur, he has not made an error *qua* collector – that is a problem to be settled between himself and his bank-manager. But if the collector pays even a moderate price for what is sold to him as an antique, but is in fact a contemporary fabrication, he has been guilty of an irremediable blunder (besides the fact that he has been made a fool of). And if such objects are deposited in a museum or some public collection, they debase the general taste and remain to trap future generations.

An imitation has, indeed, a place in a collection when the original cannot be obtained; but a fake – never, except in the rogues' gallery, for which there is a place only in major collections. Indeed, in view of recent developments, it might be desirable for synagogue and temple museums to have a display of such objects, in order to demonstrate to their supporters what not to buy when they are on their summer tour to ancient centres of Jewish life in Europe or the Holy Land – where action should have been taken by the competent authorities long before this. *Caveat Emptor Judaeus.*

First published in *Commentary*, New York, March 1967.

38 Dealings in the Higher Junk

THE ART AND CRAFT OF JEWISH COLLECTING

I imagine that I must own one of the most preposterous private collections of miscellaneous Jewish junk to be found anywhere in the world today. I have over three hundred manuscripts, dozens of Chanukkah lamps, a boxful of ancient coins, a sprinkling of bookplates, scores of illuminated marriage contracts, hundreds of engravings and caricatures, a good amount of domestic and synagogal silver and embroidery, some nice pewter – and just about enough space left over for my wife to be able to squeeze herself into the house when it is absolutely necessary. And I've managed it all on an income which I can only describe as regrettably exiguous.

Actually, I am probably not a true collector, for your true collector must be willing to thieve, lie, steal, flatter, cajole, and demean himself for the sake of an acquisition, whereas I can bring myself to do only some of these things. The classical story, I think, is that told of the late David Sassoon, a famous bibliophile, who while he was sailing through the Suez Canal found out that one of the Jewish peddlers who had come aboard at Suez or Port Said had a Hebrew manuscript at home. The peddler refused to go back to fetch it, saying he could not afford to lose his shipboard 'business'. In desperation, the plutocrat offered to look after the peddler's 'business' during his absence. I understand that a roaring trade was done. And the manuscript, as it happens, was worth having.

One of the greatest Jewish collectors of modern times, the late Elkan Adler, I knew very intimately in his old age. I learned from him two things in particular. One was that books which seem identical, frequently have some minute differences. The other was that no time, hour, or place is to be considered an unlikely one to make a find or an acquisition. Adler was intensely Orthodox, but he often got some friend who wasn't observant to make his purchases for him on the Sabbath, if they found something during a stroll together. It was Adler, of course, who first 'raided' the Cairo Genizah (the book-lumber room of the old synagogue in that city in which so many literary treasures were discovered), and who was upbraided by Solomon Schechter, when he came home, for not making a clean sweep, as the latter did later, to the great benefit of Jewish scholarship.

Even before Adler's day, however, the great Karaite forger, Firkovitch,[1] had found similar Geniza hoards in the ancient synagogues of the Crimea, especially Biblical manuscripts of immense antiquity (the scientific value of which he sometimes ruined by shamelessly altering the dates so as to add another few hundred years to their age.) I have been told of his method. He used to commiserate with the local community on having to make use of these old, crabbed, almost worn-out volumes, and would generously offer to present, as a substitute for them, clear modern texts published in London by the British and Foreign Bible Society.

The first collector on record of Jewish objects was an 18th-century German named Alexander David, Court Jew to the Duke of Brunswick, whose assemblage of curios was housed in the local synagogue. A hundred years later, a musician named Strauss, who was, I think, conductor of the private orchestra of the Emperor Napoleon III at Vichy, brought together a fine collection in France. After his death it was purchased by one of the Rothschilds and presented to the Cluny Museum in Paris, where for some years it has been inaccessibly stored in the vaults. Later a number of enthusiastic collectors sprang up, especially in Germany, where there were several synagogal and communal museums, and even a society with a periodical devoted to such questions. After 1933, some of these collections were transferred to other countries.

Today there are one or two important Jewish collections, public and private, in Amsterdam, Paris, London and (I boast) Oxford. In Israel there is, naturally, great interest in the subject, and one superb public collection is in the Bezalel Museum of Jerusalem. But America has now, I suppose, risen to first place in the field. In addition to the Jewish Museum in New York, and the somewhat smaller collection at Hebrew Union College, Cincinnati, there are half a dozen private collections of first magnitude. A few congregations and temples (e.g. Temple Emanu-El in New York) have begun to build up their own collections – partly in realization of their importance as an educational aid in connection with their Sunday schools. Moreover, some synagogues now buy ancient specimens of these objects (e.g. Torah-crowns and finials, or 'bells') for current use, to replace the tawdry achievements that flooded the market in the past century. The staffs of the New York and Cincinnati Jewish Museums – scholars trained in the exacting tradition of Continental art history – have begun to place the study of various objects, for the first time, on a new and sound basis. The sale of the Salomon Collection by auction in New York in 1949 aroused great enthusiasm (greater perhaps than it deserved), and may prove to have been a turning point in the history of Jewish collecting in the United States.

On the whole, no Jewish object that one may normally be able to purchase is likely to be of really great age. Very little comes into the market older than the year 1600, and almost nothing from before 1500. There are virtually no relics of medieval Jewish life in Spain, other than buildings, tombstones, and manuscripts. Scores of visitors who have gone there with well-lined wallets and high expectations, have returned empty handed. In a Belgian collection, there is one lamp-holder from an ancient Palestinian synagogue of classical times; in a Spanish cathedral there is a pair of silver finials from a Torah scroll of the 15th century; off-hand I can think of nothing else of comparable antiquity in any collection that I know.

By a curious contrast, ancient Hebrew coins of the Maccabean period down to Bar Kochba – i.e. from the 2nd century of the Christian Era – are still relatively cheap and common. Even now, specimens may be purchased for a few dollars. But coins aren't every collector's choice.

The majority of the relatively old objects that come into the market are either Italian or German in origin, these being the only two countries where the Jewish settlement was continuous in the post-medieval period. One would have imagined that vast masses of material, now ownerless, would have been thrown on the market after the Nazi débâcle in 1945. Inexplicably this has not happened, and in fact there is a greater scarcity – and values are higher – now than ever before.

Generally speaking, where you expect to find things, you don't, for others also expect to find things in the same place and have been there before you – and have sent up the price for any unconsidered trifles that may remain. The most improbable objects may turn up in the most unexpected places. I have acquired my most important Indian volume in New York, and one in Judeo-Greek in – of all places – Greek-sounding Minneapolis, Minnesota. (In a hundred years' time, persons inspecting my collection are certain to imagine that there was a place of that name somewhere in Greece itself.) My wife unearthed a superb Spanish manuscript prayer book of the 15th-century in Johannesburg, South Africa. But in Salonica (though this was after the virtual annihilation of the community in 1941) I did not find even a scrap of paper or piece of metal of Jewish interest.

The beginner tends to imagine that any ancient object bearing on it a Shield of David (*Magen David*) must necessarily be of Jewish origin. The reverse is the case, rather. The *Magen David* became a recognized and quasi-exclusive (though even this is rather too strong) Jewish symbol only during the last couple of centuries at the most. Previously it had been as frequently used by Jewish as by non-Jewish mystics.[2] It was very common, however, and still is, in the Moslem world. An old tray or vase bearing the characteristic intertwined triangles is, therefore, far more likely to be of Arab than of Jewish origin. (Incidentally, even the presence of Hebrew lettering is not always an indication of Jewish origin. The Hebrew characters have a high decorative value, and I have been informed that some Arab brass-workers in Syria and North Africa keep a stock of punches which they use round the edges of their manufactures without any regard to meaning.)

Conversely, the beginner often imagines that an object which looks as though it was made for Jewish ritual use – a Chanukkah lamp or a Torah breastplate, perhaps – cannot possibly be because it bears animal or human forms forbidden by Jewish religious law. Once again, this prohibition is a more or less recent convention. There have been periods in Jewish history when any portraiture was anathema. But at others – especially, for example, in 16th-century Italy and 17th-century Germany, both so prolific in Jewish ritual art – there were no inhibitions of this nature, and some of the finest Italian Chanukkah lamps and better German Torah shields are adorned not merely with representations of anges and *putti*, but with Biblical scenes or conventional figures of Moses and Aaron. It is really only in the past generation that this sort of thing was utterly banished from the synagogue.

A favourite, and likely, object for the collector's fancy is the Chanukkah lamp. I myself have made a practice of adding at least one every year to my collection. I recall a find I made when I was strolling one day round the English spa, Harrogate, with Chaim Weizmann, some years before he became president of Israel. I suggested that we cross the road so that I could look into the window of a stylish antique shop. He chaffed me: 'They'll have nothing Jewish there,' he said. But he was wrong. In the window there were a couple of Dutch Chanukkah lamps of rather fine design, but with the burners removed and replaced by single candleholders so that they could be used as wall sconces.

Chanukkah lamps have been produced for hundreds of years, were owned by every householder, and were made of metal, thus being fairly permanent if not indestructible. Moreover, some of them – especially Italian specimens of the Renaissance period – are very lovely and fully worthy of the attention of even the most discriminating connoisseur. One of my own nicest lamps I bought in a little Oxfordshire village. 'You've got a real nice thing there, sir,' the vendor told me. 'The nobleman I bought it from brought it back from a monastery in Italy; them old monks used to burn one light for every day of the week – and the eighth they kept alight perpetual, in honour of Jesus.'

But the choicest specimen in my collection is one bearing the coat of arms of a cardinal of the Holy Catholic Church of the end of the 16th century, surmounted by the conventional hat with hanging tassels. Romantics might suggest that he was a crypto-Jew. Yet there is more than one such object to be found in various collections, and presumably they were made by Jews who boasted the patronage and protection of princes of the Church.

Another likely line of collecting is illuminated marriage contracts (*ketubbot*). These (the collector's pieces, that is) are almost all Italian in origin, and are generally of the 17th and 18th centuries – though a German specimen of the 14th century is preserved, and one or two superb late examples of aristocratic Dutch Sephardi families, bearing representations of the marriage scene, have recently come to light. They are generally inscribed on large sheets of vellum, and a good deal of their beauty comes from the wonderful calligraphy. The quality varies enormously, from pathetic daubs to artistic monuments in the finest taste of the age. Frequently they are surmounted by Biblical scenes having some bearing either on the date of the marriage or on the names of the couple; for example, a marriage celebrated at Purim time might show figures of Haman and Mordecai, or if the bridegroom's name was David there would perhaps be a vignette of the overthrow of Goliath, or of David's anointing by Samuel.

I once bought a nice little collection of illuminated marriage contracts in Rome. It happened this way. In the junk market in the Campo di Fiori there was a book dealer whom my wife had spotted as a Jew, and who turned out to be immensely old. He had purveyed books to many well-known scholars of the past, and decided that he would find me something for my collection too. Thereafter he would lie in wait for me as I walked through the streets, and escort me to some insalubrious neighbourhood so that I could inspect a treasure. That was the year (1935) I had my audience with the late Pope Pius XI, and as I drove through the streets to the Vatican, in full evening dress in the middle of the morning, I huddled back in the corner of the carriage lest David Sulmoni fu Moise should pounce out on me and drag me off somewhere. One day he informed me that there was a treasure trove in the Via Reginella, the last remaining street of the original Roman Ghetto. He escorted me to the top story of an ancient and somewhat malodorous house. Here I was awaited by a typical Roman Jewish peddler named Sabbadin, together with all his family and neighbours. I glanced through Sabbadin's collection – not a very exciting one – and, turning to my guide, I named a fairly substantial amount in lire that I could pay for the lot, including his commission; he could make what bargain he pleased, I added. He thanked me, and promptly offered Sabbadin one-tenth of the sum I had stated. Sabbadin retorted by asking just fifty times as much. We (or rather David Sulmoni fu Moise) haggled, and the margin was somewhat narrowed down, but there was still a discrepancy of some 1500 per cent. We left, firmly. They sent the ice-cream man after us with a further compromise suggestion, and negotiations were continued on the street corner. Again an impasse, and again we went away. We had gone two blocks when David Sulmoni fu Moise discovered that he had missed the right turning, and we went back a little way. Once more we ran into Sabbadin, who by a curious coincidence had come out to buy some cigarettes. Negotiations were resumed, and at last we reached a compromise – Sabbadin accepted about one-fortieth of what he had asked in the first instance, while my agent generously reduced his commission from 90 to 40 per cent. I had no spare cash with me. I asked Sabbadin if he would accept a cheque. 'Of course,' he said, 'I would trust you with anything in the world. What's a cheque?' I explained, and he listened very tolerantly.

'Yes,' he said when I had finished, 'but how do I get the money?' Finally I told him to bring the parcel along to the house where I was dining that evening – I knew my host would advance me what I needed. It was an elegant dinner party, in a fashionable part of Rome. As we were finishing our dessert, there was a ring at the bell and in tramped a good portion of the Roman Ghetto. Sabbadin had told everyone what was happening, and they had decided to come along to see how the rich lived – and perhaps receive a rake-off for themselves!

Of late, I have been trying to bring together a representative collection of marriage contracts, to illustrate the style used in every country regardless of artistic importance. One, of a Sephardi family in Bayonne, France, was not signed by the bridegroom, we are informed in a docket, for two reasons – first, because he suffered from cramp, and secondly, because he did not know how to write! The pearl of my recent acquisitions, however, was the *ketubbah* of a great-grandson of Gluckel of Hameln, drawn up and decorated in the typical local fashion in India, at Cochin (but acquired in Bloomsbury). Incidentally, these documents are seldom found in the hands of the descendants of the bridal couple mentioned in them, for they were generally preserved, as a rudimentary safeguard, in the family of the bride.

The other fairly common manuscript object of artistic interest that may be picked up, is the Scroll of Esther (*megillah*). Every householder had one to follow the statutory reading in the synagogue, and since these were for private use, and it was a season of some license, they were frequently enclosed in decorated silver or ivory cases and lavishly illuminated with scenes from the Biblical story. The collector must be wary, though: certain quite authentic specimens of the 17th and 18th centuries, mainly German or Dutch, were written by hand within copper-engraved borders, sometimes hand-coloured. As a matter of fact, some of there engravings are more valuable than the hand-drawn examples. It is easy enough to date them by using a trick of the trade now set down in writing for the first time: Toward the end of the scroll, where the text speaks of the Jews' celebration of their triumph (generally under the last column but one), there is almost always a representation of the junketings *in contemporary costume*. From this, place and period can often be determined almost precisely. An antique dealer in Israel has recently put on the market a number of extremely skillful forgeries in this sphere, the illuminations being meticulously based on early models and executed in the margins of authentic early plain manuscripts of the scroll. It needs a great deal of care, even for the astute collector, not to be deceived sometimes by these very decorative modernisms.

Another often found domestic item is the spice box used in the picturesque *Havdalah* ceremony on the conclusion of the Sabbath. These are almost always Ashkenazi or North European; in the Mediterranean countries it was customary to use a branch of myrtle, or the like, to provide the sweet odour on this occasion. Sometime in the 16th century, apparently, the convention arose of manufacturing these, generally in the form of towers or steeples over-lavishly provided with pennants, and sometimes with clock-faces and movable hands, on which the pious householder could indicate the time of the conclusion of the Sabbath. Further east, these spice boxes were frequently made in the form of flowers, or even entire posies; and one interesting West German local variant combines the spice box with a taper-holder, for the light which was also used in the traditional ceremony.

Less frequently found are the Passover dishes for use in the Seder ceremony on the eve of the festival. These are, for the most part, North European and made of pewter, though in Italy, in the 17th and 18th centuries, a couple of families of craftsmen in Pesaro and Ancona manufactured them of majolica, proudly signing their names on the backs. Mine (made by Isaac Cohen, Ancona, 1672) I acquired in the only manner in which the poor man can get hold of such treasures – by buying an entire collection at a price that I couldn't afford and disposing of the other objects at the price I had paid for the lot, retaining this as my profit. These majolica dishes are now so much sought after that there are a number of palpable (and other less palpable) fakes on the market at present.

Specifically synagogal objects are, of course, less easy to acquire. There were never so many of them, and they tended to remain, naturally, in the places of worship for which they were made. To compensate for this, they are generally of finer, and sometimes of the very finest, workmanship, and are sought after by collectors quite apart from their specific interest. There was a time, I am informed, when a tip to the beadle of an almost abandoned community was enough to secure one's choice of its accumulated treasure. One bearded dealer of the past generation wrought havoc in the Italian communities by claiming that he was a rabbi from Jerusalem who was collecting books and material for the places of study in the Holy City.

One remarkable thing about these Jewish ritual objects is the strong local patriotism they sometime display. It is occasionally possible to 'place' an object by reason of the fact that it flaunts an Austrian, or even a Russian, eagle. I own a Circumcisional Chair of Elijah, of the heavy rococo German workmanship that can best be described as 'Ludwig Seize', which bears the monogram of Frederick the First of Prussia (though to be sure this may have originated as a commonplace *fauteuil* in a royal palace). More specific still is a spice box, made for one Nathan Adler in 1773 in the form of the famous City Gate of Frankfort, the Eschenheimerthurm; this was just one hundred and seventy years before the surviving Frankfort Jews were shipped to the gas chambers. A similar token of local pride is a 16th-century Hanukkah lamp, proudly adorned with the Lily of Florence; some of my best friends were murdered in 20th century Florence.

The experience of the collector who buys something as genuine, and then finds out that it is a fake, is common enough. As a matter of fact that is the only way to learn, and the man who assures you that he has never been taken in probably knows nothing whatsoever about the subject. It sometimes happens, though, that you buy something believing that it's a fake, or nearly so, and it turns out to be genuine. Indeed, in my non-Jewish collection I have a pewter tankard, sold to an uncle of mine by a store in London's West End as a reproduction, which turned out to be an admirable and genuine piece.

Some years ago I bought, from a private owner, a Scroll of Esther with illuminations in the Chinese style (the bowman, the festivities, the dance, the musicians), which I thought very amusing; but I was sure that it was of piece of *Chinoiserie*, executed in Europe with a more or less humorous intent. I showed it, however, to experts in Chinese art, and to my amazement they have told me one and all that the illuminations are without question Chinese, and could only have been executed by some person steeped in that country's artistic and cultural tradition. In fact, I had apparently picked up unwittingly, almost reluctantly, the only artistic relic that is left today of the ancient indigenous Chinese Jewish community of Kain-Feng-fu. One American enthusiast, who should know, says that this is the most remarkable piece of Jewish art in existence. In Cairo, I was once offered, at a pretty high price, a curious Hebrew document written on the shoulder-blade of a sheep (or was it a cow?). I am convinced that it was a fake, but still I sometimes have my doubts and kick myself for not having bought it.

It is perhaps worth while to point out that, especially in Holland and Italy, there are large numbers of modern reproductions manufactured in all innocence – which in all innocence are occasionally purchased by tourists and brought home in antiquarian triumph. But there are some near-forgeries which are harder to detect. I know one dealer who, when he is in doubt as to whether an object (for example, a silver goblet) was really manufactured for Jewish ritual use, settle the matter by having an apposite Hebrew inscription engraved on it, after which he is able to sell it at an enhanced price. There was once a dealer-collector in London (his collection was sold not long since by auction in New York) who never cared much if his treasures were battered and ruined. In that case, he always said that they were of Spanish origin, and had been broken up and buried at the time of the Inquisition, and in consequence of this romantic association he put a higher valuation on them. I once found him telling this tale about a fully inscribed 18th-century Polish Torah ornament, and told him so, but that didn't shake him; the Spanish Marranos must have imported it from Poland, he said.

Forgeries turn up sometimes in the most unlikely places, so that the circumstances in which you buy something which purports to be 'old' is not necessarily a guarantee of its authenticity. A venturesome dealer I know once purchased, deep in the Arabian desert, some Nabataean figures which he was told had been dug up in a ruin that he had just passed. They turned out to be hopeless fakes. Elkan Adler, himself, bought at a high price, from the library of an inaccessible monastery in Peru, bound up in a collection of ancient pamphlets, a copy of Christopher Columbus's letter to his Marrano patron, Luis de Santangel, informing him of his discovery of America, published immediately after his return to Europe. Adler only found out when he got it home that it was an extremely skilful imitation.

In due course your true collector becomes utterly ghoulish. He knows what every other collector has, and speculates on the chance of acquiring it from the estate after his death – sometimes he's on the doorstep nearly as soon as the undertaker. I recall being once at a funeral in London where, again Elkan Adler, who had come in on the way to his office, found himself standing by the side of a learned and wealthy collector who was following the recital of the Psalms out of a finely written manuscript Bible. That reminded Elkan of something. He opened his attaché case, and produced another volume from it, and while the coffin was being carried down the stairs, these two pious bibliophiles engaged in spirited negotiations for an exchange.

I know one or two people who even now are calculating my age and speculating on their chances of surviving me, in the hope of getting hold of this or that. For my part, nothing would give me greater satisfaction after my demise than to attend, in the flesh, at the auction sale of my own collections.

NOTES

1. In 1839 Abraham Firkovich, a book collector living in the Crimea, was charged by Tsar Alexander II to oversee a survey of the Karites in the Russian Empire to determine their civil status. Armed for this task with an official government document demanding complete cooperation, he used the opportunity to abstract old books and documents from the Jewish communities he visited. He built up a vast collection of some 17,000 items including others he similarly obtained during expeditions to the Middle East, so forming one of the most important collections in the world, which is now housed in the Russian State Library in St Petersburg. See Shimon M. Iakerson, *Selected Pearls: Treasures of Jewish Culture in St Petersburg*, St Petersburg, 2003, pp. 33–8.

2. See Gershon Scholem, 'The Curious History of the Six-Pointed Star', Commentary, September 1949. (CR)

39 From my Uncle's Treasure Trove
A Postscript by Joseph F. Roth

When looking through archives, you never know what gems might be uncovered. So it was when I was sorting through the contents of one of the packing cases containing the remaining parts of the private library and personal papers of my uncle Cecil Roth. To my surprise I came across a small white volume just 9 cm by 14 cm and 1 cm thick. On the front was the title in Russian and on opening the volume I found every page closely printed in Russian on specially thin paper. The little volume could be easily slipped into a pocket. There was no publisher's imprint nor any publication date to be found anywhere. What was this book and why did Cecil have it amongst his private papers?

Utilising the little Russian I could remember from having spent three weeks in Moscow at the British Exhibition in 1961 and with the help of a friend, we translated the title – 'Cecil Roth' on the first line and underneath 'History of the Jews'. I looked up Cecil's bibliography but could find no reference to a Russian translation of his history. The title page also included the sub-title 'From Ancient Times to the Six Day War' and 'Translated from English'. The short preface by Cecil on the following page is dated 'Jerusalem 1967'. Search as I may, I found references to editions in English, Japanese, French, Italian, Spanish, German and Hebrew but nothing in Russian. Comparing this volume with the various editions of Cecil's history I have in my own library, it would seem that this volume is a translation of the *The Bird's Eye View of Jewish History*. So what was the story of this volume?

Searching further I came across some other papers which indicated that the volume had been given to my aunt Irene in 1976 by a Russian émigré, a Mr U. Andres. Mulling over these items, I recalled a story my aunt had told me some years ago.

Irene was in Israel for Pesach when she went with a party to witness the Samaritan Passover on Mount Gerizim. Amongst the party was a lecturer from the Haifa Technion, a Russian emigrant and a noted mineralogist. He enquired from the host whether my aunt was indeed the widow of Cecil Roth and, when being assured that she was, asked to be introduced to her. He wanted to express his profound thanks for the help and inspiration this little volume had given him for it had allowed him to rediscover his roots and find out the history of his people. Through his reading and re-reading of the book he had become not only fascinated with Jewish history but had also decided to emigrate to Israel. Irene assumed that he had somehow obtained a copy of an English version brought in surreptitiously by a foreign visitor from the West but he assured her that he had read a Russian language version. Irene was amazed and could hardly believe the story. But some days later, Mr Andres sent her his own prized copy. And it was this that I had unearthed.

Irene remembered that some time previously she had seen a press report that in Moscow the police, in raiding homes, had confiscated many copies of Cecil Roth's *History of the Jews* and had assumed that these were English copies – now she realized that these must have been the mini volume she had just received. In June 1985 it was reported that the home of Isai and Grigory Goldshtein in Tiblisi was searched and Judaica, a Cecil Roth history book and money were confiscated by the police.

Some years after this event Irene met two brothers who had recently arrived from Kiev. They also were delighted to meet the widow of the man who had done so much in enabling them to learn of their ancestry. They went on to tell her of the many hundreds of Russians who treated this book as their 'bible' and how it was their sole source of information of their Jewish history. When copies had become scarce, the entire book had been secretly typed out time and time again and circulated through the clandestine system for reproducing and circulating banned literature in the USSR.

In another packing case I came across two similar volumes. Both had a printers name and date incorporated. In one this information was on an inside page – 'Biblos' in English and Hebrew characters with a date of 1976, whilst the other with a date of 1978 had this information boldly displayed on the front cover. These volumes were printed on low-grade normal paper and as such are somewhat thicker.

Yet there are still questions remaining to be answered – who actually printed these volumes, were they all printed in Israel or elsewhere, were there any other editions, how many copies were printed and perhaps even of greater significance, how were they smuggled into Russia and distributed so widely and without those in the West knowing anything about it at the time.

Cecil had been heard to say that 'Even if one Jew, of uncertain allegiance to Judaism, had by any one of my writings been influenced to return to his heritage to which he was born, then I would consider my work had not been in vain.' Had he lived to know how his history had achieved so much for so many, he would surely have felt that his life's labour had been amply compensated.

Glossary

Apocrypha	'Not recognised' – a collection of four books of Jewish writing which are not included in the Hebrew Bible
A priori	Reasoning from cause to effect
Aramaic	Semitic language that was common in the Middle East
Auto-da-Fe	The ceremonial of pronouncing sentence on heretics by the Spanish Inquisition and the burning of them at the stake
Avignon	Town in southern France
Buxdorf	An outstanding Hebraist of the seventeenth century
Carrierre	Ghetto
Comtat Venaissin	The former papal territory in southeastern France corresponding approximately to the present Department of Vaucluse and ceded to the Holy See from 1274 to 1791
Din (plural dinim)	Jewish law
Ecclesiastes (Hebrew *Koheleth*)	The *Megilla* (scroll) recited in Synagogue on Shemini Atzeret, consisting of observations on the purpose of life
Escola	Place of worship
Etrog	Citron, one of the 'Four Species' used in the synagogue service on the Feast of Tabernacles (Succot)
Fenugreek	A heavily scented Mediterranean vegetable plant cultivated for its aromatic seeds
Ganephs	Thief
Gemara	Explanations of the text of the Mishna including the discussions of the Rabbis, third to sixth centuries
Ibon Tibbon	One of a family of authors and translators

	from Arabic to Hebrew in the twelfth century
Juderias	Jewish quarter
Judengasse	Jewish quarter
Kapparah (Hebrew 'Atonement')	A common custom among Eastern European Jewry of symbolically substituting on the eve of the Day of Atonement an animal – usually a fowl – for the implied forfeited life of the sinner
Ladino	Common language of Jews of Spain incorporating elements of Hebrew, Arabic and Spanish, written with Hebrew characters
Lulav	The palm branch with sprigs of myrtle and willow accompanied by an Etrog used in the synagogue on the Feast of Tabernacles (Succot)
Maharil	Rabbi Jacob ben Moses Moellin (1360–1427), an eminent talmudist and head of the Jewish communities of Germany, Austria and Bohemia
Mahzor	Prayer book for the festivals
Minyan	The minimum number of ten adults for public prayer
Mishna	Originally the traditional religious and civil oral laws and traditions, written down by Rabbi Judah ha-Nasi around 200 CE
Pentateuch	The first five books of the Old Testament
Perquisition	Thorough search ordered by law for the discovery of incriminating documents
Poetasters	Writers of inferior verse
Prosody	The study of poetic metre and the art of versification
Rosh Hashanah	The New Year festival celebrated in the autumn
Seder	The home service on the first nights of Passover interrupted by the festival meal
Selichot	Penitential prayers recited on fast days
Siddur	Daily prayer book
Sumptuary Laws	Laws aimed at curbing expenditure or extravagance
Talmud	The Mishna together with the Gemara

Tashlich	A ceremony carried out at New Year in which sins are symbolically cast into running water
Vayles	Tallit or prayer shawl
Yiddish	For centuries the common language of Eastern European Jews, derived largely from German
Zante	City on the island of Zante, the main southernmost island of the Ionian islands of Greece